Department
of Health

Manual of Nutrition

Twelfth Edition

London: TSO

information & publishing solutions

Published by TSO (The Stationery Office) and available from:

Online
www.tsoshop.co.uk

Mail, Telephone, Fax & E-mail
TSO
PO Box 29, Norwich, NR3 1GN
Telephone orders/General enquiries: 0870 600 5522
Fax orders: 0870 600 5533
E-mail: customer.services@tso.co.uk
Textphone 0870 240 3701

TSO@Blackwell and other Accredited Agents

Customers can also order publications from:
TSO Ireland
16 Arthur Street, Belfast BT1 4GD
Tel 028 9023 8451 Fax 028 9023 5401

First published 2012

ISBN 978 0 11 322929 1

Contents

List of tables

Tables in appendices

Foreword

The 12th edition of the *Manual of Nutrition* is published at a time of increasing obesity, diabetes and heart disease. We continue to have concern about the population's calorie intake and intakes of saturated fat, salt and added sugars. Yet we all believe we are experts on food and nutrition; after all, we eat every day.

This manual describes the major nutrients, their roles and sources together with the mechanisms of digestion and utilisation. It also outlines how this information links to food and nutrition policy. As such, it provides a valuable contribution to ensure that we all understand the real role that food plays in our health and wellbeing.

This edition covers similar ground to the previous editions but contains updated values for the typical nutrient content of commonly eaten foods as well as the nutrient intake of the population which has been estimated from the recently published *National Diet and Nutrition Survey: Headline Results from Years 1 and 2 (Combined) of the Rolling Programme (2008/9–2009/10)* (Department of Health, 2011). The chapter on energy (Chapter 5) has been updated to include new information from the Scientific Advisory Committee on Nutrition's energy report (*Dietary Reference Values for Energy 2011*). Other updated information includes that related to iron, caffeine intake for pregnant women and recommendations on being active.

I would like to thank the Department of Health's nutrition team who have used their knowledge and skills to update this 12th edition and I hope that this new edition continues to prove a valuable source of reference to a wide range of students, teachers, health professionals and interested members of the public.

Sally C C

Professor Dame Sally C Davies
Chief Medical Officer and Chief Scientific Adviser

PART 1

Nutrients and their utilisation

1 Introduction to nutrition, and some definitions

Most people grow well and stay healthy provided that they get enough of a variety of food to eat, wherever they live in the world. The reasons for this, and the ways in which the adequacy of any diet can be assessed, form part of the science of nutrition with which this manual is concerned. A knowledge of nutrition principles is therefore important to all of us, whether we plan and provide meals for ourselves and our families; cater for large numbers of customers or vulnerable groups such as older people, children and/or the sick; provide advice about healthier eating; or teach in schools.

Before proceeding further, it is necessary to define some terms:

The science of *nutrition* is the study of all processes of growth, maintenance and repair of the living body that depend upon the digestion of food, and the study of that food.

Food is any solid or liquid that, when swallowed, can supply any of the following:

* material from which the body can produce movement, heat or other forms of energy
* material for growth, repair or reproduction
* substances necessary to regulate the production of energy or the processes of growth and repair.

Foods are considered in more detail in Part 2.

The components of foods that have these functions are called *nutrients*. They are introduced below, and considered in more detail in Chapters 2, 3, 4, 7 and 8. The *diet* consists of those foods or mixtures of foods in the amounts which are actually eaten over a period of time, for example, a week or so. A good diet provides adequate amounts of all the nutrients, without harmful excesses, from a wide range of foods.

The nutrients in food

The following types of nutrients may be present in foods:

* *Carbohydrates*, which provide the body with energy; excess may also be converted into body fat.

- *Fats*, which provide energy in a more concentrated form than carbohydrates, and may also be converted into body fat.
- *Proteins*, which provide materials (amino acids) for growth and repair. They can also be converted into carbohydrates and used to provide energy.

As they are needed in relatively large quantities, carbohydrates, fats and proteins are sometimes referred to as macronutrients.

Vitamins and minerals are required to help to regulate body processes and for growth and repair.[1] Vitamins and minerals are needed only in small quantities and are sometimes referred to as micronutrients.

Although water, like oxygen from the air, is also essential for life, it is not usually considered as a food or a nutrient. The carbohydrate compounds, known collectively as *fibre*, are not strictly nutrients but have positive effects on our health. On the other hand, alcohol would be considered a food because it provides energy, even though it has drug-like properties. Iron obtained from a cooking utensil (for example) rather than from a food, is also a nutrient since it may be used to renew substances in the blood.

Hardly any foods contain only one nutrient. Most are very complex mixtures, which consist mainly of a variety of carbohydrates, fats and proteins, together with water. Vitamins and minerals are present in very much smaller amounts. One hundred grams of potatoes, for example, contain about 18 g of carbohydrate, 2 g of protein, 80 g of water, some fibre and, if fried, will also contain fat, but less than 50 mg in total of vitamins and minerals.

Energy

Energy is needed for the body to function and be active. The body derives energy from carbohydrates, fat, protein and alcohol in the diet. Experiments show that almost exactly the same amount of energy is produced from, say, wheat when it is eaten by humans as when it is used for fuel in a railway engine (as it has been in times of excess production of wheat). The essential difference between the two chemical processes is that in an engine the energy is released immediately, whereas in the body the energy is released gradually by a series of steps, each carefully controlled by an *enzyme*.[2] This energy is used to perform muscular work and to maintain body temperature and such

---

[1] Vitamins differ from hormones (which also help to regulate body processes) in that, with the exception of vitamin D, they cannot be made in the body and must therefore be supplied in the diet; hormones are always made within the body itself.

[2] Enzymes are special proteins, each of which accelerates the rate of a specific chemical reaction without itself being affected. They enable complex changes to occur in the body that would otherwise require more extreme conditions; without them, life could not exist. To be active, many require the presence of vitamins or minerals as 'co-factors'.

processes as breathing, but a considerable amount is also lost as heat. The energy provided by carbohydrate, fat, protein and other constituents can be measured and used to calculate the energy value of any food (see 'Energy value of food' in Chapter 5).

Other constituents of food

WATER

Water comprises about two-thirds of the body's weight, and is the medium or solvent in which almost every body process takes place. The need of the body for water is second only to its need for oxygen. Adults can survive for many weeks without food but for only a few days without water. Water is lost from the body in various ways: in the form of urine, combined with the body's toxic waste products excreted by the kidneys as well as by evaporation in the breath and sweat. Water is taken into the body from solid foods as well as from drinks (see Table 9 in Chapter 5). The balance of water retained within the body is normally carefully regulated by the kidneys, but excessive losses can result from vomiting or diarrhoea in illness, or from heavy sweating due to strenuous activity or a hot climate. If water intake is not increased, dehydration may result. In temperate climates such as that of the UK we need to drink about 1.2 litres (6–8 glasses) of water or other fluids each day to maintain water balance and prevent dehydration. However, this quantity should be increased when activity increases or the external temperature rises.

FIBRE

Some foods, particularly wholegrain cereals, pulses and some fruit and vegetables, contain substantial amounts of fibre (non-starch polysaccharides – see Chapter 2). Insoluble fibre fractions are not absorbed into the body; instead they add bulk to the faeces. This property is beneficial to health, in helping to prevent constipation. Soluble fibre constituents, which may be absorbed, are found especially in fruit, vegetables and pulses and can help to reduce the amount of cholesterol in the blood. Fibre is discussed further in Chapter 2.

FLAVOURS AND COLOURS

In addition to the main nutritive and structural components, foods also contain innumerable minor constituents which give them their characteristic flavours, colours and textures. Control over the changes that occur in these constituents on ripening, and during storage, preparation and cooking, is an important consideration for both chefs and food technologists.

There is also increasing interest in this variety of biologically active compounds in relation to health. The compounds that colour foods, such as carotenoids (yellow or orange pigments), anthocyanins (red and purple pigments), the flavonoids and other phenolic compounds (found particularly in fruits, vegetables, tea and wine) have antioxidant properties, and increased consumption of some of these compounds may be associated with a reduced risk of heart disease.

Malnutrition

The maintenance of health in an individual depends upon the consumption and absorption of appropriate amounts of energy and all the nutrients. Too little or too much of some nutrients, usually over a period of months or longer, may lead to ill health or malnutrition. Although the body has considerable power to adapt to reduced dietary intakes, for example by reducing physical activity, too low an intake of food will eventually result in *undernutrition* and, in extreme cases, *starvation*.

An example is wasting (*marasmus*) in young children and the stunting of their physical, and perhaps even mental, development, which may result from inadequate breastfeeding or from a poor weaning diet in developing countries. Other examples include the 'classical' nutrition deficiency diseases such as scurvy and some anaemias which result from diets containing too little of one or more vitamins or minerals, or from a physiological inability to absorb these nutrients. Excessive fatness (*obesity*), resulting from too great a food intake for the body's needs, is also a form of malnutrition, as is the excessive consumption of any nutrient, whether fat, sugar, mineral or vitamin, if it leads to ill health.

Units of measurement

Standard units are used to calculate the energy and nutrients in various amounts of food, and to measure heights and weights of individuals. The metric system (including the form known as SI[3]) has mainly been used in this edition of the manual. The relationships between these and traditional units are given in detail in Appendix 1.

Sources of data

Sources of data in this manual are based on the most up-to-date information published by the Department of Health or other government departments. Unless stated otherwise, data sources are taken from *McCance and Widdowson's Composition of Foods Integrated Dataset* (COFIDS), published

---

[3] The SI unit for energy is the joule; however, in the UK most people are more familiar with the term 'calorie' (see Appendix 1 for the relationship between the two).

by the Food Standards Agency in 2008, and *National Diet and Nutrition Survey: Headline Results from Years 1 and 2 (Combined) of the Rolling Programme (2008/9–2009/10)*, published by the Department of Health in 2011.

2 Carbohydrates

There are three major groups of carbohydrates in food: *sugars, starches* and *non-starch polysaccharides* (NSP). All are compounds of carbon, hydrogen and oxygen only, and their chemical structures are all based on a common unit (usually glucose). The units can be linked together in varying ways and in different numbers, and classification of the carbohydrates depends primarily on the number of units, which varies from one to many thousands. Sugars and starches are a major source of food energy for humans throughout the world. Non-starch polysaccharides are known collectively as *fibre*.

Sugars

MONOSACCHARIDES (OR SIMPLE SUGARS)

Glucose (dextrose) occurs naturally in fruit and plant juices and in the blood of living animals. Most carbohydrates in food are ultimately converted to glucose during digestion. Glucose can also be manufactured from starch by the action of acid or specific enzymes. *Glucose syrups* (liquid glucose) are the product of the hydrolysis of starch (usually maize or wheat starch), and contain variable concentrations of glucose, maltose and other more complex carbohydrates depending on the end use for which they are intended. Except where the syrup is almost pure glucose, these syrups are less sweet than glucose. They are used in many manufactured foods including sugar confectionery, soft drinks and jams.

Fructose occurs naturally in some fruit and vegetables and especially in honey. It is the sweetest sugar known. It is also a component of sucrose, from which it may be derived. The conversion of some of the glucose in glucose syrup to fructose results in the production of 'high-fructose' syrups.

Galactose is a component of lactose, but also occurs in some food as an individual monosaccharide.

DISACCHARIDES

Disaccharides consist of two monosaccharides linked together (minus the elements of water).

Sucrose occurs naturally in sugar cane and sugar beet, and in lesser amounts in fruits and some root vegetables such as carrots. It is a chemical combination of glucose and fructose. Table sugar, whether white or brown, is essentially pure sucrose.

Maltose is formed during the breakdown of starch by digestion and, for example, when grain is germinated for the production of malt liquors such as beer. It is a combination of two glucose units.

Lactose occurs only in milk, including breast milk. It is less sweet than sucrose or glucose, and is a combination of glucose and galactose. In its isolated form, it is added to some food products including meat products and some infant foods.

Many individuals, particularly those of African, Asian and Indian races, have a limited ability to digest lactose. In later life some of these people may develop *lactose intolerance*, which results in digestive disturbances when the equivalent of a glass or more of milk is drunk. It is rarely found in healthy infants who receive a large amount of their energy from milk.

PROPERTIES OF SUGARS

All sugars, whether monosaccharides or disaccharides, dissolve in water but vary in sweetness. Their taste may be modified by cooking (e.g. by *caramelisation*). They usually form white (colourless) crystals when the water in which they are dissolved becomes supersaturated, but impure preparations may be brown. In addition to sweetness, they provide a readily available source of energy: monosaccharides provide 16 kJ (3.75 kcal) per gram and disaccharides 17 kJ (4 kcal) per gram. Sugars can be used for several purposes in food preparation. For example, in jam-making and bottling, they act as preservatives, and in biscuits, cakes, soft drinks and certain other foods, they also help to provide the characteristic texture and consistency.

NON-SUGAR SWEETENERS

Some other substances also taste sweet. *Sorbitol, mannitol* and *xylitol* are polyols (also known as sugar alcohols) which are made from sugars. Their energy value is similar to that of glucose, but for labelling purposes they are deemed to provide 10 kJ (2.4 kcal) per gram. In contrast, the intense sweeteners saccharin, aspartame and acesulfame K are classed as food additives as they have no chemical or nutritional relationship to sugars. They are about 200–500 times sweeter than sucrose and consequently used at a very low level so that even aspartame, which is the only one metabolised by the body, provides essentially no energy. They are used as sweetening agents to restrict the amount of sugar in the diet. Certain sweetening agents available in a granulated form (for example, to sprinkle on breakfast cereals) are mixtures of an intense sweetener and a carbohydrate diluent and as such are sources of energy, although substantially less than the equivalent amount of sugar.

Starches

Starches are *polysaccharides* composed of variably large numbers of glucose units linked together to form both straight and branched chains (*amylose* and *amylopectin*, respectively). They are found in plants. They exist in granules of a size and shape that are characteristic for each plant. In this form they are insoluble in water, and foods such as flour and potatoes, which contain large amounts of them, are indigestible if eaten raw. When heated or cooked in the presence of water, the starch granules swell and eventually gelatinise. They can then be more easily digested. One gram of starch provides approximately 17.6 kJ (4.2 kcal) of energy, but for food-labelling purposes a value of 17 kJ (4 kcal) is used. Some forms of processing, for example dry heat used in the manufacture of certain breakfast cereals, can make part of the starch indigestible. Some scientists regard this fraction, known as *resistant starch*, as fibre along with non-starch polysaccharides (see below).

Glycogen is similar to starch in composition, but is made from glucose primarily by animals, including humans. Small amounts are stored in the liver and muscles as an energy reserve. It is not a significant item in the diet because it breaks down again to glucose after an animal's death.

Non-starch polysaccharides

In addition to starch there are other polysaccharides found in the cell walls of vegetables, fruits, pulses and cereal grains where they provide part of the plant structure. This range of diverse compounds, when forming part of the human diet, is classified as *fibre* (Table 2). The non-starch polysaccharides (NSP) in wheat, maize and rice are mainly insoluble cellulose and related materials, but those in fruits, vegetables and the cereals oats, barley and rye also contain soluble forms, including pectins and gums.

Cellulose consists of many thousands of glucose units. It cannot be digested by humans, but can be used as food by cows and other ruminants whose digestive tract contains micro-organisms capable of breaking it down into glucose. Cellulose and other indigestible polysaccharides add bulk to the faeces because of their water-binding capacity, and greatly assist the passage of digestible materials and waste products through the intestines, thus helping to prevent constipation. *Pectin* is present in apples and many other fruits and in roots such as turnips and sweet potatoes. Its property of forming a stiff jelly is important in jam-making.

Pectin is not fibrous, and because it is completely digested it has little effect on the faeces. However, pectin and other soluble fibre components may help to reduce the amount of cholesterol in the blood.

As the effects of both soluble and insoluble NSP are beneficial, it is best to include a variety of NSP-rich foods in the diet. National dietary guidelines recommend consumption of a naturally high-fibre diet. Daily intakes of NSP in the UK average 14.9 g (119.2 kJ, 29.8 kcal) for men and lower, 12.8 g (102.4 kJ, 25.6 kcal), for women, being provided mainly by cereals and cereal products and vegetables and potatoes. It has been recommended, however, that population average intakes of NSP should rise to 18 g (144 kJ, 36 kcal) per day (see 'Carbohydrates' in Chapter 9). One gram of fibre provides approximately 8 kJ (2 kcal).

Sources of carbohydrates in the diet

Plants form sugars in their leaves by the action of sunlight, but store them in their stems, roots, tubers or seeds as starch (the small amount of starch stored in unripe fruits, however, turns back into glucose or sucrose on ripening). Starch forms the major energy reserve of most plants, and thus in turn provides a major part of food energy for humans. The sugar and starch contents of selected foods are shown in Table 1.

In 2008/10, the proportions of food energy provided by total sugars and starch in the UK were similar (21% and 27%, respectively). The main sources of carbohydrate in the UK adult diet are cereals and cereal products, which provide more than 40% of intake. Other sources include vegetables and potatoes, sugars, preserves, and confectionery and fruit.

The total fibre content of the average UK diet has not changed much over the past decade and adult intakes are still below the recommended 18 g per day. Cereals and cereal products continue to be the main source of fibre.

Health aspects of carbohydrates

Although all sugars and starches absorbed by the body provide similar amounts of energy, they have different physiological effects. Eating a lot of certain types of sugary foods at frequent intervals, especially between meals, is associated with increased tooth decay (dental caries). In a 1989 report, *Dietary Sugars and Human Disease*, the Government's advisory Committee on Medical Aspects of Food and Nutrition Policy (COMA)[4] considered that the type of sugar and its location within a food can affect its ability to cause dental caries, and that it is useful to classify sugars in the following way:

- *Intrinsic sugars* are those contained within the cell walls of food, e.g. sugars in whole fruits and vegetables.

---

[4] COMA was replaced in 2000 by the Scientific Advisory Committee on Nutrition (SACN), which advises the UK health departments on scientific aspects of nutrition and health.

9

Table 1. Average carbohydrate content of selected foods (edible portion)

	Available carbohydrate, as monosaccharides (g/100 g)		
	Sugars	Starch	Total
Whole milk[a]	4.5	0.0	4.5
Skimmed milk	4.4	0.0	4.4
Ice cream, vanilla (non-dairy)[b]	23.5	0.0	29.8[c]
Meat	0.0	0.0	0.0
Sugar[d]	105.0	0.0	105.0
Honey	76.4	0.0	76.4
Jam	69.0	0.0	69.0
Potatoes, old, boiled	0.7	16.3	17.0
Macaroni, boiled	0.3	18.2	18.5
Rice, long grain, cooked[e]	0.0	31.1	31.1
Bananas	20.9	2.3	23.2
Oranges	8.5	0.0	8.5
Peaches, canned, in syrup	14.0	0.0	14.0
Peaches, canned, in juice	9.7	0.0	9.7
Sultanas	69.4	0.0	69.4
Biscuits, chocolate, fully coated[f]	39.3	23.5	62.8
Bread, white	3.4	42.7	46.1
Bread, wholemeal	2.8	39.3	42.0
Flour, soft, white, plain[e]	0.6	80.3	80.9
Cornflakes[g]	7.3	72.0	85.9[h]
Muesli, Swiss-style (with added sugar)	26.2	46.0	72.2
Muesli, no added sugar	15.7	51.4	67.1
Porridge, made with water	0.1	8.0	8.1
Orange juice, unsweetened	8.8	0.0	8.8
Cola	10.9	0.0	10.9
Soup, canned, cream of tomato[b]	5.5	2.2	7.8
Milk chocolate[b]	56.0	0.0	56.0
Lager	0.0	0.0	0.0
Wine, white, medium	3.0	0.0	3.0

Source: unless otherwise stated, *McCance and Widdowson's Composition of Foods Integrated Dataset* (COFIDS), published by the Food Standards Agency, 2008.
[a] Lactose
[b] Source: *Nutrient Analysis of a Range of Processed Foods with Particular Reference to Trans Fatty Acids – Summary Report*, Department of Health, 2011.
[c] Includes oligosaccharides.
[d] Equivalent to 100 g of sucrose. 1 g of disaccharide is equivalent to 1.05 g of monosaccharide. 1 g of starch is equivalent to 1.10 g of monosaccharide.
[e] Source: *Nutrient Survey of Flours and Grains – Analytical Report*, Food Standards Agency, 2005.
[f] Source: *Nutrient Analysis Survey of Biscuits, Buns, Cakes and Pastries – Summary Report*, Department of Health, 2011.
[g] Source: *Nutrient Survey of Breakfast Cereals – Analytical Report*, Food Standards Agency, 2004.
[h] Includes oligosaccharides and maltodextrin.

- *Extrinsic sugars* are those not contained within the cell structure of a food and include milk sugars that occur naturally in milk and milk products (almost all lactose).
- *Non-milk extrinsic (NME) sugars*, e.g. sugars in fruit juices, table sugar and sugars added to food, including honey, glucose syrups, maple syrup etc.

Intrinsic and milk sugars are not considered to have adverse effects on teeth. NME sugars, on the other hand, can play a significant part in tooth decay, although regular brushing of teeth (including flossing) and the use of fluoride toothpaste can lessen this effect.

NME sugars should contribute no more than 11% of food energy on average for the population. In 2008/10 adults aged 19–64 years and children aged over 4 years exceeded this recommendation, whereas younger children and older adults were close to this recommendation. The mean percentage food energy derived from starch and intrinsic and milk sugars for the population was below the recommended 39%. The largest source of NME sugars in the adult diet was table sugar, preserves and sweet spreads, whereas the largest source in children's diets was sugary soft drinks.

As previously discussed, consumption of a high-fibre diet is recommended for good health and a daily target for NSP for the UK population is set at 18 g (see 'Non-starch polysaccharides' in this chapter). When it is desirable to reduce the sugar content of the diet, a good way of replacing the lost energy is by increasing the intake of fibre-rich starchy foods.

Because of these recommendations, it is useful to know the amounts of different types of carbohydrate in foods. Examples are shown in Tables 1 and 2.

Table 2 shows two fibre values for some selected foods. One value is fibre determined as NSP by the Englyst method, which has traditionally been used in the UK and Ireland; the other is fibre determined as NSP plus resistant starch and lignin by the Association of Analytical Chemists (AOAC) method used in other European countries. In general, the AOAC method tends to give higher values than Englyst, the magnitude of the difference varying between foods, which makes it difficult to compare fibre contents of foods produced in different countries. The Government has recommended that AOAC values be used for nutrition-labelling purposes in the UK.

Table 2. Fibre content of selected foods (edible portion), expressed as non-starch polysaccharides (NSP) and total dietary fibre (AOAC)

	Non-starch polysaccharides (NSP) (g/100 g)	Total dietary fibre (AOAC) (g/100 g)
Meat	0.0	0.0
Low-fat yogurt, fruit	0.2	0.3
Baked beans	3.7	n/a
Beans, red kidney, boiled	6.7	n/a
Beans, runner, boiled	1.9	n/a
Broccoli, boiled	2.3	n/a
Carrots, boiled	2.5	n/a
Potatoes, cooked	1.9	2.4
Tomatoes, raw	1.0	n/a
Apples with skin, eating	1.8	n/a
Bananas	1.1	n/a
Mixed nuts	6.0	n/a
Scones, fruit	2.0	2.9
Biscuits, semi-sweet, e.g. rich tea[a]	1.9	2.7
Bread, white	1.9	2.5
Bread, brown	3.5	5.0
Bread, wholemeal	5.0	7.0
Wheat flour, soft, white[b]	3.4	4.0
Wheat flour, brown[b]	6.9	7.7
Wheat flour, wholemeal[b]	8.8	10.1
Rice, egg fried, takeaway	0.8	1.1
Rice, brown, wholegrain, boiled[b]	0.9	1.5
Dried spaghetti, white, boiled[c]	1.5	1.7
Dried spaghetti, wholewheat, boiled[c]	4.4	4.2

Source: unless otherwise stated, *McCance and Widdowson's Composition of Foods Integrated Dataset* (COFIDS), published by the Food Standards Agency, 2008.
[a] Source: *Nutrient Analysis Survey of Biscuits, Buns, Cakes and Pastries – Summary Report*, Department of Health, 2011.
[b] Source: *Nutrient Survey of Flours and Grains – Analytical Report*, Food Standards Agency, 2005.
[c] Source: *Nutrient Survey of Pasta and Pasta Sauces – Analytical Report*, Food Standards Agency, 2004.

3 Fats

Fats include not only 'visible fats' such as butter and fat spreads, cooking fats and oils and the fat on meat, but also the 'invisible fats' which are found in foods such as cheese, biscuits and cakes, nuts and other foods of animal and vegetable origin. They are a more concentrated source of energy than carbohydrates, and are the form in which much of the energy reserve of animals and some seeds is stored.

Like carbohydrates, fats are compounds of carbon, hydrogen and oxygen only, but the proportion of oxygen is lower. Chemically, fats in food consist mainly of mixtures of *triglycerides*. Each triglyceride is a combination of three *fatty acids* with a unit of glycerol (glycerine), and the differences between one fat or oil and another are largely the result of the different fatty acids in each of them.

Fatty acids

Many different fatty acids are found in nature. They differ in the number of carbon atoms they contain, and the number of hydrogen atoms held by the carbon atoms. *Saturated* fatty acids have as many hydrogen atoms as they can hold, which means that they are stable and that they keep well. When hydrogen atoms are missing, carbon atoms form double bonds with each other. *Monounsaturated* fatty acids contain only one double bond (two missing hydrogen atoms). *Polyunsaturated* fatty acids have two or more double bonds (four or more missing hydrogen atoms) which react gradually with oxygen in the air and make the fat rancid. In polyunsaturated fatty acids, the hydrogen atoms can be arranged in one of two ways. One arrangement is called *cis*, and the other is called *trans*. Cis is the usual form found in nature. The position of the double bonds within the polyunsaturated fatty acid structure determines its type, the two main types being *omega-3* and *omega-6* fatty acids. A *cis* configuration means that adjacent hydrogen atoms are on the same side of the double bond. A *trans* configuration, by contrast, means that the adjacent hydrogen atoms are bound to opposite sides of the double bond.

All fats contain a mixture of these three types of fatty acid, but in widely varying proportions, depending on the source (Table 3 and Appendix 3). The presence of large amounts of unsaturated fatty acids in a mixture affects the physical as well as the chemical properties of a fat, making it liquid at room temperature (i.e. an oil). Fats that are solid at room temperature, for example beef fat, contain most of their fatty acids as saturates and monounsaturates. Some vegetable oils such as coconut and palm oils have a relatively high proportion of saturated fatty acids but, because they have a relatively low number of carbon atoms, they do not cause the oil to solidify. In nature, unsaturated fatty acids generally have their double bonds in the *cis* form. They can be changed into saturated fatty acids and a mixture of *cis* and *trans* monounsaturated fatty acids by controlled treatment with hydrogen (hydrogenation). This happens when liquid oils are hardened in the manufacture of fat spreads and cooking fats and, to a lesser extent, in the rumen of cows and sheep. The more important fatty acids in foods are as follows.

SATURATED FATTY ACIDS

Palmitic acid and *stearic acid* are major constituents of hard fats such as butter, lard, suet and cocoa butter. *Myristic acid* occurs in butter and coconut oil.

Butyric acid, although present in only small amounts, makes an important contribution to the taste of milk fat and butter. Free butyric acid is released when these fats become rancid.

UNSATURATED FATTY ACIDS

Monounsaturated fatty acids

Oleic acid occurs in substantial amounts in all fats but especially in olive oil and rapeseed (canola) oil where it provides 60–70% of the total fatty acid content.

Trans unsaturated fatty acids

Trans isomers of oleic and other monounsaturated fatty acids (*trans* fatty acids) occur in nature in ruminant fats (e.g. milk, cheese, beef, lamb). Substantial amounts of artificial *trans* fats, produced by partial hydrogenation of vegetable oils, used to be present in vegetable oils and fat spreads, as well as foods made from these products such as biscuits and pastries. However, the UK food industry has now largely removed partially hydrogenated vegetable oils from vegetable oils and fat spreads.

Meat and meat products are currently the greatest contributors to *trans* fatty acid intake in the diets of UK adults (25%), followed by milk and milk products (22%), cereals and cereal products (19%), and fat spreads (10%). *Trans* fatty acids have no known nutritional benefits. The adverse health impact of these types of fat in the diet is discussed later in this chapter.

Table 3. Average fatty acid composition of some foods

	Fat (g/100g edible portion)	Fatty acids[a] (g/ 100 g edible portion)			
		Saturated	Monoun-saturated	Polyun-saturated	Trans
Milk, cow's, semi-skimmed	1.7	1.1	0.4	0.0	0.1
Milk, human	4.1	1.8	1.6	0.5	N
Cheese, Cheddar	34.9	21.7	9.4	1.1	1.4
Eggs, chicken, raw	11.2	3.2	4.4	1.7	0.1
Beef, mince, raw	16.2[b]	6.9	6.9	0.5	0.8
Pork, chops, lean and fat, raw	21.7	8.0	8.5	3.6	0.1
Chicken, meat average, raw	2.1	0.6	1.0	0.4	0.0
Liver, lamb's, raw	6.2	1.7	1.8	0.9	0.0
Sardines, canned, in tomato sauce	9.9	2.8	2.9	3.2	0.0
Butter	82.2	52.1	20.9	2.8	2.9
Fat spread (62–75%), not polyunsaturated[c]	73.2	24.35	33.24	11.80	0.14
Reduced-fat spread (41–62%), not polyunsaturated[c]	60.6	15.61	29.80	11.90	0.15
Reduced-fat spread (41–62%), polyunsaturated[c]	59.2	13.21	17.57	25.17	0.13
Sunflower oil	99.9	12.0	20.5	63.3	0.0
Olive oil	99.9	14.3	73.0	8.2	0.0
Blended vegetable oil[d]	99.9	11.7	53.2	29.8	0.0
Potato crisps fried in high oleic sunflower oil	28.8	2.48	22.41	2.51	0.03
Peanuts, dry-roasted	49.8	8.9	22.8	15.5	0.0
Chocolate chip cookies[e]	24.9	12.15	8.96	2.47	0.03
Chocolate, milk[c]	31.1	18.71	9.44	1.13	0.16

Source: unless otherwise stated, *McCance and Widdowson's Composition of Foods Integrated Dataset* (COFIDS) published by the Food Standards Agency, 2008.
[a] The fatty acids add up to less than the total fat because fat also contains glycerol, phospholipids, sterols and other fatty compounds.
[b] Average of values that ranged from 7.8 g to 26.5 g per 100 g.
[c] Source: *Nutrient Analysis of a Range of Processed Foods with Particular Reference to Trans Fatty Acids – Summary Report*, Department of Health, 2011.
[d] Average of several kinds; fatty acid profile of any one kind will depend on the particular blend of oils used in its manufacture.
[e] Source: *Nutrient Analysis Survey of Biscuits, Buns, Cakes and Pastries – Summary Report*, Department of Health, 2011.
N – The nutrient is present in significant quantities but there is no reliable information on the amount.

Polyunsaturated fatty acids

Polyunsaturated fatty acids can be classified into two types – *omega-6* and *omega-3* – according to the position of the double bonds. Depending on the length of the fatty acid chain (i.e. the number of carbons), the fatty acids from both families can also be described as long- or short-chain.

Linoleic acid (omega-6) and *alpha-linolenic acid* (omega-3) are short-chain polyunsaturated fatty acids which cannot be synthesised by the body and are, therefore, essential in small amounts in the diet. Linoleic acid is found in sunflower and rapeseed oil and in small amounts in some animal fats such as pork, and alpha-linolenic acid is found in flaxseed, walnut and rapeseed oil.

From these short-chain fatty acids, the body can make the longer forms which are important for health. Linoleic acid is transformed in the body into longer-chain omega-6 fatty acids such as *arachidonic acid* which is used in cell membranes and is a key precursor for hormone-like compounds called *eicosanoids*.

Alpha-linolenic acid is the main short-chain omega-3 polyunsaturated fatty acid. The body can convert this to the long-chain omega-3 fatty acids *eicosapentaenoic acid* (EPA) and *docosahexaenoic acid* (DHA); however, they can also be obtained pre-formed directly through diet. The principal dietary source of these longer-chain omega-3 polyunsaturated fatty acids is oily fish such as salmon, mackerel and sardines.

There is strong evidence for a beneficial effect of long-chain omega-3 polyunsaturated fatty acid consumption by reducing cardiovascular disease mortality. The evidence was reviewed in the 2004 joint report by the Scientific Advisory Committee on Nutrition (SACN) and Committee on Toxicity (COT), *Advice on Fish Consumption: Benefits & Risks*. The short-chain omega-3 polyunsaturated fatty acids found in vegetable sources may not have the same benefits on cardiovascular health as those in fish owing to the limited ability to convert them to the longer forms in the human body.

Properties of fats

Fats are solid at low temperatures and become liquid when they are heated. Oils are simply fats that are liquid at room temperature, usually as a result of their higher content of unsaturated fatty acids, and which solidify on refrigeration (e.g. olive oil). Oils and fats do not dissolve in water, but may be *emulsified* with water by vigorous mixing as when butter and fat spreads are made. The oil and water usually separate again unless emulsifiers such as lecithin from soya beans or egg are added to the mixture.

Fats make an important contribution to food characteristics such as texture and palatability. Food fats usually contain small amounts of other fat-soluble substances, including flavour components and some of the vitamins. Animal fats may contain retinol (vitamin A) and vitamin D, and varying amounts of cholesterol, while vegetable fats may contain carotenes (which can be converted into vitamin A in the body) and vitamin E, but do not contain cholesterol.

The amount of energy obtained from a given weight of all common fats is about the same, despite the different functions and properties of many of the component fatty acids. It is more than double the energy, at 37 kJ/g (9 kcal/g), of an equal weight of carbohydrate or protein (see 'Energy value of food' in Chapter 5).

Sources of fat in the diet

VEGETABLE SOURCES

In plants, fats are formed from carbohydrate. Thus, when seeds such as sunflower and cottonseed ripen, their starch content decreases as their fat content rises. Oilseeds such as these and peanuts, coconuts, rapeseeds, palm kernels and soya beans contain about 20–40% oil and are among the chief sources of oil for the manufacture of cooking oils and fat. The fat content of flour and other cereal products (apart from oatmeal) is generally low, as is the fat content of most vegetables and fruits. The proportion of each fatty acid present varies from plant to plant, and is also quite variable within a species. Vegetable seeds are among the principal sources of omega-6 polyunsaturated fatty acids.

ANIMAL SOURCES

Animals, including humans, store excess energy almost entirely in deposits of fat, the amount of which is very variable. As in plants, this fat can be made from carbohydrate, but the dietary carbohydrate can be starch, sugar or even (in cows and sheep) cellulose. Animals also lay down fat from their dietary fat; in this case, the fatty acid composition reflects that of the diet, except for ruminants whose digestive processes normally make the fatty acids more saturated.

Fish such as salmon, mackerel, sardines, trout and herring are *oily fish*. The proportion of fat in them varies with the season of the year. Fish oils are the principal sources of long-chain omega-3 polyunsaturated fatty acids. *White fish* such as cod, haddock, plaice, pollock and coley contain little fat except in the liver. Some types of shellfish, such as mussels, oysters, squid and crab, are also good sources of long-chain omega-3 fatty acids, but they do not contain as much as oily fish. Fish liver is also a rich source of vitamins A and D.

The fat content of many foods, especially meat, varies widely. Average values for a selection of foods are shown in Table 4.

Table 4. Average fat content of foods, uncooked (edible portion)

	Fat (g/100 g)		Fat (g/100 g)
Milk, whole	3.9	Cod, filleted	0.7
Milk, semi-skimmed	1.7	Mackerel	16.1[b]
Milk, 1%	1.0[a]	Tuna, canned in oil, drained	9.0
Milk, skimmed	0.2	Tuna, canned in brine, drained	0.6
Cream, double	53.7	Butter	82.2
Yogurt, low-fat, fruit	1.1	Fat spread (62–75% fat), not polyunsaturated[a]	73.2
Ice cream, non-dairy, soft scoop[a]	7.7	Reduced-fat spread (41–62% fat), not polyunsaturated[a]	60.6
Cheese, Cheddar	34.9	Low-fat spread (26–39% fat), polyunsaturated[a]	36.9
Cheese, Edam	26.0	Vegetable oils	99.9
Cheese, cottage, plain	4.3	Lard and dripping	99.0
Eggs	11.2	Ghee, made from vegetable oil[c]	100.0
Beef, stewing steak	6.4	Potatoes, old	0.2
Lamb, leg, lean and fat	12.3	Chips, takeaway	8.4[d]
Pork, chop, lean and fat	21.7	Potato chips, oven-baked[a]	4.9
Bacon, streaky	23.6	Peanut butter, smooth	51.8
Sausages, pork	25.0	Bread, white	1.6
Ham	3.3	Bread, wholemeal	2.5
Beefburgers	24.7	Porridge oats	7.8
Chicken, dark and light meat	2.1	Biscuits, digestive, plain	21.3
Turkey, dark and light meat	1.6		

The main sources of fat in the diet are meat and meat products, cereals and cereal products (including biscuits, buns, cakes and pastries), and milk and milk products.

Source: unless otherwise stated, *McCance and Widdowson's Composition of Foods Integrated Dataset* (COFIDS), published by the Food Standards Agency, 2008.
[a] Source: average from product's label information.
[b] Levels range from 6 g to 23 g fat per 100 g.
[c] Source: *Nutrient Analysis of a Range of Processed Foods with Particular Reference to Trans Fatty Acids – Summary Report*, Department of Health, 2011.
[d] Content variable and depends on a number of factors relating to preparation.

Throughout the world, the amount of fat in the diet tends to be higher in affluent than in poor countries and, within poorer countries, it tends to be higher in the wealthier families. Less than 10% of the energy value of the diet is derived from fat in many of the world's poorest countries. In most developed countries, including the UK, fat provided about 40% of energy for many years, but this has fallen to about 35% in recent years.

The amount of dietary energy derived from saturated fatty acids has been falling in the UK and the average proportion of polyunsaturated to saturated fatty acids (the 'P/S ratio') in the whole diet is about 0.5:1, having risen from about 0.2:1 in 1970.

Health aspects of fats

Diets in poor countries are often low in energy, and the World Health Organization (WHO) has recommended an increase in fat intakes in such situations. More affluent populations need to moderate their fat intake to prevent an excess of energy intake over expenditure leading to weight gain, and particularly to decrease the saturated fatty acid content of their diets as a means of reducing the risk of heart disease.

To ensure that sufficient quantities of essential fatty acids are present in our diets, the Department of Health advises that linoleic and alpha-linolenic acids should provide at least 1% and 0.2%, respectively, of total dietary energy. At the same time, to encourage a decrease in total fat and saturated fatty acid intake, the Government recommends a set of average values for the UK population to achieve in terms of the proportion of dietary energy to be consumed as different types of fatty acid (see 'Heart disease', below).

HEART DISEASE

In the UK, in both men and women, *coronary heart disease* (CHD) is a serious health problem. The risk of heart disease is increased by various factors such as smoking, high blood pressure and raised levels of cholesterol in the blood.

All, except smoking, are influenced by the diet. Obesity can affect both blood pressure and blood cholesterol, and is discussed in Chapter 5. Blood pressure can also be increased by excessive intakes of alcohol (see 'Alcohol' in Chapter 11). It may also be raised by high intakes of sodium. High saturated fatty acid intakes can lead to increased blood cholesterol levels, particularly in susceptible individuals.

Cholesterol is mostly made in the liver and is carried in the blood by two proteins – *low-density lipoprotein* (LDL) and *high-density lipoprotein* (HDL). LDL cholesterol is considered to be undesirable because if it increases to a high level in the blood it can be deposited on the walls of the blood vessels, thereby helping to form 'plaques' which may eventually lead to narrowing of the arteries that supply the heart with blood. This is more likely to happen if the LDL is modified chemically by oxidation (see 'Vitamins and antioxidant activity' in Chapter 8). If the arteries become blocked completely with further plaques or by a blood clot, the blood supply to the heart is interrupted leading to a heart attack and, in severe cases, to death. HDL cholesterol is desirable as it is a means of transporting cholesterol from parts of the body where there is too much of it, to the liver where it is disposed of. Replacing saturated with monounsaturated or polyunsaturated fatty acids in the diet can lower LDL cholesterol in the blood. The cholesterol in food has a smaller effect on blood cholesterol than do saturated fatty acids, but the effect varies in different people. The liver can compensate for changes in dietary cholesterol by changing the amount of cholesterol it makes.

The long-chain omega-3 polyunsaturated fatty acids in fish oils may help to prevent heart disease by decreasing the tendency of the blood to clot and keeping the heart cell membranes stable. Current recommendations are that the average intake of long-chain omega-3 polyunsaturated fatty acids for the population should increase to 0.45 g/day (SACN/COT, *Advice on Fish Consumption: Benefits & Risks*, 2004). This could be achieved by consuming two portions of fish a week, one of which is oily. Recent evidence suggests that the short-chain omega-3 polyunsaturated fatty acids found in vegetable sources (see 'Unsaturated fatty acids' earlier in this chapter) may not have the same beneficial effects as the long-chain omega-3 polyunsaturated fatty acids found in oily fish.

In order to reduce heart disease, the Government advises that on average, total fat and saturated fatty acids should provide not more than 35% and 10%, respectively, of dietary energy intake; omega-6 polyunsaturated fatty acids should continue to provide about 6% of energy; and the average intake of dietary cholesterol should not increase. Between 1986 and 2008/10, total fat and saturated fatty acid contributions to food energy intake fell from about 43% to 35% and from about 18% to 13%, respectively. In spite of these encouraging trends, the top 2.5% of adults surveyed in 2008/10 were getting nearly 50% of their energy from fat. Many people therefore still need to be encouraged to make substantial changes to their diets, particularly if the average dietary intake of saturated fatty acids by the UK population is to decrease to the desired level.

Trans fatty acids have been shown to raise blood cholesterol levels and increase the risk of coronary heart disease. The adverse effect of *trans* fatty acids is similar to that of saturated fatty acids (found in animal fats and dairy produce). However, the quantity of *trans* fatty acids from partially hydrogenated vegetable oils (HVO) in the average diet is much lower than that of saturated fatty acids. In 2007, SACN published its review on the evidence regarding the health effects of *trans* fatty acids in order to determine whether current population dietary advice on *trans* fatty acids should be revised. SACN endorsed the recommendation made in 1994 by the Committee on Medical Aspects of Food Policy (COMA) that the average *trans* fatty acid intake should not exceed 2% of food energy, since there is currently no firm scientific basis for its revision (SACN, *Update on Trans Fatty Acids and Health, 2007*). The Food Standards Agency endorsed SACN's recommendation and noted that the UK food industry had responded to customers' concerns about HVOs and had taken voluntary action to reduce *trans* fatty acid levels in vegetable oils (and in processed foods that use vegetable oils) to a minimum. Actions such as this, taken across the food industry, have been successful in reducing *trans* fatty acid intakes.

Current average dietary intakes of *trans* fatty acids are lower than the 1994 COMA recommendation of about 2% of total energy, or no more than 5 g per day. In 1986/87, average intakes were 2% of total energy and, by 2008/10, this had reduced to an average intake of 0.7% of total energy.

CANCER

In its report *Nutritional Aspects of the Development of Cancer*, published in 1998, COMA concluded that there was not sufficiently strong evidence linking total fat intakes to the development of cancers to make any specific recommendations. A more recent report by the World Cancer Research Fund (WCRF) reported that there was limited evidence to suggest that high total fat intake increases the risk of cancer (World Cancer Research Fund, 2007).

4   Proteins

All proteins are compounds of carbon, hydrogen and oxygen but, unlike carbohydrates and fats, they always contain nitrogen as well. Most proteins also contain sulphur (which is present in only a few amino acids) and some contain phosphorus. Protein must be provided in the diet for the growth and repair of the body but any excess is used to provide energy.

Proteins consist of chains of hundreds or even thousands of *amino acid* units. Only about 20 different amino acids are used but the number of ways in which they can be arranged is almost infinite. It is the specific and unique sequence of these units that gives each protein its characteristic structural and enzymatic properties.

Amino acids

It is convenient to divide amino acids into two types: *indispensable* and *dispensable*. Indispensable amino acids cannot be made in the body, at least in amounts sufficient for health, and must therefore be present in the diet. Dispensable amino acids are equally necessary as components of all proteins in the body; they differ only in that it is possible for them to be made from any excess of certain other amino acids in the diet. The eight amino acids which are indispensable for adults are:

Isoleucine	Phenylalanine
Leucine	Threonine
Lysine	Tryptophan
Methionine	Valine

A further amino acid, histidine, is also indispensable for the rapidly growing infant. The remaining – dispensable – amino acids which are found in proteins are:

Alanine	Glutamine
Arginine	Glycine
Aspartic acid	Proline
Asparagine	Serine
Cysteine	Tyrosine
Glutamic acid	

Animal and vegetable proteins

The overall proportions of amino acids in cereals, nuts and seeds, potatoes, legumes (such as peas and beans) or any single vegetable differ from those needed by humans.

These proteins are therefore said to have low biological values because the quality of a protein depends on its ability to supply all the indispensable amino acids in the amounts needed. Most animal proteins (from meat, fish, milk, cheese and eggs) have a high biological value. The reason for this is that humans are part of the animal kingdom; the proteins of animals are therefore more like ours and can be utilised by us with the minimum of waste. In effect, animals have pre-selected, with varying degrees of efficiency, the plant amino acids which they and we need and have burned up the remainder for energy (see 'Proteins' in Chapter 6).

Although no single food provides all the amino acids needed by humans, mixtures of different foods complement each other and result in a greatly enhanced provision of the range of indispensable amino acids. This means that, even among those who eat little or no animal protein, deficiency is rarely a problem provided that they have enough food to eat. Nevertheless, the nutritional advantages of foods of animal origin over those of vegetable origin lie, in practice, more in the presence of associated nutrients such as vitamin B_{12}, iron and retinol (pre-formed vitamin A) than in the protein.

Because there is no way in which excess amino acids can be stored in the body, they will be most efficiently used if a complete assortment is supplied to the body at about the same time. This can be achieved by eating a mixed diet at each meal and ensuring that the total energy content of the diet is also adequate. Mixtures of vegetable protein foods, such as beans on toast,

Table 5. Proportion of some indispensable amino acids in selected proteins

	Lysine (%)	Methionine (%)	Tryptophan (%)
Milk, cow's	8.4	2.9	1.5
Eggs	6.2	3.1	1.8
Beef	9.1	2.7	1.3
Fish, cod	9.8	2.9	1.1
Lentils	6.7	0.7	0.9
Peanuts	4.0	1.3	1.3
Wheat flour	2.7	1.8	1.3
Rice[a]	3.3	1.8	1.2

[a] Some amino acids can be increased by genetic breeding.

or of animal and vegetable foods, such as tuna pasta, bread and cheese, and breakfast cereals with milk, therefore have a sound physiological basis.

Novel sources of protein

Animals convert plant protein into their own muscle slowly and inefficiently (only 5–10% being retained). There is also a demand for sources of protein that are suitable for vegetarians. Some people may also want to limit their fat intake and eat protein-rich foods which are lower in fat.

As a response to these factors, products providing alternatives to meat have been developed by the food industry. In addition to those described below, soya-based foods such as tofu (bean curd) and miso (fermented bean paste), which are traditionally used in Far Eastern cuisine, are now widely available in the UK.

Textured vegetable proteins have been developed by concentrating or isolating the proteins from a number of plants, especially soya beans, and converting them directly into products such as soya 'mince' or soya 'chunks'. If suitably fortified with the most important vitamins and minerals which meat provides, such as thiamin (vitamin B_1), riboflavin (vitamin B_2), vitamin B_{12}, iron and zinc, these products can be used instead of meat and may be acceptable to vegetarians. (Vegetarian diets are discussed in Chapter 13.)

Mycoprotein is another product which can be used as an alternative to meat. One type, made from a particular fungal micro-organism and complying with a particular specification, has been cleared for human consumption. It is manufactured commercially (Quorn®) and is produced by growing the fungal micro-organism in a fermenter and 'harvesting' the product. This is heat-processed, seasoned and cooked, and then sliced, diced or shredded. It can be used instead of meat in recipes and is also incorporated into a range of retail products such as pies and prepared meals.

It is also possible to utilise other micro-organisms such as yeast, or otherwise inedible leaves, to provide protein-rich foods. Given that such foodstuffs would have a novel composition, they would be subject to a stringent pre-market safety assessment.

Protein as a source of energy

The amount and type of protein in the diet will not exactly balance the requirements for growth, repair and maintenance: there will always be excesses of some amino acids, and usually an excess of total protein. These will be converted into glucose in the liver or will be directly oxidised to provide heat and energy. Furthermore, if the total energy available from the diet is insufficient to meet demands, this oxidation of the amino acids tends to take preference over their more fundamental use for rebuilding proteins. This is why it is important to ensure that diets contain sufficient energy in the form of carbohydrate and fat before proteins are added, for only then can these proteins be properly utilised for purposes which no other nutrient can fulfil.

Other health aspects of proteins

Newborn infants can absorb some proteins intact from their mothers' milk, including antibodies which provide protection from infection.

Susceptible individuals can react adversely to certain food proteins known as allergens: for example, those with coeliac disease react to gluten and others may react to cow's milk protein and nut proteins. Most allergic reactions to food are mild, but, if someone has a food allergy, they can react to tiny amounts of the food they are sensitive to, with fatal results in rare cases.

Certain beans, including red kidney beans and soya beans, contain proteins that are harmful unless thoroughly cooked in moist heat such as boiling water.

Properties of proteins

Some proteins dissolve in water and some in salt water. Some are insoluble and this is exploited in the preparation of wheat gluten by washing other proteins and starch from a wheat dough to improve the baking quality of wheat produced in the UK. The separated starch is used for producing glucose syrups.

The action of heat on proteins is complex. Proteins such as the albumen in egg white harden or coagulate irreversibly when heated, but are still readily digested. Individual amino acids are little affected by normal cooking procedures, although some of the lysine may react with carbohydrates in the food (e.g. in the baking of bread) and methionine may sometimes be chemically reduced. In the preparation of gelatin, however, when connective tissue from meat is boiled for many hours, all the tryptophan is destroyed.

The complex *Maillard reactions* between amino acids (usually lysine) and sugars in foods result in the attractive golden brown colour of crisps or chips and also in the formation of certain desirable food flavours. However, they may also give rise to the brown discoloration which sometimes develops during prolonged storage of concentrated or dried milk or dehydrated vegetables.

Sources of protein in the diet

About one-third of the protein in the average UK diet comes from plant sources and two-thirds from animal sources. The amount of protein in nuts and dried peas and beans is very high – about the same as in meat, fish and cheese. The proportion is reduced when these pulses are soaked in water but they remain an excellent source of protein. Cereals are also rich in protein; indeed, wheat, maize and rice are the main sources of protein for many people in the world. The amount of protein in roots and tubers is small but, as potatoes are eaten in quantity in the UK, they provide useful amounts. Many green and leafy vegetables contain some protein but, because they are often eaten in small amounts or infrequently by some sectors of the UK population, they make little contribution to average protein intakes. The concentration of protein in selected foods is shown in Table 6.

Table 6. Average protein content of selected foods, uncooked[a]

	Protein (g/100 g)		Protein (g/100 g)
Milk, cow's, whole	3.3	Beans, red kidney, dry	22.1
Milk, cow's, skimmed	3.4	Soya tofu, steamed	8.1
Soya non-dairy alternative to milk, unsweetened	2.4	Quorn® (mycoprotein)	16.1
		Peanuts, plain	25.6
Cheese, Cheddar	25.4	Peas, fresh	6.9
Cheese, feta	15.6	Sweetcorn, canned	2.9
Beef, stewing, lean and fat	22.1	Potatoes, old	2.1
Lamb, leg, lean and fat	19.0	Apples, eating	0.4
Pork, chop, lean and fat	18.6	Bread, white	7.9
Sausages, pork	11.9	Bread, wholemeal	9.4
Chicken, dark and light meat	22.3	Flour, white[b]	9.1
Turkey, dark and light meat	22.6	Cornflakes[c]	7.1
Cod, fillets	18.3	Porridge oats[c]	11.0
Prawns	17.6	Spaghetti, white, dried, cooked[d]	4.4
Baked beans, reheated	5.2	Rice, white Basmati, cooked[b]	2.8

The main sources of protein in the diet are meat and meat products, cereals and cereal products, and milk and milk products.

Source: unless otherwise stated, *McCance and Widdowson's Composition of Foods Integrated Dataset* (COFIDS) published by the Food Standards Agency, 2008.

[a] Unless otherwise stated.

[b] Source: *Nutrient Survey of Flours and Grains – Analytical Report*, Food Standards Agency, 2005.

[c] Source: *Nutrient Survey of Breakfast Cereals – Analytical Report*, Food Standards Agency, 2004.

[d] Source: *Nutrient Survey of Pasta and Pasta Sauces – Analytical Report*, Food Standards Agency, 2004.

5   Energy needs and food consumption

Uses of energy

To maintain life, our cells and tissues need a constant supply of energy, which is obtained from the breakdown and oxidation of three nutrients (carbohydrate, protein and fat) either derived from food or released from the body's stores. Energy can also be obtained from the oxidation of alcohol.

Broadly, energy is needed for three purposes:

* to maintain basic bodily processes
* for physical activity
* for growth and development during infancy, childhood and pregnancy, and for milk production during lactation.

ENERGY EXPENDITURE

The amount of energy needed depends on the amount of energy expended by the body on a daily basis. This broadly has two components: the *basal metabolic rate* (BMR) and *physical activity*, plus for pregnant women, infants and children, extra energy is needed for growth and development and, for women who are lactating, additional energy is needed for milk production.

In addition, small amounts of energy are expended in eating, digesting and absorbing nutrients from food, and in maintaining body temperature.

Basal metabolic rate

Energy is required to maintain the basic metabolic function of the cells and the physiological function of the body which are essential for life. The amount of energy needed to maintain these basic functions can be measured in people lying down at rest, after all food has been digested and absorbed, in a thermal neutral environment.[5] BMR is dependent on body size, age and sex; BMR increases as body size increases; children have lower values than adults; and women generally have lower values than men. The lower BMR seen in women is not only because of their generally smaller size but also because their bodies contain proportionally less lean tissue and more fat than men's bodies; lean tissue is more metabolically active than fat. The proportion of lean tissue in the body also declines in old age. This means that BMR declines in old age even if

---

[5] A thermal neutral environment is an environment created by any method or apparatus that maintains the normal body temperature to minimise oxygen consumption and calorific expenditure, or an environment that keeps body temperature at an optimum point at which the least amount of oxygen is consumed for metabolism.

weight remains stable. Obese adults have higher BMRs than lean adults – this is because when people gain excess weight they gain both extra lean and fat tissue.

BMR is the largest component of most individuals' energy expenditure and energy requirements. It typically accounts for 40–70% of total energy expenditure depending on age and lifestyle.

Average BMR values for the two sexes in different age groups can be estimated from body weight using the Henry equations shown in Appendix 2.

Physical activity

Physical activity increases energy expenditure. This is because extra energy is required to sustain muscle contractions and for movement.

Physical activity encompasses a wide range of behaviours including sitting, standing, walking and planned exercise. It also includes spontaneous activity associated with daily living, changes in posture and fidgeting. The energy expended in each activity depends on its intensity and duration.

Physical activity-related energy expenditure usually accounts for between 25% and 50% of an individual's total 24-hour energy expenditure. In unusual circumstances, it can reach 75%.

There is evidence to suggest that regular planned exercise, or recreational or work-related physical activity, reduces the risk of several diseases, including cardiovascular disease, and improves musculoskeletal health. For this reason, the UK Chief Medical Officers recommend increasing daily physical activity and minimising time spent being sedentary (i.e. sitting). The recommendations for each life stage are given in the report *Start Active, Stay Active* (Chief Medical Officers, 2011) where physical activity guidelines cover early years, children and young people, adults, and older adults. These are the first UK-wide physical activity guidelines and the first to cover early years (under-5s). Sedentary behaviour was also considered as there is now evidence that it is an independent risk factor for ill health. The guidance has a renewed focus on being active every day and spells out the recommended minimum levels of activity for each age group. For example, adults (19–64 years old) should aim to be active daily. Over a week, activity should add up to at least 150 minutes (2½ hours) of moderate-intensity activity in bouts of 10 minutes or more – it is suggested that one way to approach this is to do 30 minutes on at least 5 days a week.

Most people in the UK do not undertake regular exercise or take part in manual work. In 2008, the Health Survey for England reported that 39% of men and 29% of women were achieving the previous physical activity recommendations as set out in the report *At Least Five a Week* (Chief Medical

Officer, 2004). Most people would therefore benefit from increasing the amount of exercise they do.

Growth

Physical growth involves increasing body and organ size. This does not happen at a uniform rate or in a uniform way throughout infancy and childhood, e.g. in a newborn baby the brain represents 12% of body weight but in an adult it is about 2%. During growth, energy is used to synthesise new tissue and is also deposited in new tissues.

The energy required for growth is highest in the first 3 months of life when it accounts for about 35% of energy requirements; by 12 months it falls to about 3%. It remains low until mid-adolescence when it increases slightly and then is very small by the late teenage years.

Pregnancy and lactation

During pregnancy, energy is required for placental and fetal growth and for growth of maternal tissues, e.g. the uterus, breast and adipose tissues. In addition, there is also an increase in the energy cost of movement because of increases in the mother's weight, particularly over 25 weeks' gestation. However, some of this cost is offset by the mother becoming less active.

During lactation, energy is required to synthesise milk. Fat stored by the mother during pregnancy contributes to the energy cost of this.

ENERGY REQUIREMENTS

Energy requirements can be calculated from long-term measures of total energy expenditure (TEE).[6] In the absence of growth, pregnancy or lactation, TEE is primarily the sum of daily energy used to maintain BMR and the energy expended in physical activity. TEE can be expressed as a multiple of BMR and the physical activity level (PAL).

In the past, it was thought that by recording and adding together all daily activities and their duration, you could, using the energy cost of each activity, predict someone's 24-hour energy expenditure. This is now known not to be the case; modern methods of measuring TEE show that this factorial method underestimates PAL. On a population level, TEE can be reasonably estimated using an average PAL value of 1.63. This can be applied to men and women and is independent of body size. This PAL value can be used for all adults

---

[6] The use of doubly labelled water (DLW) is a method that provides data on the calories a person uses over a fixed period. It is unbiased by errors, such as forgetting activities, and monitors all activities, not just structured exercise. If a person is maintaining their weight, the number of calories they use over a period of time is, on average, equal to the number of calories they have taken in.

Table 7. Estimated Average Requirement for energy for UK adults[7]

	EAR MJ/day (kcal/day)	
Age range (years)	Men	Women
19–24	11.6 (2772)	9.1 (2175)
25–34	11.5 (2749)	9.1 (2175)
35–44	11.0 (2629)	8.8 (2103)
45–54	10.8 (2581)	8.8 (2103)
55–64	10.8 (2581)	8.7 (2079)
65–74	9.8 (2342)	8.0 (1912)
75+	9.6 (2294)	7.7 (1840)
All adults	10.9 (2605)	8.7 (2079)

Source: Scientific Advisory Committee on Nutrition, *Dietary Reference Values for Energy 2011.*

unless they are very active or activity has been impaired through ill health. When mobility is reduced, such as in extreme old age, PAL value declines.

In the UK, Dietary Reference Values (DRVs) for food energy are based on the Estimated Average Requirement (EAR). The EAR is an estimate of the average requirement for energy or a nutrient. In adults, the EAR for energy has been set at the level of energy intake required to achieve or maintain a healthy body weight at current physical activity levels.[8] Any sustained imbalance between energy intake and expenditure will lead to progressive gain or loss in body weight. Table 7 gives the EAR values for adults. For population groups who are overweight, the EAR values are lower than the energy intakes required to maintain weight. Consequently, matching energy intake to the EAR values will facilitate weight reduction towards the healthy body weight range. Chapter 9 gives EAR values for different life stages.

These values are intended for groups in health and are not for individuals. For people with specific needs, health professionals can calculate BMR using the Henry prediction equations (in Appendix 2) based on healthy body weights for height and using the appropriate PAL value.

Obesity

The prevalence of overweight and obesity in England, Scotland, Northern Ireland and Wales is shown in Table 8.

---

[7] EAR values were calculated using current average English heights (2009).
[8] During infancy and childhood, the requirement also has to meet the needs for healthy growth and development, while during pregnancy and lactation the requirement must meet the needs for carrying a healthy baby and supporting adequate lactation.

If individuals eat or drink foods which provide more energy than they use up in their daily activities, some of the fat, protein, carbohydrate or alcohol will be converted into body fat. Any kind of food or drink can therefore contribute to excess calories if the quantity consumed of the product, or the overall diet, results in energy intake in excess of expenditure. Some foods, however, are more concentrated sources of energy than others. These tend to be foods containing little water and a high proportion of fat, such as butter, fat spreads, fatty meat, fried foods, ice cream, cakes and biscuits. High palatability of foods can also encourage excessive amounts to be eaten. Obesity may occur even if energy intake is only slightly greater than output if it is consistently so over a long period of time.

Table 8. Prevalence of overweight and obesity in England, Scotland, Northern Ireland and Wales

	Overweight (%)	Obese (%)
England		
Boys (2–15 years)	29	15
Girls (2–15 years)	30	16
Adults (men, 16+ years)	66	22
Adults (women, 16+ years)	57	24
Scotland		
Boys (2–15 years)	15	16
Girls (2–15 years)	16	13
Adults (men, 16+ years)	68	27
Adults (women, 16+ years)	62	29
Wales		
Boys (2–15 years)	23	16
Girls (2–15 years)	16	18
Adults (men, 16+ years)	40	22
Adults (women, 16+ years)	31	21
Northern Ireland		
Boys (2–15 years)	38	20
Girls (2–15 years)	31	15
Adults (men, 16+ years)	64	25
Adults (women, 16+ years)	59	24

Source: *Health Survey for England – 2010; Scottish Health Survey 2010; Welsh Health Survey 2009; and Northern Ireland Health and Social Wellbeing Survey 2005/06.*

The broad range of weights found for people at different heights has been used to construct the chart shown in Figure 1. This can be used to indicate whether an individual is an acceptable weight for their height. The body mass index (BMI), calculated as weight in kilograms divided by the square of the height in metres, is also used to assess the degree to which a person is overweight. A BMI of 18.5 or below is underweight; 18.5–24.9 is desirable; 25–29.9 is overweight; and 30 or above is considered obese.[9] A BMI of 40 or more is considered morbidly obese. Whereas BMI is a measure of general obesity, waist circumference and waist-to-hip ratios provide measures of central obesity, which has a stronger relationship with the risk of chronic diseases than does general obesity or BMI. Most people underestimate the amount of food they eat, and overestimate how active they are. The majority of the UK population need to eat less and get more active.

Eating disorders

While the number of overweight and obese individuals remains high, there are also concerns about an increase in reporting of eating disorders, particularly in young people. Overcoming eating disorders is a specialist area. There are reputable UK-based organisations that are contactable for information and help for eating disorders – for example, Beat (www.b-eat.co.uk). Care should be taken that referrals are to a specialist eating disorders dietitian via the British Dietetic Association (www.bda.uk.com) or through a local health professional.

Energy value of food

The energy provided by the fat, protein and carbohydrate in food, and by alcohol, can be measured. Taking into account the small proportions of these macronutrients which are not absorbed into the body:

1 g of dietary carbohydrate (calculated as monosaccharides) provides	16 kJ or 3.75 kcal
1 g of dietary fat provides	37 kJ or 9 kcal
1 g of dietary protein provides	17 kJ or 4 kcal
1 g of alcohol provides	29 kJ or 7 kcal
1 g of dietary fibre provides	8 kJ or 2 kcal

Polyols[10] also provide energy, and small amounts of energy can be derived from organic acids such as citric acid in fruits and drinks and acetic acid in vinegar, with each gram providing approximately 13 kJ (3 kcal). The micronutrients (vitamins and minerals) and water do not provide energy.

---

[9] A quick BMI calculator can be found at www.nhs.uk/livewell/loseweight/pages/bodymassindex.aspx.
[10] Polyols are sugar alcohols commonly added to foods such as sugar-free desserts and confectionery because of their lower calorific content than sugars.

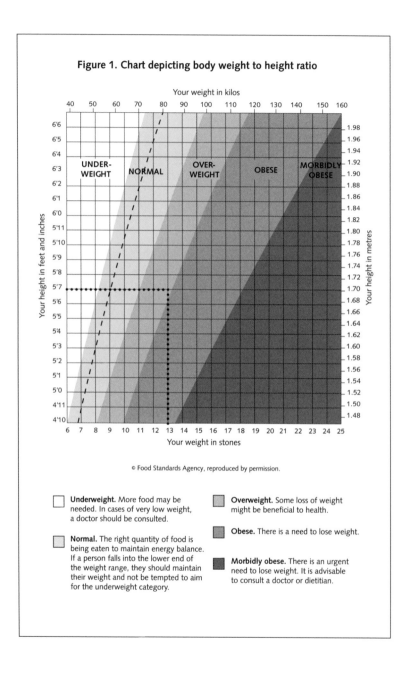

Figure 1. Chart depicting body weight to height ratio

© Food Standards Agency, reproduced by permission.

Underweight. More food may be needed. In cases of very low weight, a doctor should be consulted.

Normal. The right quantity of food is being eaten to maintain energy balance. If a person falls into the lower end of the weight range, they should maintain their weight and not be tempted to aim for the underweight category.

Overweight. Some loss of weight might be beneficial to health.

Obese. There is a need to lose weight.

Morbidly obese. There is an urgent need to lose weight. It is advisable to consult a doctor or dietitian.

The energy value of any food can be calculated when the proportions of the nutrients in it are known. For example, if 100 g of potato crisps contain 49.3 g of carbohydrate, 37.6 g of fat and 5.6 g of protein, the energy content is calculated as follows:

Carbohydrate	49.3 × 16	=	788.8 kJ
Fat	37.6 × 37	=	1391.2 kJ
Protein	5.6 × 17	=	95.2 kJ
Total energy content			2275.2 kJ
Or			
Carbohydrate	49.3 × 3.75	=	184.9 kcal
Fat	37.6 × 9	=	338.4 kcal
Protein	5.6 × 4	=	22.4 kcal
Total energy content			545.7 kcal

It is misleading, however, to imply that energy values can be obtained with such precision, and could be rounded to 2275 kJ or 546 kcal. But when performing further calculations such as for the proportion of energy derived from fat, it is wiser to use the detailed figures and round off only at the end (see also Appendix 4):

(1391.2/2275.2) × 100 = 61.15 or 61% of energy from fat

Sources of energy in the diet

Nearly all the weight of any food is made up of protein, fat and carbohydrate together with water. Foods that contain large amounts of water, such as salad vegetables and clear soups, will contain little protein, fat or carbohydrate, and consequently will provide little energy. In contrast, dry foods such as breakfast cereals, and foods rich in fat and sugar are concentrated sources of energy. The main sources of energy in the UK diet are cereal and cereal products, which provide on average 29% of energy intake, and include foods such as bread, breakfast cereals, biscuits and cakes. Bread alone provides 11%. Meat and meat products provide 17% of energy intake, drinks including alcoholic drinks provide 11%, milk and milk products provide 9%, while potatoes provide 6%. The energy (and water) contents of selected foods are shown in Table 9.

Table 9. Average energy value and water content of selected foods (edible portion)

	Energy		Water
	kJ/100 g	kcal/100 g	(g/100 g)
Milk, whole	274	66	88
Milk, semi-skimmed	195	46	90
Milk, skimmed	136	32	91
Cheese, Cheddar	1725	416	37
Yogurt, low-fat, fruit	331	78	79
Beef, stewing steak (lean and fat), stewed	852	203	59
Bacon, streaky, fried	1389	335	45
Chicken, roast, meat, average	742	177	65
Cod, fillet, baked	408	96	77
Fish fingers, grilled	838	200	56
Sardines, canned in oil, drained	918	220	59
Eggs, chicken, whole, boiled	612	147	75
Butter	3059	744	15
Reduced-fat spread (41–62%), not polyunsaturated[a]	2249	547	37
Vegetable oil, blended	3696	899	0
Sugar, white	1680	394	0
Courgettes, boiled	81	19	93
Lettuce	59	14	95
Carrots, old, boiled	100	24	91
Potatoes, old, boiled	306	72	80
Chips, fried in commercial oil, takeaway[a]	902	214	51
Apples, eating, raw	199	47	85
Bananas	403	95	75
Oranges	158	37	86
Raisins	1159	272	13
Bread, white	931	219	39
Bread, wholemeal	922	217	41
Biscuits, chocolate, fully coated[b]	2120	506	1.9
Cornflakes[c]	1526	358	3
Crispbread, rye	1312	308	6
Lager	121	29	93
Wine, white, medium	308	74	86
Spirits	919	222	68

Source: unless otherwise stated, *McCance and Widdowson's Composition of Foods Integrated Dataset* (COFIDS) published by the Food Standards Agency, 2008.
[a] Source: Calculated from *Nutrient Analysis of a Range of Processed Foods with Particular Reference to Trans Fatty Acids – Summary Report*, Department of Health, 2011.
[b] Source: *Nutrient Analysis Survey of Biscuits, Buns, Cakes and Pastries – Summary Report*, Department of Health, 2011.
[c] Source: *Nutrient Survey of Breakfast Cereals – Analytical Report*, Food Standards Agency, 2004.

6 Digestion of food and absorption of major nutrients

Food has been defined as any solid or liquid which, when swallowed, can provide the body with energy, or material for growth and repair, or certain substances for regulating body processes. However, it is clear that almost any food can be recovered virtually intact from the stomach if vomiting occurs soon after it is eaten. Therefore, food cannot really be said to have entered the body until it has been:

* *digested*, i.e. physically and chemically broken down into simple component parts which can be
* *absorbed*, i.e. passed through the walls of the digestive tract into the blood (or lymph).

Appetite and flavour

When and how much we eat is determined by a number of complex factors. The sensation of *hunger* occurs when levels of glucose and fatty acids in the blood are reduced and the stomach is empty. But people, especially overweight and obese people, do not eat only when they are hungry or stop eating when they cease to feel hungry. *Appetite* is a sensation which relates to the smell and taste of particular foods and their ingredients, and is influenced by the surroundings, habits and emotional state of the individual, all of which can also increase or decrease the flow of saliva and other digestive juices. Thus, where there is freedom of choice, more attractive foods are likely to be eaten in preference to others, and it can be seen that good cooking and pleasant surroundings are important in nutrition. It should, however, be noted that some appetising foods such as confectionery products can be relatively low in many nutrients, and that unappetising foods can provide nourishment.

The process of digestion

Although cooking softens meat fibres and the cellulose of plant materials, and gelatinises starch, digestion only begins when food enters the mouth and digestive tract. The digestive tract, illustrated in grey in Figure 2, is basically a tube about 5 m long.

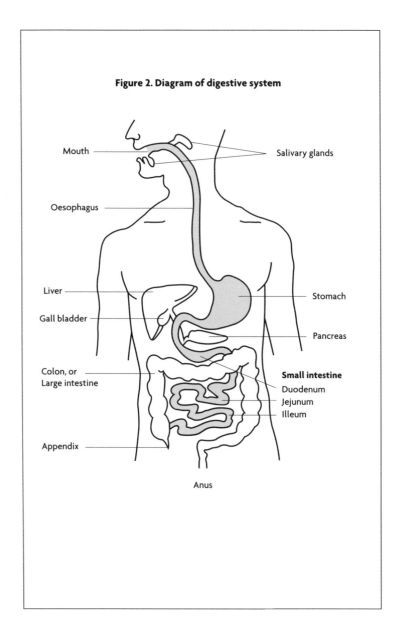

Figure 2. Diagram of digestive system

IN THE MOUTH

- Food is mechanically broken down by chewing. It is therefore important to have healthy teeth and gums.
- The food is mixed and moistened with saliva.

Saliva comes from salivary glands under the tongue and at the back of the mouth. It is usually present in the mouth but its flow is increased by the smell and taste of food and by chewing. It helps the food to be swallowed and also contains an enzyme, salivary *amylase*, which converts a small amount of the starch in food into maltose.

IN THE STOMACH

After the mixture of food particles and saliva has been swallowed – the final voluntary action – it takes about three seconds to pass down the oesophagus into the stomach, where:

- the food is mixed with gastric juice
- more mechanical breakdown results from stomach contractions.

Gastric juice is produced by the lining of the stomach in response to the same stimuli that increase saliva flow. Normally, about 3 litres are produced each day. It has three important constituents:

- the enzyme *pepsin*, which begins the digestion of protein
- about 0.2–0.4% *hydrochloric acid* which destroys most of the bacteria that could be present in food and water, and provides the acidic conditions necessary for the pepsin to be active
- *'intrinsic factor'*, which is necessary for subsequent absorption of vitamin B_{12}.

Speed of digestion in the stomach

The main function of the stomach is to act as a reservoir: digestion still proceeds if the stomach is completely removed. Food normally remains in the stomach for two to four hours before the resulting semi-liquid mixture (*chyme*) is passed little by little into the small intestine. The exact time taken for food to pass depends on many different factors including the type of food eaten: foods rich in carbohydrate (such as rice) pass most quickly and those rich in fat (such as cheese) most slowly.

IN THE SMALL INTESTINE

Despite its name, the small intestine is the longest part of the digestive tract. It is about 3 m in length (although because of the loss of tone and elasticity, it is found to be 7–8 m long after death), compared with about 1 m for the large intestine. It is, however, only 2–4 cm in diameter compared with 6 cm for the latter. The first distinct part of the small intestine is called the *duodenum*; the remainder consists of the *jejunum* and finally the *ileum*. It is in the small intestine that the main part of both digestion and absorption takes place.

In the duodenum, the digestive juices are from three sources:

- *Bile* is produced in the liver and stored in the gall bladder. Bile salts emulsify fat into microscopic droplets so that it can be digested.
- *Pancreatic* juice, from the pancreas, is an alkaline liquid which neutralises the acidic chyme, and contains a number of enzymes for breaking down fats, proteins and carbohydrates into their component parts. The most important of these are *lipase* which splits fatty acids from triglycerides of fat; *trypsin* and *chymotrypsin* which split proteins into short polymers of amino acids (peptides) and individual amino acids; and *amylase* which splits starch into maltose.
- *Intestinal juice*, from the walls of the small intestine itself, also contains digestive enzymes.

The final phase of digestion occurs in the intestinal wall after absorption, when peptides are split into their component amino acids, maltose is converted into glucose by *maltase*, sucrose into glucose and fructose by *sucrase*, and *lactose* into glucose and galactose by *lactase*. A summary of the major enzymes of digestion is provided in Table 10.

Table 10. Summary of the major enzymes of digestion

Enzyme	Where active	Action
Salivary amylase	Mouth	Some starch to maltose
Pepsin	Stomach	Protein to peptides
Rennin (in infants only)	Stomach	Milk protein to peptides
Trypsin (from pancreas)	Intestine	Protein to peptides and amino acids
Chymotrypsin (from pancreas)	Intestine	Protein to peptides and amino acids
Lipase (from pancreas and intestine)	Intestine	Fat to fatty acids
Amylase (from pancreas)	Intestine	Starch (and glycogen) to maltose
Maltase	Intestinal wall	Maltose to glucose
Sucrase	Intestinal wall	Sucrose to glucose and fructose
Lactase	Intestinal wall	Lactose to glucose and galactose

IN THE LARGE INTESTINE

Substances that have resisted digestion and absorption thus far can be used as nutrients by the bacteria present in the large intestine (*colon*). Some cellulose and other components of fibre may then be broken down, and the bacteria will form B vitamins and vitamin K which provide small amounts of additional nutrients for absorption. They also generate gas (mainly hydrogen).

DIGESTION IN INFANTS

Before birth, infants are nourished through their bloodstream via the mother's placenta. The change to intestinal digestion does not develop fully for several months after birth. Three consequences in particular may be noted:

* For a few days, some whole proteins can be absorbed without digestion. In this way, antibodies against some diseases may be absorbed intact from the mother's milk.
* The stomach contains the enzyme *rennin*, which clots the casein of milk and begins its digestion.
* Starch cannot readily be digested until the infant is several months old.

INDIGESTION

A food or food component is indigestible if it cannot be fully broken down into substances capable of absorption. Some, such as lactose from milk in lactose-intolerant individuals, will reach the large intestine and be fermented by the bacteria present; this results in the production of gas and diarrhoea. Indigestion also means discomfort or pain in the gastrointestinal tract resulting from eating. It can result as much from emotional factors as from the passage of indigestible foods.

The process of absorption

IN THE MOUTH

No significant absorption occurs through the lining of the mouth.

IN THE STOMACH

The following simple substances can pass through the lining of the stomach into the bloodstream in small quantities:

* water
* alcohol
* sugars
* minerals which are soluble in water, such as sodium chloride (salt)

- vitamins which are soluble in water, i.e. B vitamins (but not vitamin B_{12}, which can only be absorbed in the ileum with the aid of an *intrinsic factor* produced by the stomach) and vitamin C.

IN THE SMALL INTESTINE

Almost all the absorption of nutrients occurs through the walls of the small intestine. Most of the water, alcohol, simple sugars, water-soluble vitamins and minerals are absorbed here too, as well as the digestion products of the energy-producing nutrients. These are:

- peptides and amino acids from proteins
- fatty acids from fats
- disaccharides from starch.

Fat-soluble vitamins are absorbed in association with the fatty acids. Absorption into the cells of the intestinal wall is remarkably efficient; indeed, more than half of the small intestine can be removed without major consequences. The surface of the wall contains innumerable projections, called *villi*, which present a very large surface area (20–40 m^2 in total) for absorption. This process occurs both passively (by diffusion) and actively (when specific nutrients are drawn into cells already containing large amounts of those nutrients).

Absorption can, however, be impaired. In coeliac disease the villi are lost. Substances such as laxatives and fibre which speed the passage of the intestinal contents may reduce absorption in general. The fibre and phytate present in wholemeal cereals may also reduce the absorption of specific minerals including calcium and zinc.

IN THE LARGE INTESTINE

The main functions of the large intestine are to absorb water from the residue moving through it from the small intestine, and to store the resultant faeces until they are expelled through the anus. Faeces are 70–80% water but also contain the undigested materials of food. The solid portion consists of fibre, debris from the continuously replaced cells of the intestinal wall, including intestinal bacteria, and a small amount of undigested food. The entire passage of food from mouth to anus takes from one to three days but it can be decreased by disease or by antibiotics which kill the intestinal bacteria, or it can be increased to as long as a week by diets very low in fibre.

The journey of major nutrients in the body

CARBOHYDRATES

The disaccharides entering the intestinal wall are split into monosaccharides which are carried by the bloodstream directly to the liver. They may then be:

- delivered as glucose to all the cells of the body to be used directly for energy via a series of controlled steps which produce carbon dioxide and water
- converted into glycogen and stored in the liver and skeletal muscles as a readily available source of energy
- converted into fatty acids and stored in the body fat (adipose tissue) as a source of energy.

The hormone *insulin* is required for the cellular metabolism of glucose but fructose and dietary sorbitol (which is converted in the body into fructose) do not require insulin for their metabolism.

FATS

Almost all the fatty acids that enter the intestinal wall are immediately rebuilt into triglycerides which are carried to the bloodstream by lymph. Fat, in the form of microscopic particles called *chylomicrons*, circulates in the blood plasma which has a milky appearance for some time after a large meal is eaten. When fat reaches tissues requiring energy, fatty acids are released from it by enzymes and taken up into the cells. Fat may be further transformed by the liver, and most is finally deposited in the adipose tissue. Dietary fat is more easily converted into body fat than is the carbohydrate in food. The body's reservoir of fat is constantly available as a source of energy via another series of controlled steps which also give rise to carbon dioxide and water.

PROTEINS

When peptides enter the intestinal wall, they are split into amino acids which are carried in the blood directly to the liver. They may then be:

- passed into the general circulation where they enter the body's 'pool' of indispensable and dispensable amino acids. These are then built into the structural proteins and specific enzymes which each cell needs
- converted into those amino acids which are in short supply
- oxidised for energy, in some cases after conversion into glucose, if there is a residual excess of amino acids. *Urea* is also formed and excreted through the kidneys. If the diet as a whole is inadequate in energy, then a greater proportion of the protein will be used for this purpose in order to keep the body functioning.

Control of nutrients in the blood

Blood is the means by which most nutrients are carried to and from the cells where they are needed. The concentration of most nutrients in the blood is normally controlled automatically as described in Chapters 7 and 8. In addition, when carbohydrate is eaten, the resulting slight increase in blood glucose is soon reduced by the hormone insulin. In *diabetes*, however, the blood glucose levels are not kept within the normal range. In the case of Type I or insulin-dependent diabetes, the pancreas does not secrete sufficient insulin, and the blood glucose concentration increases until the excess is excreted by the kidneys into the urine. This imbalance is so severe that insulin must be injected. Type II or non-insulin-dependent diabetes occurs when the tissues develop resistance to the effects of insulin. It is strongly related to overweight/ obesity and low levels of physical activity as well as genetic predisposition. This form of diabetes can often be controlled by dietary regulation. The prevalence of Type II diabetes is increasing among adults in the UK as the incidence of overweight and obesity increases, and it is now found in children in whom it was previously rarely seen. Dietary advice for people with diabetes is similar to that for the population in general: maintenance of a healthy weight and consumption of a diet that is:

- low in fat (particularly saturated fat)
- low in sugars
- low in salt
- high in fruit and vegetables (at least five portions of a variety a day). However, drinking large amounts of fruit juice could cause problems with controlling blood sugar for some people with diabetes because it contains high levels of fruit sugar (fructose)
- high in starchy carbohydrate foods (especially wholegrain types) such as bread, chapati, rice, potatoes, pasta and yams. These should form the basis of meals.

There are not any foods that people with diabetes should not eat. Nor do they need to cut out all sugars. However, people with diabetes, like the rest of the population, should try to eat only small amounts of foods that are high in fat and sugar or both. For example, cakes and biscuits can be eaten infrequently and in small amounts as part of a balanced diet.

The Department of Health and Diabetes UK (www.diabetes.org.uk) do not recommend products aimed at diabetics. Foods that are labelled 'diabetic' are not necessarily healthier or more suitable for diabetics than other foods. They also tend to be more expensive than other products (see 'Diabetics' in Chapter 13).

7   Minerals

Most, if not all, of the inorganic elements or minerals can be detected in the body, but only about 15 of them are known to be essential and must be derived from food.

Minute amounts of a further five or more are necessary for normal life in other animal species, and may well prove to be necessary for humans; it is difficult, however, to conceive of a dietary deficiency of these.

Minerals have three main functions:

* as constituents of the bones and teeth. These include *calcium*, *phosphorus* and *magnesium*
* as soluble salts which help to control the composition of body fluids and cells. These include *sodium* and *chloride* in the fluids outside the cells (e.g. blood), and *potassium*, *magnesium* and *phosphorus* inside the cells
* as essential adjuncts to many enzymes and other proteins, such as haemoglobin, which are necessary for the release and utilisation of energy. *Iron*, *phosphorus* and *zinc*, and most of the other elements described at the end of this chapter, act in this way.

The elements mentioned above are in general needed in the greatest amounts in the diet or are present in the largest amounts in the body tissues (Table 11); calcium, iron, magnesium, phosphorus, potassium and sodium are generally considered as the *major minerals*. The remainder – including zinc, chromium, cobalt, copper, fluoride, iodine, manganese, molybdenum and selenium – are equally important but are needed, or are present in the body tissues, in smaller quantities. They are called *trace elements*. The amounts of selected elements needed to maintain the health of various age groups in the population are discussed in Chapter 9.

However, many minerals and trace elements can be toxic in excess. In 2003, the Expert Group on Vitamins and Minerals (EVM), an independent advisory committee, was asked by the UK Government to advise on the safety of intakes of minerals used in food supplements and fortified foods. The Group's recommendations (published in *Safe Upper Levels for Vitamins and Minerals*) for levels of minerals and trace elements taken as supplements each day that are unlikely to be harmful are given below either as a *Safe Upper Level* or a *Guidance Level*. Safe Upper Levels are given if supported by adequate data and Guidance Levels are given when it is not possible to establish a Safe Upper Level. The Safe Upper Level represents an intake that can be consumed daily over a lifetime without significant risk to health or medical supervision on the basis of available evidence. For the majority of minerals, the available data were inadequate to establish Safe Upper Levels. Guidance Levels have been given as approximate indications of levels that would not be expected to cause adverse effects, but have been derived from limited data and are less secure than Safe Upper Levels.

Table 11. Daily intake and total body content of minerals for an adult man

	Daily intake[a]	Total body content[c]
Major minerals		
Calcium	0.9 g	1200 g[d]
Iron	13 mg	4.2 g
Magnesium	0.3 g	19 g
Phosphorus[e]	3.2 g	780 g
Potassium	3.4 g	140 g
Sodium	3.8 g	140 g
Trace elements		
Chromium	0.1 mg[b]	<2 mg
Cobalt	0.01 mg[c]	1.5 mg
Copper	1.31 mg	72 mg
Fluoride	1.2 mg[b]	2.6 g
Iodine	197 µg	13 mg
Manganese[e]	3.4 mg	12 mg
Selenium	56 µg	>15 mg
Zinc	10.8 mg	2.3 g

Intakes are likely to be far greater than requirements. A variable proportion is actually absorbed into the body (ranging from almost 100% for sodium and chloride down to 5–10% for iron, copper, manganese and probably chromium and cobalt too); the amount absorbed normally balances the amount lost in urine and sweat, except where increased retention is necessary during growth.

[a] From all sources, unless otherwise indicated, values for the years 2008/10 from *National Diet and Nutrition Survey: Headline Results from Years 1 and 2 (Combined) of the Rolling Programme (2008/9–2009/10*, Department of Health, 2011.
[b] Food Standards Agency, *1997 Total Diet Study*, 2000. Intakes of fluoride may be much higher in those people who drink large volumes of tea made with fluoridated water.
[c] Ministry of Agriculture, Fisheries and Food, *Manual of Nutrition*, 10th edition, 1995.
[d] Expert Group on Vitamins and Minerals, *Safe Upper Levels for Vitamins and Minerals*, Food Standards Agency, 2003.
[e] These values are still based on 2000/01 National Diet and Nutrition Survey data.

Where possible, Safe Upper Levels or Guidance Levels are expressed in terms of total micronutrient intakes (from all sources, including foods that are currently fortified). However, for the majority of nutrients considered by the EVM, the data were inadequate to establish total intakes. The advice will clearly state whether the Safe Upper Levels or Guidance Levels relate to total intake or supplemental intake.

Major minerals

IRON

Function, and effects of deficiency

The healthy adult body contains 3–4 g of iron. More than half of body iron is present as a component of *haemoglobin* in red blood cells where it is essential for transporting oxygen from the lungs to the tissues. It is also present in the muscle protein *myoglobin* where it is required for storage and use of oxygen in muscle. Iron is also a component of a number of enzymes which are needed for many metabolic processes in the body. Iron is stored in tissues as *ferritin*; the highest concentrations are found in the liver, spleen and bone marrow.

Iron deficiency results when iron stores are depleted and is characterised by low concentrations of ferritin in the blood. Iron deficiency is not always caused by inadequate intakes of foods containing iron. Other causes include impaired absorption of dietary iron or increased blood loss due to menstruation or gastrointestinal blood loss. Gastrointestinal blood loss is associated with use of non-steroidal anti-inflammatory drugs (such as aspirin), and may be an important cause of iron deficiency in older people. Progressive iron deficiency leads to *iron deficiency anaemia*. Anaemia is a condition in which the body does not have sufficient healthy red blood cells to carry enough oxygen to the tissues. However, there are a number of other causes of anaemia. In addition to iron, vitamin B_{12} and folate are required for production of haemoglobin. Deficiency in any of these may cause anaemia because of inadequate production of red blood cells. Other types of anaemia include inherited blood disorders (e.g. sickle cell anaemia and thalassaemia). The 2010 report by the Scientific Advisory Committee on Nutrition (SACN) on *Iron and Health* highlights that, while most population groups in the UK have sufficient levels of body iron, health professionals need to be alert to the risk of iron deficiency anaemia and give appropriate nutritional advice on how to increase iron intakes by consuming more iron-rich foods and also taking iron supplements if required.

Absorption and excretion

Iron in the diet exists in two forms: *haem* and *non-haem* iron. More than 90% of dietary iron intake in Britain is from non-haem iron (iron salts) and less than 10% is from haem iron (from the red pigments of meat and offal). The main determinant of how much iron is absorbed from the diet is the amount needed by the body: more is absorbed when the body's stores are depleted and when needs are greatest, for example in growing children, or menstruating or pregnant women. The extent to which dietary iron is absorbed depends on its chemical form: the absorption of haem iron is more efficient (20–30%) than that of non-haem iron (5–15%). Homeostatic control of non-haem iron is greater than that of haem iron. Additionally, certain dietary constituents have been shown to increase (e.g. meat, fish) or reduce (e.g. calcium, phytates in cereals and legumes, polyphenols in tea and coffee) the amount of non-haem iron that is absorbed from the diet. However, dietary inhibitors and enhancers of non-haem iron absorption do not appear to have a substantial influence on iron status in the UK. This may be because UK diets include a broad range of foods containing a variety of enhancers and inhibitors, and their individual effects may be modulated by interactions between them. A healthy, balanced diet, which includes a variety of foods containing iron, is important for achieving adequate iron status. Individuals who may be at risk of iron deficiency (e.g. women who have heavy periods) may need iron supplements prescribed by their GP.

Sources and intakes

Currently in Britain, all wheat flour, other than wholemeal, is fortified with iron by law (see 'Nutrient losses in milling and the composition of wheat flour' in Chapter 11). Other foods, including many breakfast cereals, are fortified voluntarily by manufacturers. About 40% of the iron in the British diet comes from cereals and cereal products, with about 20% from breakfast cereals alone, 17% comes from meat and meat products, and 10% from vegetables, not including potatoes. The total amounts of iron in selected foods are shown in Table 12.

In Britain, average daily intake of iron from food sources and supplements was about 12 mg for men and women (19–64 years) in 2008/10. The average daily iron intake from food sources alone was about 12 mg for men and 10 mg for women. Women obtained about 17% of their total iron intake from dietary supplements while men obtained only 5% from supplements. Mean daily iron intakes were above the Reference Nutrient Intake (RNI) (see Chapter 9) for men and boys (4–18 years) but were 58% of the RNI for girls (11–18 years) and 79% of the RNI for women (97% of the RNI when supplements were included). About 44% of girls and 22% of women (20% when supplements were included), but only 1% of men, had average daily intakes of iron from food sources below the Lower Reference Nutrient Intake (LRNI) (see Chapter 9). While large proportions of the UK population appear to have iron intakes below dietary recommendations for iron, this is not consistent with the low prevalence of iron deficiency anaemia in the UK. This might be because of uncertainties in the dietary recommendations for iron intake which are based on limited evidence. SACN has suggested in *Iron and Health* (2010) that the RNI and LRNI for iron intake in girls and women of reproductive age are too high.

Most people should be able to get all the iron they need by eating a varied and balanced diet. High doses of iron supplements can cause gastrointestinal problems such as constipation, nausea, diarrhoea and vomiting. In the UK, supplemental doses above the Guidance Level of 17 mg per day are not advised. Iron supplements are usually taken as a short-term measure to provide extra iron when levels in the body are low.

Table 12. Total iron content of selected foods (edible portion)

	Iron (mg/100 g)		Iron (mg/100 g)
Milk, semi-skimmed	0.02	Potatoes, old, boiled	0.4
Eggs, chicken, whole, boiled	1.9	Watercress	2.2
Beef, stewing steak, stewed	2.3	Okra, boiled	0.6
Beefburgers, grilled	2.5	Apricots, semi-dried, as eaten	3.4
Chicken, roast, meat only, average	0.8	Bananas	0.3
Kidney, pig's, stewed	6.4	Bread, white	1.6
Liver, lamb's, fried	7.7	Bread, wholemeal	2.4
Liver pâté	5.9	Cornflakes, fortified	8.0
Cod, fillet, baked	0.1	Curry powder	58.3
Sardines, in tomato sauce	2.9	Soy sauce	2.4
Broccoli, boiled	1.0	Cocoa powder	10.5
Lettuce	0.7	Chocolate, plain	2.3
Cabbage, boiled	0.3	Chocolate, milk	2.1
Lentils, green, dried, boiled	3.5	Wine, red	0.9
Red kidney beans, dried, boiled	2.5	Wine, white, dry	0.5
		Spirits	0.0

The main sources of iron in the diet are cereals and cereal products (especially breakfast cereals and white bread), meat and meat products, and vegetables (excluding potatoes).

CALCIUM

Function

Calcium is the most abundant mineral in the body. All but about 1% of it is found in the bones and teeth, together with more than three-quarters of the body's phosphorus, in the form of calcium phosphates deposited in an organic framework. In addition to giving strength to the bones, these minerals act as a reserve supply for other needs and the calcium is constantly withdrawn into and replaced from the blood at carefully controlled rates. The remaining 5–10 g of calcium is essential for the contraction of muscles, including the heart muscle; for nerve function; for the activity of several enzymes; and for normal clotting of the blood.

The effects of deficiency

Rickets and osteomalacia

Rickets (softening and weakening of the bones during bone formation) may result in children when intakes of calcium are very low. In adults, the deficiency may show as *osteomalacia* (softening of the bones). The primary deficiency in rickets and osteomalacia, however, is of vitamin D which means too little calcium is absorbed. It occurs among some ethnic groups, older people aged 65 years and over, and people who are not exposed to much sun (such as people who cover up their skin when outdoors or those who are confined indoors for long periods). Such people have a low exposure to sunlight and consequently form little or no vitamin D in their skin (see 'Vitamin D' in Chapter 8). They may also be eating diets low in calcium or high in *phytate* (see below). Women who lose large quantities of calcium through repeated pregnancies and lactation are also at risk of osteomalacia.

Osteoporosis

Osteoporosis is a reduction in bone density and strength which causes bones to become brittle and fracture easily, and is caused by progressive loss of bone components as people age. Bone density increases until it reaches a peak bone mass at around the age of 30. The extent of peak bone mass depends on how well nourished young people have been during childhood and early adulthood. As people age beyond 30 their bone density decreases. This decline is particularly rapid in women around the time of the menopause. The most common sites of osteoporotic fracture are the vertebrae (resulting in curvature of the spine), wrist and hip. This condition causes a great deal of suffering, particularly for elderly women, and can result in the loss of independence. The resulting health care required for the elderly is also costly for the health services.

The causes of osteoporosis are multifactorial. Lifestyle factors, such as diet and exercise, play an important role and are amenable to change so may help people to reduce their risk of fracture. Studies are continuing into the role of nutrition, but the importance of calcium and vitamin D (see 'Vitamin D' in Chapter 8) for bone health has been known for some time. A healthy, balanced diet, including plenty of fruit and vegetables, along with weight-bearing physical activity, such as brisk walking, spending time outdoors to encourage vitamin D formation in the skin and the avoidance of smoking seem to promote healthy bones.

Possible protective effects of calcium

It is thought that calcium may help to lower high blood pressure and may help to protect against colon and breast cancer, although more evidence is needed to support these suggestions.

Absorption and excretion

Only 30–40% of the calcium in the diet is absorbed and the remainder is lost in the faeces. But without adequate amounts of vitamin D, little or no calcium can be absorbed, and when fibre, phytate (present mainly in the outer layers of cereals) or oxalate (present in spinach and rhubarb) is added to the diet, calcium absorption is also reduced. It was partly to compensate for this that calcium carbonate was added to the high-extraction flour used during and after World War II; it is still added to all flour except wholemeal, although it is now known that the body can adapt to the presence of phytates.

Excretion of absorbed calcium is mainly through the kidneys, and is increased when the diet contains large amounts of protein; some calcium is also lost in sweat. Adults normally absorb enough calcium to balance these losses until middle age, unless they have restricted movement, but lactating women, and growing children who are forming new bone, must consume more.

Sources and intakes

Good sources of calcium include milk, cheese and other dairy foods; green leafy vegetables such as broccoli, cabbage and okra; soya drinks with added calcium; and fish with edible bones, such as sardines and pilchards.

Reduced-fat milks contain essentially the same quantity of calcium as whole milk (see Table 13). However, children under the age of 2 need an energy-dense diet and should always be given whole milk and full-fat dairy products. Over the age of 2, semi-skimmed milk may be gradually introduced as a main drink, as long as a child is eating a varied and balanced diet and growing well. Skimmed or 1%-fat milks are not suitable for children under the age of 5, as they do not contain enough energy.

Table 13. Calcium content of selected foods (edible portion)

	Calcium (mg/100 g)		Calcium (mg/100 g)
Milk, whole	118	Baked beans	53
Milk, semi-skimmed	120	Courgettes, boiled	19
Milk, skimmed	122	Cabbage, boiled	33
Milk, dried, skimmed	1280	Okra, boiled	120
Milk, 1%	126[a]	Onions, fried	47
Yogurt, low-fat, fruit	140	Potatoes, old, boiled	5
Fromage frais, plain	110	Watercress, raw	170
Cheese, Cheddar	739	Apples (eating)	4
Cheese, cottage	127	Oranges	47
Ice cream, non-dairy, vanilla	80	Raisins	46
Eggs, chicken, whole, boiled	57	Peanuts, dry-roasted	52
Beef, stewing steak, stewed	15	Bread, white	177
Cod, fillet, baked	11	Bread, wholemeal	106
Sardines, canned in oil, drained	500	Rice, white basmati, boiled	14

The main sources of calcium in the diet are milk and milk products (especially semi-skimmed milk and cheese), and cereals and cereal products (especially white bread). For some people, hard water and the bones in canned sardines and salmon can be important sources.

[a] Data are an average of supermarket label information.

Most people should be able to get all the calcium they need by eating a varied and balanced diet. No additional intake is considered necessary for pregnancy, although an increase is recommended during lactation. The average adult intake of calcium from food in the UK is 830 mg per day, which is adequate for the needs of most people. Adult men and women consumed on average about 920 mg and 740 mg per day, respectively, from food in 2008/10. If calcium supplements are taken, it is important that they are not taken in excessive amounts as this could be harmful. Guidance suggests that taking 1500 mg or less of calcium per day in the form of supplements is unlikely to cause any adverse effects.

PHOSPHORUS

Phosphorus is the second most abundant mineral in the body. Most phosphorus in the body is linked to calcium in the bones and teeth. About 80% of the phosphorus in the human body is present in bones as a calcium salt or *calcium phosphate* which gives rigidity to the skeleton. Phosphorus has an essential role in energy release and other metabolic processes. It is present in *phospholipids* which are incorporated in neural tissue in early life and in all cell membranes.

An excess of phosphorus (high phosphate to calcium ratio) can trigger *tetany* (involuntary muscle convulsion). A varying calcium to phosphorus ratio can be tolerated by adult populations with no effect on the calcium balance; however, young infants can be more sensitive to a varying ratio. High intakes of phosphorus in the first few days of life, resulting from the use of unmodified cow's milk, may produce low levels of calcium in the blood and tetany.

Phosphorus is present in nearly all foods, largely as phosphates (Table 14). Furthermore, phosphates are added to a number of processed foods. Consequently, most people should be able to get all the phosphorus they need as long as they eat a varied diet. No additional intake is considered necessary for pregnancy, although an increase is recommended during lactation. A deficiency in phosphorus is rare as it is so readily found in foods.

Table 14. Phosphorus and magnesium content of selected foods (edible portion)

	Phosphorus (mg/100 g)	Magnesium (mg/100 g)
Milk, semi-skimmed	94	11
Cheese, Cheddar	505	29
Eggs, chicken, whole, boiled	200	12
Beef, stewing steak, stewed	180	19
Chicken, roast, meat only	200	23
Ham	340	24
Cod, fillets, baked	190	26
Sardines, canned, in tomato sauce	420	39
Cabbage, boiled	25	4
Baked beans, reheated	100	31
Potatoes, old, boiled	31	14
Oranges	21	10
Peanuts, dry-roasted	420	190
Bread, white	95	23
Bread, wholemeal	202	66
Chapati, made without fat	120	37
Yeast extract	950	160

The main sources of phosphorus in the diet are cereals and cereal products (especially bread and breakfast cereals), milk and milk products (especially semi-skimmed milk), and meat and meat products. The main sources of magnesium are cereals and cereal products (especially bread and breakfast cereals), drinks (including beer and lager, coffee and tea), meat and meat products, milk and milk products, and potatoes and savoury snacks.

In 2000/01, the average daily intake from food was about 1500 mg for men and 1100 mg for women, well above the RNI (see Chapter 9). High intakes have been associated with mild gastrointestinal symptoms. However, guidance suggests that taking up to 250 mg of phosphorus per day in the form of supplements is unlikely to cause any adverse effects.

MAGNESIUM

Most of the magnesium in the body is present in the bones but it is also an essential constituent of all cells and is necessary for the functioning of some of the enzymes that are involved in energy utilisation. It is thought that magnesium may help to lower high blood pressure. Magnesium is widespread in foods (Table 14), especially those of vegetable origin because it is a constituent of chlorophyll. Less than half of magnesium that is ingested is normally absorbed. In 2008/10, food provided on average about 290 mg and 230 mg magnesium per day for men and women, respectively. Deficiency is rare, and results from excessive losses in diarrhoea rather than from low intakes. No additional magnesium is required during pregnancy, but an extra 50 mg per day is needed during lactation to offset secretion in breast milk. Most people should be able to get all the magnesium they need by eating a varied and balanced diet. Guidance suggests that people are unlikely to experience adverse effects if they take 400 mg or less per day of magnesium in the form of supplements.

SODIUM AND CHLORIDE

Functions

Sodium and chloride are found in those body fluids outside the cells, such as blood. They are both essential in small amounts in the diet for maintaining the water balance of the body, and for muscle and nerve activity.

Absorption and excretion

The concentrations of sodium and chloride in the body are maintained within close limits and are controlled by the kidneys, through excretion and conservation. The ability of the kidneys to regulate the body's sodium content is dependent on a number of factors, including age. For example, older adults and very young infants cannot tolerate high sodium intakes because their kidneys cannot excrete the excess.

Sources and intakes

Sodium and chloride are often added to the diet as salt, which is the main source of sodium in the diet. Habitually high salt intakes have been associated with high blood pressure, also called *hypertension*, which can increase the risk of stroke and heart disease. The evidence for the association between salt and blood pressure relates to sodium.

Some additives used in food (e.g. the flavour enhancer monosodium glutamate) contain sodium, but these make a comparatively small contribution to intakes. The main categories of food that contribute to sodium intakes in the UK are bread and meat products. Table 15 shows the amount of sodium in selected foods. The sodium content of unprocessed foods is comparatively low, but salt is added to many prepared foods. The salt added during cooking or at the table, and the salt found naturally in most foods, makes up only a quarter of the salt in our diets. The rest (75%) comes from processed foods. For example, salt is low in pork and other meats, but high in bacon, sausages and other meat products; it is low in herrings, but high in kippers. Foods where some products will be high in salt include soups, sauces, some ready meals, some breakfast cereals, pizzas, baked beans and savoury snack foods (e.g. crisps, salted nuts).

The average daily adult sodium intake in 2008, as estimated by measuring sodium excreted in the urine, was about 3.9 g for men and about 3.1 g for women, equivalent to dietary intakes of about 9.7 g and 7.7 g of salt per day, respectively. This method of indirectly estimating sodium intake is used because it is not possible to measure intake directly since the amount of salt added to food in cooking or at the table cannot be accurately assessed.

In May 2003, SACN made recommendations on the amount of salt that the population should be eating. In order to help lower the average blood pressure of the population, and so decrease the prevalence of coronary heart disease and stroke, current recommendations are that the average sodium intake of the adult population should not exceed 2.4 g of sodium (6 g of salt) per day. In 2008, 82% of men and 65% of women had salt intakes greater than this (average dietary intakes of salt for adults were 8.6 g per day). The recommended maximum intake of 6 g per day is higher than the RNI (see Chapter 9) and substantially greater than the salt intake needed to maintain the sodium content of the body in a temperate climate. This amount is not an optimal level of salt intake but is considered to be an achievable population goal.

The maximum amount of salt that babies and children should be having varies by age:

- Up to 6 months old – less than 1 g per day
- 7 to 12 months – 1 g per day
- 1 to 3 years – 2 g per day
- 4 to 6 years – 3 g per day
- 7 to 10 years – 5 g per day

Babies who are breastfed receive the right amount of sodium through breast milk, and infant formula is manufactured to contain a similar amount. Babies should not be given processed foods, such as breakfast cereals and pasta sauces, which are not made specifically for them because these can be high in salt.

There is currently no reliable estimate of the amount of salt consumed by children but available information suggests that it is substantially higher than these targets. From the age of 11, children should be having no more than about 6 g per day. This is the same level that is recommended for adults.

In the UK, salt targets have been developed for 80 food categories to help businesses achieve a further salt reduction by the end of 2012.[11] In England, these have been included in the Public Health Responsibility Deal.

POTASSIUM

Function, and effects of deficiency

Potassium is present largely in the fluids within the body cells where its concentration is carefully controlled. The total amount in the body is closely related to the amount of lean tissue. Potassium has a complementary action with sodium in the functioning of cells.

As potassium is found so widely in foods, deficiency is unlikely to occur. Like sodium, most of the potassium in the diet is absorbed and the excess is excreted through the kidneys. Losses may be large if diuretics or laxatives are frequently taken and in cases of protein-energy malnutrition (*kwashiorkor*) where tissue breakdown as well as diarrhoea occurs. Potassium is essential to the correct functioning of heart muscle and, in severe cases of potassium depletion, heart failure may result unless supplements are given.

Potassium, as well as calcium and magnesium, has been shown to have beneficial effects on reducing blood pressure.

---

[11] The 2010 targets relate to targets set previously by the Food Standards Agency before responsibility for nutrition passed to the Department of Health in 2010. The Public Health Responsibility Deal targets for 2012 were developed from targets previously set by the Food Standards Agency.

Table 15. Sodium and potassium content of selected foods (edible portion)

	Sodium (mg/100 g)	Potassium (mg/100 g)
Milk, semi-skimmed	43	156
Cheese, Cheddar	723	75
Eggs, chicken, whole, raw or boiled	140	130
Beef, mince, raw	80	260
Corned beef, canned	860	140
Bacon, streaky, grilled	1680	330
Sausages, pork, grilled	1080	190
Ham	1200	340
Chicken, meat, average, raw	77	380
Haddock, fresh, raw	67	360
Haddock, smoked, steamed	990	440
Butter, unsalted	9	27
Butter, salted	606	27
Reduced-fat spread (62–75%), not polyunsaturated	747	17
Low-fat spread (26–39%), not polyunsaturated	692	61
Potatoes, old, raw	7	360
Potato crisps	450[a]	810[b]
Cauliflower, boiled, unsalted	4	120
Baked beans, reheated	530	310
Baked beans, reduced salt	330	270
Peanuts, dry-roasted	790	730
Tomatoes, raw	9	250
Bananas	1	400
Peaches, canned in juice	12	170
Raisins	60	1020
Bread, white	461	137
Bread, wholemeal	487	253
Cornflakes	500	90
Muesli, no added sugar	47	530
Tomato soup, cream of, canned	245	179
Yeast extract	4300	2100
Soy sauce	7120	180
Gravy, instant granules	6330	150

[a] Average of values ranging from 30 mg to 850 mg per 100 g.
[b] Average values ranging from 600 mg to 1330 mg per 100 g.

Sources and intakes

Potassium is widespread in foods but is particularly abundant in fruit (especially bananas), vegetables (including potatoes) and juices (Table 15). Most people should be able to get all the potassium they need by eating a varied and balanced diet. The average daily adult intake of potassium from foods in 2008/10 was about 3000 mg. Guidance suggests that taking up to 3700 mg of potassium in the form of supplements per day is unlikely to be harmful. However, older people may be more at risk. This is because, as people get older, the kidneys may become less able to remove potassium from the blood. Therefore, older people should not take potassium supplements except on medical advice.

Trace elements

Though they are essential nutrients that the body requires in order to function properly, trace elements are needed in much smaller amounts than vitamins and minerals. Trace elements are found in small amounts in a variety of foods such as meat, fish, cereals, milk and dairy foods, vegetables and nuts.

ZINC

Zinc helps with the healing of wounds, and is also associated with the activity of a wide variety of enzymes; about one-third of the comparatively large amount which is present in the body is in the bones. Zinc is present in a wide range of foods; good sources include meat, shellfish, milk and dairy foods. About one-third of the zinc in the diet is absorbed but this is reduced if large amounts of wholegrain cereals rich in dietary fibre and phytates are eaten, although the amount of zinc present in wholegrain cereals is enough to offset the limited bioavailability of the metal. Average adult daily intakes from food sources in 2008/10 were 10 mg for men and about 8 mg for women, which is adequate for most people. Some 8% of men and 3% of women had intakes below the LRNI (see Chapter 9) for zinc. Most people should be able to get all the zinc they need by eating a varied and balanced diet. When supplements are taken, advice is that taking no more than 25 mg of zinc as supplements per day (the Safe Upper Level) should not be harmful. If a higher dose is being taken under medical advice then this should be continued. High intakes from water stored in galvanised containers have caused toxicity. The zinc content of selected foods is shown in Table 16.

Note to Table 15

The sodium content of vegetables is much higher if they are cooked in salted water. Apart from this, the main sources of sodium in the UK diet are cereals and cereal products, especially white bread, meat products including bacon and ham, milk and milk products, and food such as soups, sauces and condiments. The main sources of potassium are potatoes and savoury snacks, meat and meat products, milk, cereal products, vegetables and various drinks. Fruit and fruit juices are also noteworthy as being much richer in potassium than sodium.

Table 16. Zinc content of selected foods (edible portion)

	Zinc (mg/100 g)
Milk, semi-skimmed	0.4
Cheese, Cheddar	4.1
Beef, stewing steak, stewed	7.5
Chicken, roast, meat only	2.2
Ham	1.8
Pâté, liver	2.8
Cod, fillets, baked	0.5
Eggs, chicken, whole, boiled	1.3
Potatoes, old, boiled	0.3
Bread, white	0.8
Bread, wholemeal	1.6
Chapati, made without fat	1.0

The main sources of zinc in the diet are meat and meat products, cereal products (especially white bread and breakfast cereals), and milk and milk products (especially semi-skimmed milk and cheese).

COBALT

Cobalt is a trace element found widely in the environment. It can be utilised by humans only as part of vitamin B_{12} (see 'Vitamin B_{12}' in Chapter 8). Good food sources of cobalt include fish, nuts, green leafy vegetables and cereals. Most people should be able to get all the cobalt they need from eating a varied and balanced diet. Average daily intakes from food are 0.012 mg per day.[12] Currently, cobalt is not used in supplements in the UK and intake levels from food are not harmful. However, for guidance purposes, having 1.4 mg or less per day of cobalt supplements is unlikely to cause harm.

COPPER

Copper is a component of a number of enzymes. Deficiency has occasionally been observed in malnourished infants, particularly if their initial stores were depleted by prolonged feeding of cow's milk alone (which contains less copper than most foods). Good sources include nuts, shellfish and offal (such as liver), but copper in the British diet mainly comes from cereal products, especially white bread, meat and meat products, potatoes, savoury snacks, drinks, fruit and nuts. The average daily intake of copper by British adults in 2000/01 was about 1.2 mg per day from food. Most people should be able to get all the

[12] Ministry of Agriculture, Fisheries and Food, *Total Diet Study 1994* (TDS), 1997. The TDS is a model of the average diet in the UK. Foods representing the average diet, based on the Expenditure and Food Survey (formerly the National Food Survey) are purchased from retail outlets across the UK, prepared and combined, for analysis, into 20 groups of similar foods. Analysis of TDS samples is used to estimate population average intakes of mineral elements and other dietary constituents.

copper they need by eating a varied and balanced diet. If copper is taken as a supplement, guidance suggests that having 1 mg or less per day is unlikely to cause harm.

CHROMIUM

Chromium is involved in the utilisation of glucose. It is fairly widely distributed in foods; those with a high content include brewer's yeast, meat, wholegrain cereals, legumes and nuts. A safe and adequate intake for an adult is thought to be about 0.025 mg of chromium per day. Most people should be able to get all the chromium they need by eating a varied and balanced diet. The average daily intake from food is 0.1 mg (*1997 Total Diet Study*). Guidance suggests that having 10 mg or less per day of chromium from food and supplements combined is unlikely to be harmful.

FLUORIDE

Fluoride is thought to be essential, though this has been difficult to demonstrate experimentally. Fluoride is associated with the structure of bones and teeth, and increases the resistance of the latter to decay. Drinking water is an important source but the natural content is variable and is often below the optimum level of 1 mg per litre (1 part per million). The only other important sources of fluoride in the diet are tea and seafood (especially fish whose bones can be eaten).[13] The use of a fluoridated toothpaste and mouthwash helps to prevent dental caries. It is not clear how much fluoride is needed for good health. But it is known that people whose drinking water contains fluoride at about 1 part per million tend to have less tooth decay than similar groups of people where the concentrations of fluoride are much lower. The Department of Health and the British Dental Association recommend that fluoride should be added to drinking water, but it is up to individual local health authorities (together with local health groups and the local community) to decide. Fluoride supplements are only available as licensed medicines and dentists may advise their use if an individual is prone to dental decay. However, it is important that they are only taken on the advice and instruction of the dentist.

IODINE

Iodine is an essential constituent of hormones produced by the thyroid gland in the neck, and most of the iodine in the body is in this gland. Deficiency causes the thyroid gland to enlarge – a condition known as *goitre*. The richest source of iodine is seafood. The amount of iodine in vegetable and cereal foods depends on the level in the soil, and the amount in foods from animal sources

---

[13] The EVM concluded that it is inappropriate to comment on fluoride with regard to food fortification since this is carried out as a public health measure.

depends on the level in their diet. Because of the widespread use of iodine in animal feed, milk and milk products are the main sources of iodine in the British diet, and cereals and cereal products and fish are also important. Most people should be able to get all the iodine they need by eating a varied and balanced diet. The average adult intake in the UK from food sources in 2008/10 was about 167 micrograms (μg) per day (above the RNI [see Chapter 9]), with milk and milk products being the most important sources. Low average intakes of about 80 μg per day have been found in vegans. Edible seaweeds, which are rich in iodine, can be a useful source for vegans if consumed in moderation. Guidance suggests that having 500 μg or less per day of additional iodine in the form of supplements is unlikely to be harmful. However, excessive intakes of iodine can negatively affect thyroid function, which can lead to a wide range of different symptoms, for example weight gain.

MANGANESE

Manganese is present in a number of enzymes and activates others. It is found in a variety of foods including bread, nuts, cereals and green vegetables (such as peas and runner beans). The principal sources in the British diet are cereals and cereal products, especially bread and breakfast cereals, vegetables (excluding potatoes) and drinks, particularly tea. Most people should be able to get all the manganese they need by eating a varied and balanced diet. Average daily adult intakes from food sources in 2000/01 were about 3 mg per day. Guidance suggests that taking 4 mg or less of manganese per day as a supplement is unlikely to cause any harm. For older people, taking 0.5 mg or less per day of manganese as a supplement is unlikely to cause any harm. This is a lower amount because older people may be more sensitive to manganese.

MOLYBDENUM

Molybdenum is found in a wide variety of foods. Those originating from plants that grow above ground – such as peas, leafy vegetables (including broccoli and spinach) and cauliflower – tend to be higher in molybdenum than roots or tubers that grow below the ground, or than meat. Foods particularly high in molybdenum include nuts, canned vegetables and cereals such as oats. Molybdenum is essential for the functioning of enzymes involved in DNA metabolism. Deficiency has not been reported in the UK and people should be able to get all the molybdenum needed by eating a varied and balanced diet. Average daily intakes from food are about 0.1 mg (Ministry of Agriculture, Fisheries and Food, *Total Diet Study 1994*). There is insufficient evidence about the safety or otherwise of molybdenum intakes above those from the diet but the molybdenum intake from the UK diet is not likely to be harmful.

SELENIUM

Selenium is found in foods such as Brazil nuts, fish, meat, offal, eggs and cereals. It plays a key role in the control of thyroid hormone metabolism, immune function and in reproduction, and also helps to protect cells by promoting the body's antioxidant defences. The average adult daily intake of selenium from food is about 48 µg. The selenium status of the UK population, although not as low as that found in regions of the world that suffer severe selenium deficiency, may be marginal for the maintenance of good health. The National Diet and Nutrition Survey shows that 89% of adults have intakes that are below the LRNI (see Chapter 9) of selenium from food sources.

Selenium has been claimed to reduce the incidence of a range of cancers, although the COMA report on *Nutritional Aspects of the Development of Cancer* (1998) considered there to be insufficient evidence for such a link. Dietary advice on selenium remains that most people should be able to meet their selenium requirements by eating a varied and balanced diet. The Safe Upper Level for intake of selenium from supplements is 350 µg per day.

8   Vitamins

Until the beginning of the 20th century, it was believed that the only components of a diet necessary for health, growth and reproduction were proteins, fats, carbohydrates and a number of inorganic elements. This view had to be changed when it was found that minute amounts of additional materials were also essential. These could be extracted from a variety of foods and appeared to be of two types: fat-soluble ('A') and water-soluble ('B'). They were later each discovered to contain several active components, or vitamins. Fat-soluble vitamins are mainly associated with fatty foods and include vitamins A, D, E and K. Water-soluble vitamins comprise the B vitamins and vitamin C. The vitamins of the B complex include thiamin (B_1), riboflavin (B_2), niacin (or nicotinic acid) (B_3), folate (B_9), vitamin B_6 (pyridoxine), vitamin B_{12} (cobalamin), biotin (B_7) and pantothenic acid (B_5). Vitamin C often occurs in different foods from the B vitamins. Many of these vitamins exist in more than one chemical form.

Vitamins are used by the body every day. Water-soluble vitamins are not stored by the body, so need to be consumed more frequently than fat-soluble vitamins which can be stored. The absence of a vitamin from the diet or, more usually, its presence in insufficient amounts, leads to both general and specific symptoms. The most common general symptoms are, as with deficiencies of many other components of the diet, a feeling of malaise and, in the case of children, restriction in their growth. The specific symptoms of deficiency in humans are discussed separately for each vitamin and the amounts needed to maintain health are discussed in Chapter 9. Excessive intakes of most water-soluble vitamins are rapidly excreted in the urine and, because the body doesn't store water-soluble vitamins, these are generally not harmful. However, very high intakes of some, such as vitamin B_6 and niacin, can have adverse effects. Excessive intakes of fat-soluble vitamins accumulate in the body and can also be harmful. For example, high levels of pre-formed retinol (vitamin A) may have undesirable effects on the unborn child if consumed during pregnancy (see below). As with the minerals discussed in Chapter 7, the recommendations of the Expert Group on Vitamins and Minerals (EVM) for levels of vitamins taken as supplements (and/or food) each day that are unlikely to be harmful are given below, either as a Safe Upper Level or a Guidance Level.

Safe Upper Levels are given if supported by adequate data and Guidance Levels are given when it is not possible to establish a Safe Upper Level. The Safe Upper Level represents an intake that can be consumed daily over a lifetime without significant risk to health or medical supervision on the basis of available evidence. For the majority of vitamins, the available data were inadequate to establish Safe Upper Levels. Guidance Levels have been given as approximate indications of levels that would not be expected to cause adverse effects, but have been derived from limited data and are less secure than Safe Upper Levels.

Where possible, Safe Upper Levels or Guidance Levels are expressed in terms of total micronutrient intakes (from all sources, including foods that are currently fortified). However, for the majority of nutrients considered by the EVM, the data were inadequate to establish total intakes. The advice will clearly state whether the Safe Upper Levels or Guidance Levels relate to total intake or supplemental intake.

Factors affecting the stability of vitamins in foods are discussed elsewhere (see 'Stability of individual nutrients' in Chapter 10).

Vitamin A

The chemical name of vitamin A is *retinol* and it is found, pre-formed, only in foods of animal origin. *Beta-carotene* (ß-carotene – see section below) is found in foods of plant origin and can be converted to vitamin A in the body. The most convenient way of expressing the total vitamin A activity of a diet is as *retinol equivalents*: by convention, 1 microgram (μg) retinol equivalents is equal to 1 μg retinol or 6 μg ß-carotene.[14] This average value takes into account the conversion losses and the lesser absorption of ß-carotene compared with retinol in the general diet.

FUNCTION, AND EFFECTS OF DEFICIENCY OR EXCESS

Vitamin A is essential for vision in dim light; thus, prolonged deficiency (sufficient to deplete any stores in the liver, which in previously well-nourished people will last for one to two years) results in night blindness. In children in many parts of the world, deficiency also results in severe eye lesions (*xerophthalmia* or *dry eye syndrome*) and complete blindness (*keratomalacia*). Vitamin A is also necessary for the maintenance of healthy skin and surface tissues, especially those that excrete mucus. ß-carotene and other related compounds known as carotenoids can act as antioxidants (see also 'Vitamins and antioxidant activity' later in this chapter), which, along with vitamins C, E and flavonoids, and as components of fruit and vegetables, may have beneficial health effects.

---

[14] The amounts of vitamin A in foods are sometimes quoted in International Units (IU). To convert these to μg retinol equivalents, multiply the IU of retinol (in foods of animal origin) by 0.3, and divide the IU of ß-carotene (in foods of plant origin) by 10. (This is because 1 IU vitamin A = 0.3 μg retinol or 0.6μg ß-carotene, and 1 μg retinol equivalents = 1 μg retinol or 6 μg ß-carotene.)

Excessive doses, for example from taking large amounts of retinol (pre-formed vitamin A) preparations for long periods, accumulate in the liver and can be toxic. There is also an association between very high levels of retinol consumption during pregnancy and the incidence of some birth defects. As a precaution therefore, women in the UK who are, or who might become, pregnant are advised not to take vitamin A supplements, including fish liver oil supplements, except on the advice of their doctor and, as an additional precaution, are advised not to eat liver or liver products since these can also be very rich sources of retinol.

SOURCES AND INTAKES

Vitamin A is not widely distributed in food. Animals store vitamin A in their livers which are often extremely concentrated, but very variable, sources of retinol. Fish liver oils are also very rich sources of retinol. Vitamin A is now added to reduced-fat spreads in the form of synthetic retinol and ß-carotene. Other good sources of vitamin A include cheese, eggs, oily fish (such as mackerel), milk and yogurt.

Average intakes of vitamin A (retinol equivalents) from food in 2008/10 were about 1010 μg and 980 μg per day for men and women, respectively. The UK diet as a whole provides well above the Reference Nutrient Intake (RNI) (see Chapter 9) of this vitamin. However, 13% of 11–18-year-olds had intakes from food which were below the Lower Reference Nutrient Intake (LRNI) (see Chapter 9). On average, men and women obtained almost half of their vitamin A from retinol itself, with 15% of overall vitamin A from liver alone. The amounts of vitamin A in selected foods are shown in Table 17. The main sources of vitamin A in the diet are meat and meat products, vegetables, milk and milk products, and fat spreads. The contribution from liver and its products is higher in older people than in the younger age groups.

Most people should be able to get all the vitamin A they need by eating a balanced diet. Some concern has been raised about the large amounts of vitamin A that some people get from their diet and/or from supplements. There is some inconclusive evidence that having large amounts of vitamin A over a long time may adversely affect bone health, making bones more liable to fracture. As a precaution, therefore, the Scientific Advisory Committee on Nutrition (SACN) has advised consumers who eat liver once a week or more frequently not to increase their intake or to take supplements containing retinol, including fish liver oils. It also advises post-menopausal women and older people at risk of osteoporosis not to consume more than 1500 μg of pre-formed vitamin A (i.e. not including ß-carotene) per day from diet and supplements combined.

Guidance suggests that having an average of 1500 µg per day or less of vitamin A from food and supplements combined is unlikely to cause harm.

Beta-carotene

The *carotenes* are responsible for the yellow or orange colours of many fruits and vegetables. They can be converted in the body to retinol and are therefore sources of vitamin A. Beta-carotene (ß-carotene) is the most common of them. The main food sources of ß-carotene are red, yellow and green (leafy) vegetables such as carrots, red peppers and spinach, and yellow fruits such as mango, papaya and apricots. Variable amounts of ß-carotene are found in carrots and dark green or yellow vegetables, roughly in proportion to the depth of their colour; thus dark plants such as spinach contain more than cabbage, and the dark outer leaves of a cabbage contain more than the pale inner heart.

Most people should be able to get all the ß-carotene they need by eating a varied and balanced diet. If ß-carotene supplements are taken, advice is to take not more than 7 mg per day of ß-carotene from supplements (the Safe Upper Level[15]) as more could be harmful. If a high dose is being taken as a result of medical advice, this should be continued. ß-carotene supplements have been found to increase the risk of lung cancer developing in smokers and in people heavily exposed to asbestos at work. It is also possible that taking large amounts of ß-carotene supplements could increase the risk of cancer in other people. People who smoke or have been exposed to asbestos are advised not to take any ß-carotene supplements. There is no evidence to suggest that the average ß-carotene intake from food is harmful.

Table 17. Vitamin A content of selected foods (edible portion)

Foods of animal origin	Retinol only (µg/100 g)	Retinol equivalents (µg/100 g)[a]
Milk, whole	33	36
Milk, semi-skimmed	19	21
Milk, skimmed	1	1
Cheese, Cheddar	364	388
Eggs, whole, boiled	190	190
Beef, stewing steak, stewed	0	1
Liver, lamb's, fried	(19700)[b]	(19710)[b]
Kidney, pig's, stewed	46	46
Cod, fillets, baked	2	2

[15] The Safe Upper Level is the dose of a vitamin that potentially susceptible people could safely take every day of their lives without medical supervision. In the case of those vitamins where there is not enough evidence to set a Safe Upper Level, Guidance Levels have been set instead.

Table 17. Vitamin A content of selected foods (edible portion) *continued*

Foods of animal origin	Retinol only (µg/100 g)	Retinol equivalents (µg/100 g)[a]
Mackerel, smoked	31	31
Sardines, canned in oil, drained	7	7
Butter	958	1059[c]
Reduced-fat spread (62–75%), not polyunsaturated[d]	807	920[c]
Cod liver oil	18000	18000

	Carotene fractions			
Foods of vegetable origin	Alpha-carotene (µg/100 g)	Beta-carotene (µg/100 g)	Beta-cryptoxanthin (µg/100 g)	Retinol equivalents (µg/100 g)[f]
Sweetcorn, kernels, canned, reheated, drained	0	22	180	18
Green beans, frozen, boiled	52	494	0	87
Lettuce, average of dark and light leaves	0	1020	0	171
Spinach, boiled	0	3820	39	640
Peas, fresh, boiled	7	245	0	41
Peas, frozen, boiled	26	558	0	95
Carrots, old, boiled	4170	11300	0	2230
Tomatoes, raw	0	564	0	94
Peppers, capsicum, red, raw	135	3170	1220	640
Peppers, capsicum, green, raw	9	260	0	44
Apricots, raw	2	405	0	68
Mango, raw	0	682	27	116
Bread		0		0
Potatoes, old boiled		0		0

The main sources of vitamin A in the diet are liver, vegetables (especially carrots), milk and milk products, and butter and fat spreads.

[a] Retinol plus (ß-carotene equivalents/6)
[b] Figures in brackets are estimated values.
[c] Some types which do not contain ß-carotene have lower levels than this.
[d] Data from *Nutrient Analysis of a Range of Processed Foods with Particular Reference to Trans Fatty Acids – Summary Report*, Department of Health, 2011. Macronutrients only.
[e] The carotene content of many vegetables and fruit varies widely depending on variety and season.
[f] ß-carotene/6 plus other carotenoids/12

B vitamins

Although the chemical structure of each of the B vitamins is quite different, they have several features in common. They act as *co-factors* in different enzyme systems in the body. They tend to occur in the same foods and, being water-soluble, they are not stored for long in the body. These characteristics mean that diets containing too little of the B vitamins can lead to multiple deficiency diseases within a few months.

THIAMIN (VITAMIN B₁)

Function, and effects of deficiency

Thiamin is necessary for the steady and continuous release of energy from carbohydrate. Thiamin requirements are thus related to the amount of carbohydrate, and more or less to the amount of energy, in the diet. The deficiency disease, *beriberi*, results from a diet that is not only poor in thiamin but also rich in carbohydrate, such as one based almost entirely on polished rice from which the thiamin-rich seed coat has been removed. In developed countries, most cases of thiamin deficiency are associated with alcoholism, where intake of the vitamin may be low and absorption and utilisation impaired.

Sources and intakes

Thiamin is widely distributed in both animal and vegetable foods (Table 18). Good sources are pork, vegetables, milk, cheese, fresh and dried fruit, eggs, wholegrain breads and some fortified breakfast cereals. It should, however, be noted that cooking may result in considerable losses from these foods (see 'Stability of individual nutrients' in Chapter 10). Fats, sugars and alcoholic drinks contain no thiamin at all.

Wheat in the form of bread has long been a major source of carbohydrate in the British diet, but much of the thiamin is removed with the bran in the milling necessary to produce white bread. Thus, a 30 g (about 1 oz) slice of wholemeal bread provides about 0.10 mg of thiamin, while 30 g of unfortified white bread would provide only about 0.03 mg of thiamin. It is therefore a legal requirement in the UK that all flour (except wholemeal) be fortified with thiamin to at least 0.24 mg per 100 g (equivalent to 0.07 mg per 30 g slice; see 'Nutrient losses in milling and the composition of wheat flour' in Chapter 11).

Most people should be able to get all the thiamin they need from a varied and balanced diet. In 2008/10, average intakes from food were 1.7 mg and 1.3 mg per day for men and women, respectively – well above average requirements.

Guidance suggests that having 100 mg or less of thiamin per day as supplements is unlikely to be harmful.

Table 18. Thiamin content of selected foods

	Thiamin (mg/100 g)	Thiamin (mg/1000 kJ)
Milk, semi-skimmed	0.04	0.21
Bacon, streaky, fried	0.75	0.54
Beef, stewing steak, stewed	0.03	0.04
Corned beef, canned	0.00	0.00
Ham	0.80	1.77
Chicken, roast, meat only	0.07	0.09
Pork chop, grilled, lean	0.78	1.01
Sausage, pork, grilled	0.00	0.00
Sugar	0.00	0.00
Peas, frozen, boiled	0.26	0.89
Potatoes, old, boiled	0.18	0.59
Lentils, red, boiled	0.11	0.26
Oranges	0.11	0.70
Pineapple, canned in juice	0.09	0.45
Peanuts, dry-roasted	0.18	0.07
Bread, white, average	0.24	0.26
Bread, wholemeal, average	0.25	0.27
Chapati, made without fat	0.23	0.27
Cornflakes, fortified[a]	0.60	0.75
Basmati, white easy-cook rice, cooked[b]	0.06	0.10
Brown, wholegrain rice, cooked[b]	0.11	0.20
Dried white spaghetti, cooked[c]	0.08	0.13
Dried wholewheat spaghetti, cooked[c]	0.11	0.19
Yeast extract	4.10	5.37

The main sources of thiamin in the diet are cereals and cereal products (especially fortified breakfast cereals and white bread), meat and meat products (especially bacon and ham), vegetables, and potatoes and savoury snacks.

[a] Manufacturer label data from market leader in cornflakes.
[b] Source: *Nutrient Survey of Flours and Grains – Analytical Report*, Food Standards Agency, 2005.
[c] Source: *Nutrient Survey of Pasta and Pasta Sauces – Analytical Report*, Food Standards Agency, 2004.

RIBOFLAVIN (VITAMIN B$_2$)

Function, and effects of deficiency

Riboflavin is a bright yellow substance, which is essential for the utilisation of energy from food. Specific deficiency signs are rarely seen in humans but include sores in the corners of the mouth.

Sources and intakes

Riboflavin is found in small amounts in many foods (Table 19). Good sources include milk, eggs, fortified breakfast cereals, rice and mushrooms. About one-third of the average intake in Britain is derived from one source alone – milk and its products.

UV light can destroy riboflavin, so ideally these foods should be kept out of direct sunlight (e.g. bottled milk should not be allowed to stay too long on the doorstep). Some people in the UK, such as vegans, who avoid milk, have low intakes.

Most people should be able to get all the riboflavin they need by eating a varied and balanced diet. In 2008/10, average intakes from food were about 1.8 mg and 1.4 mg per day for men and women, respectively. This was well above the RNI (see Chapter 9), although a significant proportion of girls aged 11–18 years (17%) and adult women aged 19–64 years (11%) had intakes below the LRNI.

Table 19. Riboflavin content of selected foods (edible portion)

	Riboflavin (mg/100 g)
Milk, semi-skimmed	0.24
Cheese, Cheddar	0.39
Beef, stewing steak, stewed	0.15
Chicken, roast, meat only	0.11
Liver, lamb's, fried	5.65
Kidney, pig's, stewed	2.10
Eggs, chicken, whole, boiled	0.35
Red kidney beans, canned, reheated, drained	0.06
Potatoes, old, boiled	0.01
Brussels sprouts, boiled	0.09
Mushrooms, fried	0.34
Bananas	0.06
Apricots, ready-to-eat	0.16
Basmati rice, white, cooked	0.03
Bread, white	0.08
Cornflakes, fortified	1.30
Yeast extract	11.90

The main sources of riboflavin in the diet are milk and milk products (especially semi-skimmed milk), fortified breakfast cereals, meat and meat products, and drinks (especially beer and lager).

Guidance suggests that taking 40 mg or less of riboflavin per day as supplements is unlikely to be harmful. There is not enough evidence to comment on the safety of taking high doses of riboflavin supplements each day.

NIACIN (VITAMIN B$_3$)

Function, and effects of deficiency

Nicotinic acid and *nicotinamide* are two forms of another B vitamin (known collectively as *niacin*), which is involved in the utilisation of food energy. Nicotinamide can be synthesised from the amino acid *tryptophan*. Both forms are found in food. It is therefore convenient to express the niacin content of foods in terms of equivalents: on average, 1 mg of niacin equivalents equals 1 mg of available niacin or 60 mg of tryptophan, and this is accepted as a definition. The amounts of both forms in selected foods are shown in Table 20. Deficiency results in *pellagra*, in which the skin becomes dark and scaly especially where it is exposed to light. There are two apparent anomalies associated with pellagra: it occurs when the diet consists largely of maize, a cereal which contains nicotinic acid; and it can be cured by eating milk or eggs, which are not rich sources of this vitamin. The reasons for these anomalies are firstly, that the nicotinic acid in maize and other cereals is largely present in a bound form which is unavailable to humans (although it can be released by alkali as in the preparation of Mexican tortillas), and secondly, that proteins of milk and eggs are especially rich in tryptophan – the amino acid which can be converted to nicotinic acid in the body.

Sources and intakes

Good sources of niacin include beef, pork, wheat flour, maize flour, eggs and cows' milk. Most people should be able to get all the niacin they need by eating a varied and balanced diet. Average intakes in 2008/10 from food were about 45 mg and 32 mg per day for men and women, respectively – well above the RNI (see Chapter 9).

Pharmacological doses of nicotinic acid (but not nicotinamide) can cause flushing, itching and burning sensations of the skin, and nausea and gastrointestinal disturbance. Taking high doses of niacin for a long time could lead to liver damage. Evidence of the effects of taking high doses of nicotinamide supplements is sparse. Guidance suggests that taking 17 mg or less of nicotinic acid as supplements per day or taking 500 mg or less of nicotinamide as supplements per day is unlikely to be harmful.

Table 20. Niacin equivalents in selected foods (edible portion)

	Total niacin (mg/100 g)	Tryptophan (mg/100 g)	Niacin equivalents[a] (mg/100 g)
Milk, semi-skimmed	0.1	48	0.9
Cheese, Cheddar	0.1	408	6.9
Beef, stewing steak, stewed	2.4	372	8.6
Pork chop, grilled	9.1	372	15.3
Chicken, roast, meat only	6.2	318	11.5
Salmon, farmed, grilled	8.6	250	12.8
Eggs, chicken, whole, boiled	0.1	222	3.8
Baked beans	0.5	48	1.3
Peas, frozen, boiled	1.6	54	2.5
Potatoes, old, boiled	0.5	24	0.9
Bread, white[b]	1.6	120	3.6
Bread, wholemeal	3.8	138	6.1
Cornflakes, fortified[d]	13.5	0.4	13.9
Wheatgerm[c]	6.7	364	12.7
Tea, infusion	0.2	12	0.4
Coffee, infusion	0.7	0	0.7

The main sources of niacin in the diet are meat and meat products, cereals and cereal products (especially fortified breakfast cereals), and drinks (especially beer and lager).

[a] Available niacin plus (tryptophan/60).
[b] White flour is fortified to at least 1.6 mg of niacin per 100 g by law.
[c] Source: *Nutrient Survey of Flours and Grains – Analytical Report*, Food Standards Agency, 2005.
[d] Based on the 13.9 mg/100 g data for niacin provided by Kellogg's.

PYRIDOXINE (VITAMIN B$_6$)

Function, and effects of deficiency

Vitamin B$_6$, or pyridoxine, is involved in the metabolism of amino acids, including the conversion of tryptophan to niacin; the requirements are thus related to the protein content of the diet. The vitamin is also necessary for the formation of haemoglobin. Deficiency is rare in humans. It has been claimed that women taking oral contraceptives may have an increased requirement for pyridoxine; however, there is no evidence to support this.

Sources and intakes

Vitamin B$_6$ deficiency is unusual in humans since the vitamin occurs widely in food, for example: chicken, fish, liver, kidney, pork, eggs, wholegrain cereals (such as oatmeal, wheatgerm and brown rice), soya beans, peanuts and walnuts (Table 21). Micro-organisms in the intestine synthesise the vitamin, and some of this may be available to the body.

Table 21. Vitamin B$_6$ content of selected foods (edible portion)

	Vitamin B$_6$ (mg/100 g)
Milk, semi-skimmed	0.06
Beef, stewing steak, stewed	0.23
Chicken, roast, meat only	0.27
Turkey, roast, meat only	0.49
Tuna, canned in brine, drained	0.47
Baked beans	0.14
Cauliflower, boiled	0.15
Peas, frozen, boiled	0.09
Potatoes, old, boiled	0.33
Yam, boiled	0.12
Tomatoes, raw	0.14
Oranges	0.10
Bananas	0.29
Raisins	0.25
Bread, white	0.08
Bread, wholemeal	0.11
Cornflakes, fortified	1.20
Basmati rice, white, cooked	0.03
Wheatgerm	2.58

The main sources of vitamin B$_6$ in the diet are cereals and cereal products (especially fortified breakfast cereals), meat and meat products (especially poultry), and potatoes (especially potato chips) and savoury snacks.

Most people should be able to get all the vitamin B$_6$ they need from eating a varied and balanced diet. Average intakes from food in 2008/10 were 2.8 mg and 1.9 mg per day for men and women, respectively – well above the RNI (see Chapter 9).

If vitamin B$_6$ supplements are taken, it is important not to take too much as this could be harmful. Taking large amounts of vitamin B$_6$ (more than 200 mg per day), or taking it for a long time, can lead to a loss of feeling in the arms and legs – known as *peripheral neuropathy*. Generally these symptoms are reversible, so once the supplements are stopped, the symptoms usually disappear. However, in a few cases when people have taken large amounts of vitamin B$_6$, especially for more than a few months, the effect has been irreversible. Taking doses between 10 mg and 200 mg per day, for only short periods of time, might not cause any harm. But there is not enough evidence to say how long these doses can be taken safely. The UK Government advises against taking more than 10 mg of vitamin B_6 (the Safe Upper Level) as supplements per day. If people are taking a higher dose under medical advice, then this dose should be continued.

COBALAMIN (VITAMIN B_{12})

Function, and effects of deficiency

Vitamin B_{12} or cobalamin is a mixture of several related compounds, all of which contain the trace element *cobalt*. Together with folate, it is needed by rapidly dividing cells such as those in the bone marrow which form blood cells.

Because vitamin B_{12} does not occur in foods of vegetable origin, deficiency may occur in vegans who do not consume meat, milk, eggs or any supplement. It more usually arises, however, in those few individuals whose gastric juice contains no *intrinsic factor* (see 'The process of digestion' in Chapter 6) and who therefore cannot absorb this vitamin. Deficiency leads to a characteristic (*pernicious*) anaemia and the degeneration of nerve cells, and occurs most frequently in older people. If a state of vitamin B_{12} deficiency occurs, taking supplements of folic acid can mask it. An early symptom of vitamin B_{12} deficiency is anaemia. Taking large amounts of folic acid treats the anaemia without treating the vitamin B_{12} deficiency. If vitamin B_{12} deficiency is not diagnosed, it can eventually lead to damage of the nervous system (neurological damage). This is a concern particularly for older people, in whom vitamin B_{12} absorption can become more difficult.

Sources and intakes

Vitamin B_{12} occurs only in foods of animal origin, and in micro-organisms including yeast. Liver is the richest source, but useful amounts also occur in meat, fish, cheese and some fortified breakfast cereals, as shown in Table 22. If meat, fish or dairy foods are consumed then people should be able to get enough vitamin B_{12} from the diet. In 2008/10, average intakes from food were 6.1 µg and 4.7 µg per day for men and women, respectively. Adverse effects due to high doses in humans are rare and there is little evidence to show what the effects might be of taking high doses of vitamin B_{12} supplements for long periods. Guidance suggests that taking 2 mg or less of vitamin B_{12} as supplements per day is unlikely to be harmful.

Table 22. Vitamin B_{12} content of selected foods (edible portion)

	Vitamin B_{12} (µg/100 g)
Milk, whole	0.9
Milk, semi-skimmed	0.4
Cheese, Cheddar	2.4
Eggs, chicken, whole, boiled	1.1
Beef or lamb, mince, stewed	2
Pork chop, grilled	1
Liver, lamb's, fried	83
Pâté, liver	8
Kipper, grilled	12
Cod, fillets, baked	2
Tuna, canned in brine, drained	4
Cornflakes, fortified	2.1
Yeast extract	1

The main sources of vitamin B_{12} in the diet are milk and milk products (especially semi-skimmed milk), meat and meat products (especially liver and liver products), and oily fish.

FOLATE

Function, and effects of deficiency

Folate (vitamin B_9) is not naturally present in significant amounts in foods. The synthetic form of folate known as *folic acid* is used for food fortification and in supplements. Folate has several functions, including its action with vitamin B_{12} in rapidly dividing cells. Deficiency leads to a characteristic (*megaloblastic*) form of anaemia, which must be distinguished from that caused by a deficiency of vitamin B_{12}. Folate deficiency can result not only from a poor diet but also from increased needs for the synthesis of red blood cells in pregnant women, from increased requirements arising from certain medical conditions in the elderly, and when there is decreased absorption of folate in gastrointestinal disease.

Folate is important for pregnancy as a higher folate status in the mother has been associated with a reduced risk of her child developing a *neural tube defect*, such as spina bifida or anencephaly.

It is very difficult for women to meet increased requirements for folate from food alone. Therefore, taking a folic acid supplement is important when trying to get pregnant and in the early stages of pregnancy. All women of child-bearing age are advised to take 400 µg of folic acid per day as a supplement prior to conception and until they are 12 weeks pregnant. If folic acid supplementation was not taken before conception, it is important to start taking it as soon as the woman is aware of the pregnancy.

Table 23. Folate content of selected foods (edible portion)

	Folate (µg/100 g)
Cornflakes, fortified	166
Weetabix	170
Bread, wholemeal	40
Bread, white	25
Potatoes, old, boiled	19
Peas, frozen, boiled	47
Broccoli, boiled	64
Brussels sprouts, boiled	110
Lettuce	55
Okra, boiled	46
Apples, eating	1
Bananas	14
Oranges	31
Raisins	10
Almonds	48
Peanuts, plain, unsalted	110
Peanuts, dry-roasted	44
Black-eyed beans, boiled	210
Chickpeas, boiled	66
Eggs, chicken, whole, boiled	39
Kidney, ox, stewed	130
Beef, stewed	11
Cheese, Cheddar	31
Milk, semi-skimmed	6

The main sources of folate in the diet are cereals and cereal products (especially fortified breakfast cereals), vegetables, potatoes and drinks (especially beer and lager).

Women who have already had a pregnancy affected by a neural tube defect need to take 5 mg of folic acid each day until the 12th week of their pregnancy. In addition, women who have diabetes and those taking anti-epileptic medicines should consult their GP for advice, as it is likely that they will also need to take a higher dose of folic acid.

Sources and intakes

Folate occurs in small amounts in many foods. Good sources include green leafy vegetables (such as broccoli and Brussels sprouts), peas, chickpeas, yeast extract, brown rice and some fruit (such as oranges and bananas). Other useful sources include fortified breakfast cereals and some breads. Liver and its products are very rich sources but are not suitable for enhancing intakes by women who are, or might become, pregnant (see 'Vitamin A' earlier in this chapter). Folate is readily destroyed in cooking, with much being lost in the water used for cooking vegetables, and it is also readily oxidised to unavailable forms of the vitamin. Thus care should be taken to include several good sources of folate in the diet and to cook vegetables in only a little water for a short time to minimise the risk of deficiency. Selected sources of folate are shown in Table 23.

Apart from women who are planning a pregnancy or who are pregnant, most people should be able to get all the folate they need by eating a varied and balanced diet. In 2008/10, average intakes from food were about 310 µg and 230 µg per day for men and women, respectively, which are above the RNI (see Chapter 9).

Guidance suggests that taking 1 mg or less of folic acid supplements per day is unlikely to be harmful (see above).

PANTOTHENIC ACID

Pantothenic acid (vitamin B_5) is necessary for the release of energy from fat and carbohydrate. Dietary deficiencies of this vitamin are unlikely in humans because it is so widespread in food. Good sources include chicken, beef, potatoes, porridge, tomatoes, liver, kidney, yeast, eggs, broccoli and wholegrains such as brown rice and wholemeal bread. Breakfast cereals are also a good source if they have been fortified with pantothenic acid. Most people can get all the pantothenic acid they need by eating a varied and balanced diet. Average daily intakes from food in 2000/01 were about 7 mg for men and about 5 mg for women, which is within the range considered adequate. There is not enough evidence at present to know what the effects might be of taking high doses of pantothenic acid supplements for an extended period of time. Guidance suggests that taking a supplement of 200 mg or less of pantothenic acid per day is unlikely to be harmful.

BIOTIN

Biotin (vitamin B_7) is essential for the metabolism of fat. Very small amounts are required, and sufficient amounts may well be made by the bacteria normally inhabiting the large intestine. It is therefore probable that no additional biotin need be provided in the diet, except in the very unusual situation when large quantities of raw eggs are consumed. This is because raw, but not cooked, egg white contains a substance (*avidin*) which combines with biotin making it unavailable to the body.

Biotin occurs naturally in a wide range of foods, but at very low levels compared with other water-soluble vitamins. Relatively good sources include meat such as kidney and liver, egg yolk, some vegetables and dried mixed fruit. Most people should be able to get the amount of biotin they need from a varied and balanced diet. Average daily intakes from food in 2000/01 were 41 µg and 29 µg for men and women, respectively, which are within the ranges considered safe and adequate. There is little evidence to establish the extent of risk associated with supplemental biotin. Guidance suggests that taking 0.9 mg or less of biotin as supplements per day is unlikely to be harmful.

Vitamin C (ascorbic acid)

FUNCTION, AND EFFECTS OF DEFICIENCY

Vitamin C is necessary for the maintenance of healthy connective tissue. It is a powerful antioxidant and is involved in preventing damage to the body by free radicals. Humans are among the few animals (along with monkeys and guinea pigs) unable to form their own vitamin C, and must therefore obtain it from food. Deficiency soon results in bleeding, especially from small blood vessels (*capillaries*) under the skin and from the gums, and wounds heal more slowly. *Scurvy* follows and, if the deficiency is prolonged, death results. Mild deficiencies may occur in infants who are given unsupplemented cow's milk, in people eating poor diets (for example some elderly people), and in people who have very restricted diets that contain little besides wholegrain cereals which lack vitamin C. Claims that extremely large amounts of vitamin C cure colds and other minor ailments have little scientific basis.

SOURCES AND INTAKES

Vitamin C is not widely distributed in foods. Small amounts occur in milk, especially breast milk, and liver, but virtually all the vitamin C in most diets is derived from vegetables, potatoes and fruit. Many people do not eat enough vegetables and fruit, and vitamin C is readily lost from these foods during storage, preparation and cooking. Care should be taken to include good sources of the vitamin in the diet to minimise the risk of deficiency. The average vitamin C content of selected foods is shown in Table 24.

Citrus fruits and blackcurrants are particularly good sources but some tropical fruits, such as guavas and West Indian cherries, are even richer. Synthetic vitamin C, which is equally valuable, may be added to fruit juices to compensate for losses during storage and to juice drinks which are only partially composed of fruit juice.

The amount of vitamin C in any particular fruit or vegetable may differ considerably from the value shown in Table 24. This is because of the natural variations that occur, the variable losses during the time between harvesting and consumption in the home, and the variations in cooking methods that may be used. As an example, fresh peas may contain between 10 mg and 30 mg of vitamin C per 100 g; the higher values would tend to occur in the spring and early summer when the plants are growing most rapidly, and may be preserved by freezing. The loss which can occur after harvesting is illustrated in Table 24 by the average change in vitamin C content of potatoes during storage; it can also be substantial in the days that elapse between the harvest of leafy vegetables and their consumption in the home. Vitamin C, like riboflavin, is also rapidly lost when milk is allowed to stand on the doorstep; this may be important for young children and those older people with restricted diets for whom milk may be one of the few sources of this vitamin.

The highest contributions to vitamin C intake in the UK are made by drinks in the form of fruit juices and soft drinks with added vitamin C, fruit and vegetables, and potatoes also contribute a significant amount as the large

Table 24. Vitamin C content of selected foods (edible portion)

	Raw (mg/100 g)	After boiling (mg/100 g)
Courgettes	21	11
Carrots, old	6	2
Cabbage, average	49	20
Cauliflower	43	27
Lettuce	5	
Pepper, capsicum, green, raw	120	69
Plantain (green banana)	15	9
Potatoes, new, average	16	15
Potatoes, old, freshly dug	21	
Stored 3 months	9	
Stored 9 months	7	
Average	11	6
Sweet potatoes	23	17
Tomatoes	17	12 (canned)
Apples	6	
Bananas	11	
Blackcurrants	200	115 (stewed)
Grapefruit juice	31	
Kiwi fruit	59	
Mangoes	37	
Melon, cantaloupe	26	
Oranges	54	

The main sources of vitamin C in the diet are drinks in the form of fruit juices and soft drinks with added vitamin C, vegetables, fruit and potatoes. The vitamin C content of many vegetables and fruits varies widely, depending on variety, season and freshness.

quantities eaten more than compensate for their comparatively modest content of this vitamin. The only vegetable materials containing no vitamin C are cereal grains (unless they are allowed to sprout) and dried peas and beans.

Most people should be able to get all the vitamin C they need from a varied and balanced diet. Average daily intakes from food in 2008/10 by men and women, respectively, were about 91 mg and 88 mg – well above the RNI (see Chapter 9). Taking large doses (more than 1000 mg per day) can cause gastrointestinal disturbances. However, guidance suggests that taking 1000 mg or less of vitamin C supplements per day is unlikely to cause any significant adverse effects.

Vitamin D

FUNCTION, AND EFFECTS OF DEFICIENCY AND EXCESS

Vitamin D helps to maintain bone mineralisation by ensuring an appropriate supply of calcium in the blood. It achieves this primarily by enhancing the absorption of dietary calcium from the intestine, but it may also have a direct positive effect on the deposition of calcium in bone. Most people should be able to get all the vitamin D they need by eating a healthy, balanced diet and getting some summer sun.

However, infants and children who are deprived of vitamin D develop *rickets*, with deformed bones which are too weak to support their weight. In extreme cases, low blood levels of vitamin D, resulting in low blood levels of calcium, can cause heart failure.

Some adults are at risk from bone softening (*osteomalacia*), resulting in skeletal pain and bone fractures, because they absorb too little calcium from a diet low in calcium and vitamin D. Because these changes readily become permanent, it is important to prevent their development; hence, in the UK, supplements containing vitamin D are recommended for some groups of the population at risk of not getting enough vitamin D, and many fat spreads and some breakfast cereals are fortified.

The groups of the population who are at risk of not getting enough vitamin D are:

- all pregnant and breastfeeding women
- babies and young children under 5 years of age
- older people aged 65 and over
- people who are not exposed to much sun, such as people who cover up their skin when outdoors or those who are confined indoors for long periods

- people who have darker skins, such as people of African, African-Caribbean and South Asian origin.

The Department of Health recommends that:

- all pregnant and breastfeeding women should take a daily supplement containing 10 µg of vitamin D, to ensure that the mother's requirement for vitamin D is met and to build adequate fetal stores for early infancy
- all babies and young children aged 6 months to 5 years should take a daily supplement containing vitamin D in the form of vitamin drops, to help them to meet the requirement set for this age group of 7–8.5 µg of vitamin D per day. However, those babies who are fed infant formula will not need vitamin drops until they are receiving less than 500 ml (about a pint) of infant formula per day, as these products are fortified with vitamin D. Breastfed infants may need to receive drops containing vitamin D from 1 month old if their mother has not taken vitamin D supplements throughout pregnancy
- people aged 65 years and over and people who are not exposed to much sun should also take a daily supplement containing 10 µg of vitamin D.

Excessive intakes of vitamin D cause more calcium to be absorbed than can be excreted; the excess is then deposited in, and can damage, the kidneys. Vitamin D also encourages calcium to be removed from bones which can soften and weaken them. Guidance suggests that, for the general population, taking 25 µg or less per day of vitamin D as supplements is unlikely to cause adverse effects.

Infants are vulnerable to the *hypercalcaemia* associated with excess vitamin D. As a guide, supplementation should not take the infant much above current recommendations for nutritional need.

SOURCES AND INTAKES

Most vitamin D comes from sunlight on the skin. The vitamin forms under the skin in reaction to sunlight. The best source is summer sunlight; however, care should be taken to cover up or protect the skin before it turns red or burns.

Vitamin D is also found in a small number of foods (Table 25). All those which contain vitamin D naturally are products of animal origin and exhibit seasonal variations in the amounts present. Good sources are oily fish, liver and eggs. Vitamin D can also be used to fortify foods; the different forms used – vitamin D_2 (*ergocalciferol*) and vitamin D_3 (*cholecalciferol*) – both appear to be active in humans and can readily be manufactured using plant materials. Vitamin D is added to most fat spreads and some breakfast cereals. Cod liver oil supplements can also provide a source. Average daily intakes from food in 2008/10 were 3.1 µg and 2.6 µg for men and women respectively.

Table 25. Vitamin D content of selected foods (edible portion)

	Vitamin D (µg/100 g)
Milk, whole	0.0
Milk, skimmed, dried, fortified	2.1
Evaporated milk, whole, fortified	4.0
Cheese, Cheddar	0.3
Eggs, chicken, whole, boiled	1.8
Beef, stewing steak, stewed	0.6
Liver, lamb's, fried	0.9
Herring, grilled	16.1
Salmon, grilled, farmed	7.8
Sardines, canned in tomato sauce	8.0
Tuna, canned in oil, drained	3.0
Butter	0.9
Reduced-fat spread (62–75%), not polyunsaturated	8.4
Vegetable oil	0.0
Cornflakes, fortified[a]	4.2

The main sources of vitamin D in the diet are oily fish, meat and meat products, cereals and cereal products (especially fortified breakfast cereals), fat spreads, and eggs.

[a] Vitamin D is only in breakfast cereals if it is added.

Single vitamin D supplements or vitamin drops containing vitamin D (for use by under-5s) can be purchased at most pharmacies and supermarkets, or can be prescribed. Women, babies and children who qualify for, or already participate in, the Healthy Start Scheme (www.healthystart.nhs.uk) can get free supplements containing vitamin D.

Vitamin E

FUNCTION, AND EFFECTS OF DEFICIENCY AND EXCESS

A number of related compounds (*tocopherols*) show vitamin E activity, the most potent being alpha-tocopherol.[16] Its major activity in the body is as an antioxidant. Vitamin E occurs widely in foods, mainly those of plant origin, and like other fat-soluble vitamins it is stored in the body. People who cannot absorb or utilise the vitamin can also be deficient.

---

[16] Vitamin E activity is expressed as alpha-tocopherol equivalents; 1 IU of alpha-tocopherol is equivalent to 0.67 mg alpha-tocopherol.

SOURCES AND INTAKES

Most foods contain vitamin E. Good sources are plant oils such as soya, corn and olive oil. Other good sources include nuts, seeds and wheatgerm (found in cereals and cereal products). Meat, poultry and dairy products also provide small amounts. The main sources of vitamin E in the diet are fat spreads; breakfast cereals; biscuits, buns, cakes and pastries; potato chips and savoury snacks fried in oil; vegetables; and meat.

Average daily intakes of vitamin E from food in 2000/01 were about 10 mg and 8 mg for men and women, respectively, which are above what is considered adequate. Large doses of the vitamin may make the effects of vitamin K deficiency worse and hence affect blood coagulation (see below), and may cause a range of symptoms including headache and nausea. The UK Government advises that taking 800 IU (540 mg, the Safe Upper Level) or less of vitamin E from supplements each day is unlikely to be harmful.

Vitamin K

Vitamin K is a group of compounds necessary for the normal clotting of blood. Deficiency can occur in a very few newborn babies so, to counteract this possibility, all babies should be given a supplement of vitamin K at birth. It also occurs in rare individuals who cannot absorb or utilise the vitamin. A dietary deficiency is unlikely, partly because the vitamin is widespread in vegetable foods such as spinach, cabbage and cauliflower, peas and cereals, and partly because certain bacteria present in the intestine can synthesise it. Guidance suggests that a daily supplement of 1 mg of vitamin K is unlikely to be harmful.

Vitamins and antioxidant activity

Some carotenes, vitamin C and vitamin E are among the many substances in food that can have antioxidant properties. This attribute can help to counter the effects of *reactive oxygen species* (free radicals), which are produced by the body's normal metabolic processes. If free radicals accumulate, they can damage key cellular molecules such as DNA and proteins. Cells which do not repair all the damage to DNA may be more prone to developing cancer. Free radicals can also readily oxidise polyunsaturated fatty acids in foods and in cell membranes in the body to produce lipid peroxides which can also damage cells. Peroxides, for example those formed by the oxidation of low-density lipoprotein (LDL) cholesterol (see 'Health aspects of fats' in Chapter 3) may play a part in the formation of the 'plaque' which can build up on the walls of arteries and eventually cause heart disease.

Experts suggest that there may be evidence that high intakes of fruit and vegetables are protective against heart disease and some cancers. However, there is currently not enough evidence to identify any single component, or mixture of components, that protects against the development of these diseases; this also relates to individual vitamins, for example in the form of dietary supplements (vitamin pills). There is also evidence that high levels of ß-carotene in the form of supplements can actually increase the risk of cancer in smokers, who are already at high risk. As well as vitamins, fruits and vegetables contain a wide range of other compounds with varying levels of antioxidant activity and it is possible that the range and mix of antioxidant vitamins and other compounds found in fruits and vegetables are necessary for effective protective activity. Research is continuing into the possible role of these compounds in the prevention of heart disease and cancer.

9 Dietary Reference Values for nutrients

An adequate intake of all the essential nutrients is needed to maintain health, and there are additional requirements for growth, pregnancy and lactation. The exact amounts needed are different for each individual, and depend on factors such as age, height, weight, sex and physical activity throughout the day.

As these requirements can only be determined after lengthy experimentation, it is impracticable to determine them exactly for each individual. Instead, a number of national and international bodies have set standards in the form of recommended nutrient intakes for various groups of the population. These recommendations have generally been designed to ensure that the needs of most healthy people will be covered and are therefore higher than estimates of average requirements (except for energy). The actual nutrient requirements of almost all individuals are less than recommended intakes. Therefore, if a person's diet consistently contains more of a nutrient than is recommended, they are almost certainly obtaining more than their requirements. Consistently consuming less than the recommendations is not a good indicator of risk of deficiency. As a result, while Recommended Daily Intakes (RDIs) or Recommended Daily Amounts (RDAs) were useful for minimising the risk of dietary deficiency in a population, they were often used wrongly to assess the adequacy of the diet of an individual.

The Dietary Reference Values (DRVs) replaced RDAs in the UK in 1991 (see Appendix 9). However, the RDAs are used in nutrition labelling across Europe (see 'Uses of the Dietary Reference Values' later in this chapter).The DRVs cover a range of intakes for most nutrients and can therefore be used not only for assessing the adequacy of the diets of groups of people but also, in some circumstances, as a useful reference for those of healthy individuals in the UK. There are three values for most nutrients:

1 *Estimated Average Requirement* (EAR) of a group of people for energy or protein or a vitamin or mineral. About half of the group will usually need more than the EAR, and half less. The EARs for energy in the UK are shown in Table 26.

2 *Reference Nutrient Intake* (RNI) for protein or a vitamin or mineral. This is an amount of the nutrient that is enough, or more than enough, for about 97% of people in a group. If the average intake of a group is at RNI, then the risk of deficiency is very small. The RNIs for protein and selected vitamins and minerals are shown in Table 27.

3   *Lower Reference Nutrient Intake* (LRNI) is the amount of a nutrient that is enough for a small number of people in a group with the smallest needs. Most people will need more than this.

Since individual needs vary so widely, DRVs can only provide a guide to the adequacy or otherwise of a diet. Even when intakes are below the LRNI, biochemical measures of adequacy may be needed to determine whether there is really a problem.

As well as those nutrients shown in Table 27, the Committee on Medical Aspects of Food Policy (COMA) also gives DRVs for riboflavin, niacin, vitamin B_{12}, vitamin D, phosphorus, magnesium, potassium, chloride, copper, selenium and iodine.

A *safe intake* is used when there is not enough evidence to set an EAR, RNI or LRNI. The safe intake is the amount judged to be enough for almost everyone, but below a level that could have undesirable effects. These include pantothenic acid, biotin, vitamin E, vitamin K, manganese, molybdenum, chromium and fluoride (see Chapters 7 and 8).[17]

There are also DRVs for total fat, fatty acids, starch and sugars, and fibre (as non-starch polysaccharides – NSP). However, apart from certain fatty acids (see Chapter 3), none of these nutrients is essential. Since there is no actual requirement for them, EARs could not be set. Instead, desirable population average intakes were recommended for adults (see Table 28) with a view to improving health and reducing the incidence of diseases such as heart disease and some cancers in the UK. DRVs for fat, carbohydrate and NSP have not been set for children because research has not yet established the scientific basis for their needs. Children under the age of 5, who need energy-dense diets, should not be restricted in their fat intakes; however, from the age of 2 they can cut down on fat by gradually being introduced to foods such as low-fat dairy products.

---

[17] Note that, in 2003, the Expert Group on Vitamins and Minerals (EVM) was asked by the UK Government to advise on the safety of intakes of vitamins and minerals used in food supplements and fortified foods. The results are published in *Safe Upper Levels for Vitamins and Minerals* (Food Standards Agency, 2003).

Table 26. Estimated Average Requirements for energy in the UK (per day)

Infants	Breastfed	Breast milk substitute-fed	Mixed feeding or unknown
Age	(MJ/day) (kcal/day)	(MJ/day) (kcal/day)	(MJ/day) (kcal/day)
Boys			
1–2	2.2 (526)	2.5 (598)	2.4 (574)
3–4	2.4 (574)	2.6 (622)	2.5 (598)
5–6	2.5 (598)	2.7 (646)	2.6 (622)
7–12	2.9 (694)	3.1 (742)	3.0 (718)
Girls			
1–2	2.0 (478)	2.3 (550)	2.1 (502)
3–4	2.2 (526)	2.5 (598)	2.3 (550)
5–6	2.3 (550)	2.6 (622)	2.4 (574)
7–12	2.7 (646)	2.8 (670)	2.7 (646)

Children and adults	EAR (MJ/day) (kcal/day)	
Age	Male	Female
Children		
1	3.2 (765)	3.0 (717)
2	4.2 (1004)	3.9 (932)
3	4.9 (1171)	4.5 (1076)
4	5.8 (1386)	5.4 (1291)
5	6.2 (1482)	5.7 (1362)
6	6.6 (1577)	6.2 (1482)
7	6.9 (1649)	6.4 (1530)
8	7.3 (1745)	6.8 (1625)
9	7.7 (1840)	7.2 (1721)
10	8.5 (2032)	8.1 (1936)
11	8.9 (2127)	8.5 (2032)
12	9.4 (2247)	8.8 (2103)
13	10.1 (2414)	9.3 (2223)
14	11.0 (2629)	9.8 (2342)
15	11.8 (2820)	10.0 (2390)
16	12.4 (2964)	10.1 (2414)
17	12.9 (3083)	10.3 (2462)
18	13.2 (3155)	10.3 (2462)
Adults		
19–24	11.6 (2772)	9.1 (2175)
25–34	11.5 (2749)	9.1 (2175)
35–44	11.0 (2629)	8.8 (2103)
45–54	10.8 (2581)	8.8 (2103)
55–64	10.8 (2581)	8.7 (2079)
65–74	9.8 (2342)	8.0 (1912)
75+	9.6 (2294)	7.7 (1840)
All adults[a]	10.9 (2605)	8.7 (2079)

[a] In the last trimester of pregnancy, an increment of 191 kcal/day (or 0.8 MJ/day) is recommended. For lactation, an increment of 335 kcal/day (or 1.4 MJ/day) in the first six months is recommended.

Table 27. Reference Nutrient Intakes for selected nutrients for the UK (per day)

Age range	Protein (g)	Calcium (mg)	Iron (mg)	Sodium (mg)	Zinc (mg)	Vitamin A (µg)	Thiamin (mg)	Vitamin B$_6$ (mg)[a]	Folic acid (µg)	Vitamin C (mg)
0–3 months (formula-fed)	12.5	525	1.7	210	4.0	350	0.2	0.2	50	25
4–6 months	12.7	525	4.3	280	4.0	350	0.2	0.2	50	25
7–9 months	13.7	525	7.8	320	5.0	350	0.2	0.3	50	25
10–12 months	14.9	525	7.8	350	5.0	350	0.3	0.4	50	25
1–3 years	14.5	350	6.9	500	5.0	400	0.5	0.7	70	30
4–6 years	19.7	450	6.1	700	6.5	500	0.7	0.9	100	30
7–10 years	28.3	550	8.7	1200	7.0	500	0.7	1.0	150	30
Males										
11–14 years	42.1	1000	11.3	1600	9.0	600	0.9	1.2	200	35
15–18 years	55.2	1000	11.3	1600	9.5	700	1.1	1.5	200	40
19–50 years	55.5	700	8.7	1600	9.5	700	1.0	1.4	200	40
50+ years	53.3	700	8.7	1600	9.5	700	0.9	1.4	200	40
Females										
11–14 years	41.2	800	14.8[b]	1600	9.0	600	0.7	1.0	200	35
15–18 years	45.0	800	14.8[b]	1600	7.0	600	0.8	1.2	200	40
19–50 years	45.0	700	14.8[b]	1600	7.0	600	0.8	1.2	200	40
50+ years	46.5	700	8.7	1600	7.0	600	0.8	1.2	200	40
Pregnant	+6.0	[c]	[c]	[c]	[c]	+100	+0.1[d]	[c]	+100	+10
Lactating										
0–4 months	+11.0	+550	[c]	[c]	+6.0	+350	+0.2	[c]	+60	+30
Over 4 months	+8.0	+550	[c]	[c]	+2.5	+350	+0.2	[c]	+60	+30

[a] Based on protein providing 14.7% of the EAR for energy.
[b] These RNIs will not meet the needs of approximately 10% of women with the highest menstrual losses, who may need iron supplements.
[c] No increment.
[d] Last trimester only.

Table 28. Dietary Reference Values for fat and carbohydrate for adults as a percentage of daily energy intake

	Population average	
	Percentage of total energy[a]	Percentage of food energy
Saturated fatty acids	10	11
Polyunsaturated fatty acids	6	6.5
Monounsaturated fatty acids	12	13
Trans fatty acids	2	2
Total fat	33	35
Non-milk extrinsic sugars	10	11
Intrinsic and milk sugars, and starch	37	39
Total carbohydrate	47	50
Fibre as non-starch polysaccharides (g/day)[b]	18 g	18 g

[a] Includes energy from alcohol.
[b] COMA proposed that adult diets should contain an average for the population of 18 g per day of non-starch polysaccharide (NSP) from a variety of foods whose constituents contain it as a naturally integrated component.

Energy

Energy balance and weight maintenance are achieved when energy intake is equal to total energy expenditure over time. Progressive weight gain or loss results from energy intakes that either exceed or do not meet energy expenditure, even as a small fraction of energy needs, over a prolonged period. The recommendation for different sections (age and gender) of the population was therefore set at the EAR. Energy needs are calculated using basal metabolic rates (BMR – see Appendix 2) and physical activity levels (PAL – see 'Activity' in Chapter 5).

$$EAR = BMR \times PAL$$

During pregnancy, energy is required for placental and fetal growth and for growth of maternal tissues, e.g. the uterus, breast and adipose tissues. In addition, there is also an increase in the energy cost of movement because of increases in the mother's weight, particularly over 25 weeks' gestation. However, some of this cost is offset by the mother becoming less active. Ideally, women should begin pregnancy at a healthy body weight. Women who are underweight or overweight at the beginning of pregnancy are at risk of poor maternal and fetal outcomes. Women who are underweight benefit from greater weight gain during pregnancy. For women who are overweight and obese, the consequences of weight change during pregnancy are not completely understood. Given this uncertainty, a precautionary approach has been adopted and weight loss during pregnancy is not advised. Energy is also needed for lactation, as breast milk contains enough energy to supply the needs of the growing infant. The EARs for pregnancy and lactation defined in the report *Dietary Reference Values for Energy 2011* by the Scientific and Advisory Committee (SACN) are estimates of the incremental energy intakes likely to be associated with healthy outcomes for mother and child, for women consuming energy intakes that match energy expenditure at the commencement of pregnancy. That is, for women who are overweight, the incremental energy intakes should be added to EAR values calculated at pre-conception body weights, rather than at healthy body weights for non-pregnant women or men.

Fat

DRVs for fatty acids and total fat are given as their percentage contributions to energy intake (Table 28). These can be translated into quantities of fat or saturates per day for the average adult; around 100 g and 80 g of fat per day and around 30 g and 20 g of saturated fatty acids per day for men and women, respectively. These should be regarded only as guidelines to desirable intakes, rather than estimates of individual requirements, and are average values for the population consistent with good health. Apart from the essential fatty acids (see 'Unsaturated fatty acids' in Chapter 3), there is no absolute need for these nutrients individually. A breakdown of the different types of fat (e.g. into saturated, unsaturated etc.) has been included because their varying effects on health (see 'Health aspects of fat' in Chapter 3) are as important to take into account as is total fat intake. The DRV for saturated fatty acids has been set with the intention of reducing the average blood cholesterol level of the population in order to help decrease the incidence of heart disease. To meet this target intake, there needs to be a considerable change in people's diets; current recommendations are that present average intakes of saturates should be reduced from about 13% to no more than about 11% of food energy. It is recommended that average intakes of polyunsaturated fatty acids (PUFAs) do not increase. If monounsaturated fatty acid intakes also stay the same, or increase at the expense of PUFAs, total fat intakes must decrease to bring about a decreased intake of saturates. Average total fat intakes for the population are currently at the recommended level of about 35% of dietary energy for the population as a whole. A small proportion of the population still have fat intakes of nearly 50% of dietary energy.

Carbohydrates

DRVs for carbohydrates are also given as their percentage contributions to energy intake. It is recommended that 50% of food energy should come from carbohydrates. Carbohydrates are expressed in the following terms: sugars, starches, intrinsic and non-milk extrinsic (NME) sugars, and milk sugars (see Chapter 2 for definitions of terms).

NME sugars are more detrimental to dental health than other forms of sugar, and it is currently recommended that the target population average intake be no more than 10% of dietary energy (11% of food energy). As the present average intake of NME sugars for adults is about 13% (15% in children) of food energy, many people will need to reduce their intakes of certain foods such as table sugar, confectionery, cakes, jam, honey and sugary soft drinks. Starch and intrinsic and milk sugars should therefore provide most of the 50% of dietary energy to be derived from carbohydrate.

Average adult intakes of NSP (see 'Non-starch polysaccharides' in Chapter 2) should increase from the present level of about 14 g per day to about 18 g per day. Children should eat proportionately less. Small children under 2 years of age should not eat fibre-rich foods in place of other energy-rich foods or they may not be able to satisfy their energy needs. The amount of NSP in selected foods is shown in Table 2 (Chapter 2).

SACN is reviewing the evidence on carbohydrates and health; it is anticipated that the report will go to consultation in 2013.

Protein

The DRVs are based on estimates of need. The protein RNI for adults aged 19 or over is 0.75 g per kg (of body weight) per day. Extra protein is allowed for growth in children, growth of the fetus and maternal tissue in pregnant women, and producing breast milk during lactation. The current average adult protein intake is about 18% of food energy which is above the RNI but not likely to have an adverse effect on health. Since very high intakes will increase the rate at which kidney function is lost with age, it is recommended that protein intakes should not exceed twice the RNI.

Calcium

DRVs allow for the limited absorption of calcium from the diet and for the high needs of growing children and adolescents. There is no recommended increase in the intake of calcium for the period of pregnancy as calcium absorption is known to increase during this time, but extra may be needed during lactation to provide for milk production (see Table 27).

Iron

DRV values assume that only 15% of iron is absorbed from a mixed diet. The RNI for women of child-bearing age is higher than for other groups to take account of the higher iron requirements of women with high menstrual blood losses. However, women with very high menstrual blood losses may require intakes above the RNI and may need to take iron supplements.

Sodium

The RNI for adults of 1.6 g per day of sodium (about 4 g of salt) is enough to meet the physiological needs of almost everyone and there is no advantage in exceeding this amount. Habitually high intakes of sodium have been associated with high blood pressure which is a major risk factor for heart disease and premature death. In 1994, COMA, in its report *Nutritional Aspects of Cardiovascular Disease*, recommended a reduction in the average salt intake of the population from 9 g per day (the average level at that time) to 6 g per day to reduce the population's blood pressure. Analysis of salt in urine samples indicates an average adult intake of about 3.44 g of sodium per day (equivalent to about 8.6 g of salt per day) (Food Standards Agency urinary sodium survey, 2008) which is considered too high, and current recommendations are that the average adult population intake of sodium should not exceed 2.4 g (6 g of salt) per day to help to decrease the incidence of high blood pressure and therefore reduce the risk of heart disease and stroke.

In its 2003 report *Salt and Health*, SACN endorsed COMA's[18] 1994 recommendation to consume no more than an average of 6 g per day of salt. It also made recommendations on the maximum amounts of salt intake for babies and children (see Table 27 and 'Sodium and chloride' in Chapter 7). The maximum salt intakes set for adults and children do not represent ideal or optimum consumption levels (they are above the RNIs) but are considered achievable population goals.

Niacin

DRVs allow for the contributions made by tryptophan to the niacin intake in addition to pre-formed nicotinic acid (see 'Niacin' in Chapter 8).

Vitamin A

DRVs allow for the contributions made by carotenes to the vitamin A intake in addition to pre-formed retinol. Pregnant women and women thinking of having a baby should not take supplements containing vitamin A or fish liver oil (which contains high levels of vitamin A) (except on medical advice) and should not eat liver or liver products, which are extremely rich sources of vitamin A. High intakes of retinol in pregnancy can harm the unborn baby.

---

[18] COMA was replaced by the SACN in 2000.

Some evidence suggests that vitamin A intakes over 1500 µg per day may increase the risk of bone fracture (SACN, *Review of Dietary Advice on Vitamin A*, 2005). As a precaution, regular consumers of liver (once a week or more) are advised not to increase liver intakes or take vitamin A supplements. Post-menopausal women and older people at risk of osteoporosis are also advised not to consume more than 1.5 mg of vitamin A per day from food and supplements combined (SACN, 2005).

Folate

The extra quantity of folate (or folic acid as a supplement) required by women who are or who may become pregnant, in relation to reducing the risk of neural tube defects in their offspring, is described in 'Folate' in Chapter 8.

Vitamin C

Opinions differ about the quantity of vitamin C required for health. It is generally agreed that 10 mg daily will not only prevent, but also cure, scurvy. The RNI of 40 mg for adults is thought to provide a reasonable safety margin. This is recommended to increase to 50 mg per day during pregnancy and to 70 mg per day during lactation. The evidence for possible benefits of significantly higher general intakes is still conflicting. (See 'Vitamin C (ascorbic acid)' in Chapter 8 for guidance on high intakes.)

Vitamin D

For most people in the UK, the main source of vitamin D is from the action of summer sunlight on the skin. Therefore, no DRVs have been set for 4–65-year-olds, as it is assumed that their exposure to summer sun and eating a healthy, balanced diet will result in an adequate vitamin D status. However, there are some groups of the population who are at risk of not getting enough vitamin D. These groups are:

- all pregnant and breastfeeding women
- babies and young children under 5 years of age
- older people aged 65 and over
- people who are not exposed to much sun, such as people who cover up their skin when outdoors or those who are confined indoors for long periods
- people who have darker skins, such as people of African, African-Caribbean and South Asian origin.

The Department of Health recommends that:

- all pregnant and breastfeeding women should take a daily supplement containing 10 µg of vitamin D, to ensure that the mother's RNI is met and to build adequate fetal stores for early infancy
- all babies and young children aged 6 months to 5 years should take a daily supplement containing vitamin D in the form of vitamin drops, to help them to meet the RNI set for this age group of 7–8.5 µg of vitamin D per day. However, those babies who are fed infant formula will not need vitamin drops until they are receiving less than 500 ml (about a pint) of infant formula per day, as these products are fortified with vitamin D. Breastfed infants may need to receive drops containing vitamin D from 1 month old if their mother has not taken vitamin D supplements throughout pregnancy
- people aged 65 years and over and people who are not exposed to much sun should also take a daily supplement containing 10 µg of vitamin D to meet their RNI for the same amount.

Single vitamin D supplements or vitamin drops containing vitamin D (for use by under-5s) can be purchased at most pharmacies and supermarkets, or can be prescribed. Women, babies and children who qualify for, or already participate in, Healthy Start[19] (www.healthystart.nhs.uk) can get free supplements containing vitamin D.

Excessive intakes of vitamin D cause more calcium to be absorbed than can be excreted; the excess is then deposited in, and can damage, the kidneys. Vitamin D also encourages calcium to be removed from bones which can soften and weaken them. Guidance suggests that, for the general population, taking 25 µg or less per day of vitamin D as supplements is unlikely to cause adverse effects.

Infants are vulnerable to the *hypercalcaemia* associated with excess vitamin D. As a guide, supplementation should not take the infant much above current recommendations for nutritional need.

Regulation of nutrient intakes

Excessive intakes of many of the minerals can be harmful, as can excessive intakes of some of the vitamins – especially vitamin A. Such intakes may result from the excessive consumption of certain foods (liver and fortified foods) and/or excessive use of dietary supplements (see also Chapters 7 and 8). Although our storage capacity for most nutrients apart from energy (as fat) is limited, the healthy body nevertheless contains enough reserves to last for many weeks or

---

[19] Healthy Start replaced the Welfare Food Scheme in 2006. It covers the whole of the UK.

months, even when few or no nutrients are consumed. Thus, while DRVs are most conveniently expressed in daily terms, it is not necessary for the diet to contain these quantities every day. It is sufficient if the requirements are met over a period of time.

Uses of the Dietary Reference Values

ASSESSMENT OF DIETS OF GROUPS OF PEOPLE

For population groups, the EAR for energy and the population averages for fat, carbohydrates and fibre are used. If the average intake of protein, vitamins and minerals of the group is at or above the RNI, there will be very little risk of deficiency within the group. Conversely, the greater the percentage of the population below the RNI, the greater is the risk that insufficiencies or even deficiencies will occur.

ASSESSMENT OF AN INDIVIDUAL'S DIET

Since most estimates of an individual's nutrient intakes are not very accurate, great care needs to be taken in using DRVs for assessing the adequacy of the diet of an individual. An intake above the RNI is almost certainly adequate. Whether a person consuming an intake somewhere between the RNI and the LRNI is getting sufficient amounts will depend on their level of need, but the closer the intake is to the LRNI, the more likely insufficiency becomes. However, because people's physiological needs vary considerably, deficiency of a nutrient cannot be diagnosed on the basis of dietary assessment alone.

PLANNING FOOD SUPPLIES FOR LARGE GROUPS

Those preparing foods for large groups of people have a great opportunity to help them to meet their DRVs. Owing to the diversity of foods on menus, there is a range of ways to meet the needs of large groups (such as in schools and prisons). For some groups, e.g. schools, the various education departments of the UK have set statutory standards or issued voluntary guidance. This may vary by country but, in general, the aim is for lunch to meet about a third of the day's nutrient requirements. See, for example:

- *Eat Better Do Better. A Guide to Introducing the Government's Food-based and Nutrient-based Standards for School Lunches*, School Food Trust, 2007.
- *Hungry for Success: A Whole School Approach to School Meals in Scotland. Final Report of the Expert Panel on School Meals*, Scottish Government, 2002.
- *Appetite for Life Action Plan*, Welsh Assembly Government, 2008.

- *School Meals, Top Marks. Nutritional Standards for School Lunches: A Guide for Implementation*, Health Promotion Agency for Northern Ireland, 2007.

For other care settings, there is less consistency and government policy only states that wholesome and nutritious food be provided. An example of an approach to meeting the needs of adults in major institutions can be found in *Healthier and More Sustainable Catering: A Toolkit for Serving Foods to Adults* (Department of Health, 2011). This publication includes information on buying, cooking and serving foods as well as useful guidance for organisations aiming to meet the Government's buying standards for food and catering services.

NUTRITION LABELLING

DRVs are not a single figure and they vary according to age and gender and between EU member states. This level of detail is inappropriate for food labelling, as it is impractical to provide more than a single reference amount for intake. Within the EU, the approach used for nutritional labelling is known as Recommended Daily Amounts (RDAs), which is why RDAs are used on food labels. RDAs may not necessarily be the same as DRVs. Currently within the EU the numbers to be used for *nutrition labelling* are defined in a 1990 Council Directive (90/496/EEC).

However, new EU food-labelling regulations have just been harmonised across Europe. RDAs will be replaced with Nutrient Reference Values under the new Food Information Regulations (FIR), defined in Regulation 1169/2011. Although the FIR is in place, it will not become mandatory until December 2014. Therefore, at the time of publication of this manual, there will be businesses still complying with the existing legislation while moving slowly towards the FIR format. For more information on the new Nutrient Reference Values to be used for nutrition labelling, see Annex XIII to EU Regulation 1169/2011 at: http://eur-lex.europa.eu/LexUriServ/LexUriServ.do?uri=OJ:L:2011:304:0018:0063:EN:PDF

PART 2

Nutritional value of food and diets

10 Introduction to, and general effects of, preparation and processing

Introduction

This part of the manual discusses the nutritional importance of particular foods in the context of the diet as a whole.

The nutritional importance of any food depends upon:

* the composition of the raw food or ingredients as grown or purchased
* the extent to which its nutrients are lost during storage, processing or cooking
* the composition of the cooked food as consumed, including any addition of nutrients during manufacture
* the amount that is usually eaten
* each individual's own nutritional needs and the extent to which they have already been met by other foods in the diet.

Many factors combine to produce variations in the nutrient content of foods. Representative values for the most important nutrients in a wide selection of foods are given in tables throughout this manual and in Appendix 3, and these should constantly be referred to when using this part of the book. It must be remembered, however, that individual samples or brands may differ considerably from the values quoted here. A wider selection of foods and nutrients can be found in *McCance and Widdowson's Composition of Foods Integrated Dataset* (COFIDS) for those who wish to estimate nutrient intakes in more detail.

The general effects of storage, processing and cooking are discussed below, and the application of these principles to specific foods and menus is described in Chapters 11 and 12.

Average percentage contributions made by major types of food to energy and nutrient intakes from food consumed by adults in the UK during 2008/10, and the average daily intakes of energy and these nutrients, are shown in Table 29. This table was derived from the first two years of the National Diet and Nutrition Survey Rolling Programme, which included a nationally representative sample

Table 29. Percentage contribution made by food groups to the nutrient content of the average adult diet in 2008/10

	Energy	Protein	Fat	Saturated fatty acids	Carbohydrate
Cereal and cereal products, of which	29	23	19	19	43
Bread	11	10	4	3	20
Breakfast cereals	3	3	1	1	6
Biscuits, buns, cakes, pastries and fruit pies	6	2	7	8	8
Milk and milk products, of which	9	14	13	22	5
Semi-skimmed milk	2	4	2	4	2
Cheese	3	5	6	10	0
Egg and egg dishes	2	3	4	4	0
Fat spreads and oils, of which	3	0	10	10	0
Butter	1	0	3	5	0
Meat and meat products, of which	17	37	24	25	6
Beef, veal and dishes	3	8	4	5	1
Chicken and turkey dishes	4	12	5	4	1
Coated chicken and turkey	1	2	1	1	0
Liver and liver dishes	0	0	0	0	0
Meat pies and pastries	2	1	2	3	1
Burgers, kebabs and sausages	3	4	4	4	1
Bacon and ham	1	4	2	2	0
Fish and fish dishes	3	7	5	3	1
Vegetables and potatoes, of which	11	8	10	7	14
Chips, fried and roast potatoes and potato products	4	2	5	3	5
Savoury snacks	2	1	3	1	2
Fruit	3	1	1	0	6
Nuts and seeds	1	1	2	1	0
Sugar and preserves, of which	5	1	3	5	8
Chocolate and confectionery	2	1	3	4	2
Sugars, including table sugar, preserves and sweet spreads	2	0	0	0	5
Alcoholic and non-alcoholic beverages, of which	11	2	1	1	11
Beer, lager, cider and perry	4	1	0	0	3
Soft drinks, not low calorie	2	0	0	0	5
Fruit juice	1	0	0	0	2
Miscellaneous	3	2	5	3	3
Average daily nutrient intake (from food sources only)	8 MJ	77 g	71 g	26 g	227 g

Source: Department of Health and Food Standards Agency, *National Diet and Nutrition Survey: Headline Results from Years 1 and 2 (Combined) of the Rolling Programme (2008/9–2009/10)*
Figures have been rounded to the nearest final digit so there may be an apparent slight discrepancy between the sum of the constituent items and the total shown.

NMES	Fibre (NSP)	Calcium	Iron	Sodium[a]	Vitamin C	Vitamin A	Folate	Vitamin D
20	38	29	38	31	3	5	25	9
0	19	16	16	18	0	0	11	0
4	6	2	12	2	1	0	9	5
12	5	3	5	4	0	2	2	2
6	1	41	1	9	4	12	7	4
0	0	14	0	2	2	2	3	0
0	0	13	0	4	0	6	2	2
0	0	2	3	2	0	4	2	12
0	0	0	0	3	0	9	4	19
0	0	0	0	1	0	3	0	1
1	11	6	17	27	2	18	6	24
0	3	1	5	4	0	1	2	5
1	3	1	3	5	1	1	1	3
0	0	0	1	1	0	0	0	1
0	0	0	1	0	0	15	1	1
0	1	1	1	2	0	0	0	2
0	3	2	2	5	1	0	1	5
0	0	0	1	7	0	0	0	3
0	1	2	3	5	0	1	2	30
3	32	7	18	9	37	45	28	1
0	7	1	3	1	5	0	5	0
0	2	0	1	2	1	0	1	0
1	9	2	3	1	21	1	4	0
0	1	0	1	0	0	0	1	0
27	1	2	2	1	0	0	1	0
7	1	2	1	0	0	0	1	0
17	0	0	0	0	0	0	0	0
36	0	6	8	2	31	3	15	0
9	0	2	2	1	0	0	10	0
15	0	1	0	0	8	1	0	0
8	0	1	1	0	20	1	4	0
5	3	3	5	9	1	4	5	2
62 g	14 g	830 mg	11 mg	2.4 g	90 mg	995 µg	268 µg	2.9 µg

[a] These values are for intakes from food sources only and do not include further additions of salt in cooking or at the table.

of about 1000 adults and 1000 children aged 18 months upwards from private households across the UK.[20]

Figures have been rounded to the nearest final digit so there may be an apparent slight discrepancy between the sum of the constituent items and the total shown. These values are for percentages from food and dietary supplements only. However, the average total daily sodium intake figure includes salt used in cooking and at the table.

Cooking and preservation

Most foods have to be prepared and cooked before they can be eaten. For some foods the process may be simple, as in the peeling of an orange. For others it may be complex: for example, wheat grains must be separated from the inedible parts of the plant and milled into flour, which in turn may need to be treated before being baked into bread. At each stage, some of the nutrients will be discarded or destroyed, whether the process takes place in a factory or in the home.

Nutrients may be further reduced if the food is stored for long periods, particularly if conditions are not ideal.

Although these losses are usually not of major significance if overall a balanced diet as depicted by the eatwell plate (Appendix 6) is being eaten (as this will still provide a considerable excess of nutrients over the Reference Nutrient Intakes (RNIs)), it is nevertheless desirable that the losses are kept to a minimum.

A discussion of the main methods of cooking and preserving foods is therefore followed by descriptions of the factors that tend to reduce the stability of each nutrient. Applications to specific foods are discussed in Chapter 11.

Cooking can also modify the nutrient content through the addition of nutrients when creating composite foods or through processes such as frying or roasting (see Chapter 12).

HOME COOKING

Heat is generally applied to food in one of three ways:

* directly, with or without additional fat – as in roasting, grilling and baking (120–250°C; 250–475°F), and microwave cooking

---

[20] The National Diet and Nutrition Survey (NDNS) is a continuous cross-sectional survey designed to assess the diet, nutrient intake and nutritional status of the general population aged 18 months upwards living in private households in the UK. Results are used by the Government to develop policy and monitor progress on diet and nutrition, and to assess whether the UK population is meeting expert recommendations for particular nutrients. Data from the first two years of this survey have been used extensively throughout this manual.

- with water – as in boiling, steaming, stewing and braising (100°C; 212°F)
- with fat – as in frying (155–225°C; 310–435°F).

Heat causes chemical and physical changes in food which in general make the flavour, palatability and digestibility of the raw product more acceptable and may improve its keeping quality. Heat may also increase the availability of some nutrients by destroying enzymes and anti-digestive factors. But cooking more usually results in the loss of nutrients, this being greatest at high temperatures with long cooking times, or if an excessive amount of liquid is used. The losses of soluble vitamins and minerals are, of course, reduced if meat juices and cooking water are not discarded but used in (for example) soups or gravies.

The effects of microwaves and infrared cooking on nutrients are similar to the effects of the more traditional methods they replace. When used for reheating, they cause little additional destruction of nutrients.

HOME FREEZING

This method of food preservation may result in some loss of thiamin and vitamin C when vegetables are blanched in water before freezing, but less than would otherwise result from the continuing action of enzymes in the plant tissues during storage. In general, differences between the nutrient content of cooked fresh foods and cooked frozen foods as served on the plate are small.

INDUSTRIAL PROCESSING

Processing in a factory is mainly intended to preserve food so that the choice is greater and independent of geographical area or the season of the year, and to reduce the time spent on preparing food in the home. The main commercial processes which cause some loss of nutrients are blanching, heat processing, and drying or dehydration.

Blanching or scalding in water or steam is done mainly to minimise enzyme activity, and is a first step in the preservation of most vegetables for subsequent freezing, canning or dehydration. The process is usually carefully controlled, but small amounts of some minerals and water-soluble vitamins dissolve in the water or steam and are lost.

Freezing itself has little effect on nutritional value and, since the delay after harvesting is minimal, the nutrients in the high-quality fresh foods that are used are generally well retained and can be present at a higher level than that of 'fresh' produce that has been stored for some time.

Heat processing in metal cans or bottling in glass jars will reduce the amounts of heat-sensitive vitamins, especially thiamin, folate and vitamin C. The losses will depend on the length of time needed to destroy any harmful organisms and to cook the food, and will be greater for larger cans and in foods of a solid consistency, such as ham, because of the slow transfer of heat from the outside to the centre. They will also depend on the acidity of the food and the presence of light and air, so that it is difficult to give precise values for expected losses. In addition, the process of canning tuna reduces the level of long-chain omega-3 fatty acids to a low level.

Dehydration (in air) in carefully controlled conditions has little effect on most nutrients, but destroys about half the vitamin C. Thiamin is completely lost if sulphur dioxide is added as a preservative. Prolonged sun drying as in the production of raisins allows substantial changes to occur. Suitable packaging of dried foods is essential to prevent nutrient losses during their prolonged storage life.

High Pressure Processing (HPP) has emerged as a relatively new low-temperature process, which destroys bacteria but has little effect on the sensory and nutritional quality of the product. Food products are subjected either in a batch or continuous process to a pressure of 4000 to 7000 times atmospheric pressure for around 10 minutes. There is a small temperature rise under the high pressure, and protein denaturation occurs. As bacterial spores may survive this process, products on the market processed by HPP have been restricted to acid foods such as fruit juices, smoothies and dips. The process can be used to destroy pathogens in oysters and assist removal from the shell.

Stability of individual nutrients

PROTEIN

Protein is denatured by heat and when cooking conditions are severe it becomes less available for utilisation within the body. This is partly because the changes in structure make the protein more difficult to digest and partly because some of the component amino acids are destroyed – most notably lysine, which can react with carbohydrates in the food. These losses can also occur during prolonged storage even at room temperature.

VITAMIN A

Both retinol and beta-carotene are stable throughout most cooking procedures, although there will be some loss at high temperatures and in the presence of air (e.g. when butter is used in frying or when vegetables are canned). Some loss also occurs during prolonged storage if light and air are not rigorously excluded.

B VITAMINS

The *B vitamins* are all water-soluble and most are also sensitive to heat. *Thiamin* is one of the least stable vitamins. It is readily dissolved out of foods into the cooking water and is easily lost in the juices from meat. It is fairly stable when heated if the food is acidic, but a considerable amount can be lost under alkaline conditions, especially if sodium bicarbonate is added during cooking. It has been calculated that, on average, about 20% of the thiamin content of all the food brought into the home is lost during cooking and reheating, but the loss is greater in some foods than in others. Any foods that have been preserved by the use of sulphur dioxide, such as sausages, will contain very little thiamin.

Riboflavin can be lost in discarded cooking water and meat juices; it is also unstable in alkaline conditions, and is especially sensitive to light.

Niacin is an exceptionally stable vitamin, and will be lost only through its solubility in water.

Other B *vitamins* are all soluble in water. Vitamin B_6, folate and pantothenic acid are also sensitive to heat, and can therefore be lost in cooking and canning.

VITAMIN C

Vitamin C is perhaps the least stable of all the vitamins. In addition to being water-soluble, it is very readily destroyed by air. This destruction is accelerated by heat, by alkali and by the presence of certain metals, e.g. copper or iron. Vitamin C is also rapidly oxidised when an enzyme present in fruit and vegetables is released by any physical damage to the plant such as cutting. Thus, poor cooking practices, such as prolonged boiling of green vegetables in large amounts of water (especially if sodium bicarbonate has been added to improve the colour) followed by keeping them hot, can result in destruction of all the vitamin C originally present. Vitamin C is, however, partly protected by sulphur dioxide.

OTHER VITAMINS AND MINERALS

Vitamin D is stable during normal cooking procedures.

Vitamin E is not soluble in water and is stable when heated. It is, however, oxidised in the presence of air.

Minerals are unaffected by heat processing but can be lost by leaching into water during moist cooking or processing.

Table 30 summarises the sensitivity of the most important nutrients.

Table 30. Summary of factors (✓) which may reduce the nutrients in food

Nutrient	Heat	Light	Air	Water	Acid	Alkali	Other
Protein	✓ (if prolonged)						
Minerals				✓			
Vitamin A	✓ (with air)		✓ (with heat)				Metals
Thiamin[a]	✓		✓	✓		✓	Sulphur dioxide
Riboflavin		✓		✓		✓	
Folate	✓		✓ (but protected by vitamin C)	✓		✓	
Vitamin C[a]	✓	✓	✓ (but protected by sulphur dioxide)	✓		✓	Enzymes, metals

[a]Least stable during cooking and storage.

11   Foods

The balanced diet

The UK Government advises that a healthy, balanced diet has plenty of fruit and vegetables (at least five portions of a variety every day); plenty of starchy foods, such as potatoes, bread, rice and pasta, choosing wholegrain varieties whenever possible; some milk and dairy foods; some meat, fish, eggs, beans and other non-dairy sources of protein; and just a small amount of foods and drinks that are high in fat and/or sugar. Across the UK, health departments encourage organisations and individuals to use the eatwell plate (Appendix 6) to help to ensure that people receive consistent messages about the balance of foods in a healthy diet.

Milk

IMPORTANCE IN THE DIET

Cow's milk is the most complete of all foods, containing nearly all the constituents of nutritional importance to humans; it is, however, comparatively deficient in iron and vitamins C and D. Unlike other foods of animal origin, milk contains a significant amount of carbohydrate, in the form of the disaccharide *lactose* (see 'Disaccharides' in Chapter 2).

Typical amounts of the major nutrients present in 1 pint (568 ml) of whole milk and of semi-skimmed, 1%-fat and skimmed milks are given in Table 31. Milk from the Jersey and Guernsey breeds of cow contains rather more fat than milk from other breeds (1 pint providing 26.7 g of fat) as well as more beta-carotene and calcium.

Average milk consumption is now a quarter of a pint (141 ml) per day, 82% of which is reduced-fat milk (skimmed, 1%-fat or semi-skimmed milk).

The contribution that milk makes to the nutrient content of the average adult diet is shown in Table 29. It can be seen that, in a mixed diet, milk is particularly valuable for its content of protein and easily assimilated calcium; it is also a rich source of riboflavin.

Unmodified cow's milk is not suitable for infants under 1 year old as their main drink because it doesn't contain the correct balance of nutrients, but small amounts can be used in cooking foods for infants over 6 months old. It is important that young children are given concentrated sources of energy, therefore whole milk, not reduced-fat milks, should be given to children between the ages of 1 and 2 years. Those aged over 2 but under 5 can be

Table 31. Nutrients per pint in various types of cow's milk[a]

	Whole	Semi-skimmed	1%-fat milk[b]	Skimmed
Energy (kJ)	1605	1146	981	801
Energy (kcal)	387	270	233	188
Protein (g)	19.3	20.0	18.6	20.0
Fat (g)	22.9	10.0	5.7	1.2
Carbohydrate (g)	26.4	27.6	26.7	25.9
Calcium (mg)	691	705	718	718
Iron (mg)	0.18	0.12	–	0.18
Sodium (mg)	252	253	340	259
Vitamin A (retinol equivalents) (µg)	213	120	–	6
Thiamin (mg)	0.18	0.24	–	0.18
Riboflavin (mg)	1.35	1.41	–	1.30
Niacin equivalents (mg)	4.7	5.3	–	4.7
Vitamin B_{12} (µg)	5.3	2.4	–	4.7
Vitamin B_{12} (µg)	5.3	2.4	–	4.7
Vitamin C (mg)	12	6	–	6
Vitamin D (µg)	0	0	–	0

Source: *McCance and Widdowson's Composition of Foods Integrated Dataset (COFIDS)* published by the Food Standards Agency, 2008.
[a] To convert values to nutrients per litre multiply by 1.76. Values decline on storage in the home.
[b] Values are an average of supermarket label information; '–' where nutrient data are not available.

given semi-skimmed milk, provided that they have a good appetite and are eating a varied diet. Semi-skimmed milk contains less fat than whole milk but has a similar content of protein and calcium. Skimmed or 1%-fat milks do not contain enough calories for a child under 5. Reduced-fat milks are, however, useful for adults who wish to reduce their fat intake (see Chapter 3).

It is important that bottled milks are not left on the doorstep exposed directly to sunlight for more than an hour, since a substantial amount of the riboflavin and vitamin C can be destroyed.

EFFECTS OF COOKING

The bubbles of steam formed as milk is heated are stabilised by the protein and this gives rise to the characteristic 'boiling over'. Food such as fish or vegetables, when baked in milk, can cause coagulation of milk proteins, but this does not affect their digestibility. Some caramelisation of the sugars in milk may occur with long cooking in a very slow oven, as for example in milk puddings or in the production of sterilised or evaporated milk.

EFFECTS OF PROCESSING

When milk is homogenised, the fat globules are broken up mechanically and distributed throughout the milk so that they no longer rise to form a creamy layer at the top of the milk bottle. The nutritional value of homogenised milk is similar to that of pasteurised milk.

Skimmed milk has almost all of its fat removed, and *semi-skimmed milk* must by law contain only between 1.5% and 1.8% fat. The fat-soluble vitamins A and D are reduced proportionately (only traces remain in skimmed milk) but the calcium content remains almost unchanged (see Table 31). *Dried skimmed milk*, and similar products with added vegetable fat, may be fortified with vitamins A and D. 1% milk contains 1% fat, tastes similar to semi-skimmed milk and has just as much calcium and B vitamins as higher fat versions, but contains almost half the fat of semi-skimmed milk.

A variety of heat treatments can be used to improve the keeping quality of liquid milk. The fat, fat-soluble vitamins, carbohydrates and minerals in milk are not affected by heat but, when the heat treatment is relatively harsh, slight changes occur in the availability of some of the amino acids in the milk proteins.

The vitamins in milk that are partially destroyed by heat processing are vitamin C, thiamin, vitamin B_6, vitamin B_{12} and folate.

Most of the liquid milk supply in the UK is pasteurised by the high temperature short time (HTST) method. During this relatively mild form of heat treatment, the milk is heated to 72°C (162°F) for at least 15 seconds, killing any disease-causing bacteria. Between 0% and 10% of the thiamin, riboflavin, vitamin B_{12} and folate, and about 10% of the vitamin C are destroyed. The ultra-high temperature (UHT) treatment of milk, in which a temperature of at least 135°C (275°F) is maintained for at least 2 seconds, destroys all bacteria; it also causes some vitamin losses, which are similar to the losses in pasteurisation. UHT or 'long-life' milk is packed aseptically into special containers that protect it from light and from oxygen. It will keep satisfactorily for several months without refrigeration, but variable losses of vitamin C and folate (up to 50%) may occur during prolonged storage. Once opened, however, UHT milk is as perishable as fresh milk.

Evaporated milk is prepared by the concentration of liquid milk at low temperatures; the milk is subsequently sterilised in cans at, for example, 115°C (239°F) for 15 minutes. About 60% of the vitamin C of the raw milk and 20% of the thiamin are destroyed during the process.

Sweetened condensed milk is prepared similarly to evaporated milk but, since it contains added sucrose, the processing temperature needed for an adequate storage life is lower. Nutrient losses are therefore lower too, and are generally similar to those that occur in pasteurisation.

Milk products

CHEESE

When *rennet* is added to warm acidified milk, the milk protein *casein* coagulates to form a firm curd which is treated in various ways to make different kinds of cheese. Most of the protein, fat and vitamin A and much of the calcium in the milk remain in the curd, while a large part of the lactose and B vitamins are lost with the whey as it drains away. Further minor changes in vitamin content occur during ripening and storage – processes that are greatly affected by the amount of salt present. Cheddar cheese consists very roughly of one-third protein, one-third fat and one-third water. Although methods of preparation differ, the amounts of protein and fat in whole-milk cheeses are fairly similar. Reduced-fat cheeses are also available. *Hard cheeses*, such as Cheddar and Double Gloucester, in general contain more nutrients per 100 g than *soft cheeses*, such as Camembert, because they contain less moisture. Some cheeses are not ripened, such as cottage cheese, cream cheese, fromage frais and quark. *Fromage frais* is a very soft cheese with a mild and fresh taste. Although its fat content varies according to the starting material, most products sold have a relatively low fat content compared with hard and soft cheeses. *Cottage cheese* is made from skimmed milk and therefore contains very little fat; *cream cheese* has a high fat content. Certain cheeses are made from milk other than cow's milk; for example, *feta cheese* is traditionally made from goat's or sheep's milk and *mozzarella* from buffalo milk.

Pregnant women are advised not to eat mould-ripened soft cheese (such as Brie, Camembert and others with a similar rind), as well as soft blue-veined cheeses, like Danish blue or Gorgonzola. These cheeses can sometimes contain bacteria which could harm their unborn baby.

YOGURT

The nutritional value of yogurt is similar to that of the milk and minor ingredients used in its preparation, except that in products with added sugar or added fat the energy content is increased. Most commercial yogurts are based either on whole milk or on skimmed milk that is inoculated with a selected culture of *lactic acid bacteria* under controlled conditions. Dried skimmed milk, pectin or modified starch may be added to produce a firmer or more 'creamy' consistency; flavourings, fruit juices, fruit, nuts and sugar or non-sugar sweeteners are often incorporated to give a varied product. Some varieties of yogurt are fortified with vitamins such as A and D. There is also a yogurt available on the market containing a constituent made from plant stanols (see 'Fat spreads and oils' later in this chapter) which may help to lower blood cholesterol. Depending on the type of milk from which it is made, the fat content of yogurt can vary from about 0.2 g per 100 g in low-calorie yogurt to about 10 g per 100 g in Greek yogurt made with cow's milk.

CREAM

Cream is derived from fresh milk either by skimming off the fatty layer which rises to the surface or in a mechanical separator. The minimum fat content for different types of cream is specified in government regulations – these include *half cream*, 12% by weight as milk fat; *single cream*, 18%; *whipping cream*, 35%; *double cream*, 48%; and *clotted cream*, 55% fat. These compare with an average of 3.9% fat in whole milk. The energy value of different types of cream varies directly with the fat content. *Sour cream* is made by adding a bacterial culture to the cream to slightly sour it and give it a thicker consistency. Sour cream is nutritionally similar to the cream from which it is made.

BUTTER

Churning cream in a rotating drum so that the fat globules separate from the liquid buttermilk makes butter. Butter must contain between 80% and 90% milk fat, not more than 2% milk solids other than fat, and not more than 16% water. During manufacture, 1–2% salt is added to salted butter. The amounts of vitamins A and D in butter vary; representative values are shown in Appendix 3. *Ghee* is made by the prolonged heating of butter. The emulsion breaks down and, on cooling, the pure fat can be separated from the water so that ghee contains virtually no water. Vegetable ghee, made from vegetable oil, can also be obtained.

ICE CREAM

The nutrient composition of dairy ice cream varies with the amounts of sugar, milk, dried milk, butterfat and cream that it contains. Most ice cream in the UK is based on skimmed milk with non-dairy fats instead of, or as well as, milk fat. *Sorbets* (water ices) are not based on milk but consist of a mixture of water, fruit and variable amounts of added sugar.

Meat

Muscle tissue is composed of bundles of muscle fibres surrounded by connective tissue and associated with intramuscular fat. Each separate muscle fibre is a tube composed largely of water, and containing soluble proteins, mineral salts, vitamins and other components which give rise to flavours when meat is cooked. The eating quality of meat is largely determined by the relative proportions of connective tissue and muscle fibres in a particular cut and the amount of 'marbling' fat that is present, but the overall nutrient content of lean meat from the more expensive cuts is not significantly different from that in other parts of the carcass.

The average nutrient composition of various types of meat is shown in Appendix 3. Genetic breeding and changes in methods of animal husbandry have resulted in leaner meat, particularly in the case of sheep and pigs, than that of 20 years ago. More of the external fat may also be trimmed off prior to sale.

IMPORTANCE IN THE DIET

Meat is a good source of high-quality protein, of available iron and zinc, and of all the B vitamins except folate. Pork, bacon and ham in particular are rich in thiamin. Liver and, to a lesser extent, kidney, are also rich in vitamin A and folate (thus differing from carcass meat) and in iron, riboflavin and other B vitamins. Sweetbreads and tripe are useful and easily digestible sources of animal protein. Tripe also contains more calcium than other meats; this is derived from the lime with which it is treated during preparation. Liver and kidney and chicken and turkey meat (especially if the skin is removed) contain less fat than most carcass meat and their energy content is therefore lower. Much of the fat can nevertheless be trimmed from beef, lamb and pork before or after cooking. Mince may be heated and the melted fat poured off before further cooking takes place.

Consumption of poultry meat more than doubled between 1986/87 and 2008/10 and is greater than the consumption of beef.

However, people who eat a lot of red or processed meat – around 90 g or more cooked weight per day – are at greater risk of getting *bowel (colorectal) cancer*. The Department of Health recommends that high consumers cut down to the UK average of 70 g per day which can help to reduce the risk; this can be achieved by eating smaller portions or by eating red and processed meat less often (SACN, *Iron and Health*, 2010).

A reduction in intakes of red and processed meat by high consumers may also help to reduce their intakes of salt and saturated fat, particularly by reducing the consumption of processed meats which tend to contain higher levels of both. Cutting down on red meat consumption can help to reduce saturated fat intakes.

Since there is an association between high intakes of retinol (vitamin A) during pregnancy and the incidence of some birth defects, women who are, or who might become, pregnant are advised not to eat liver or liver products or take fish liver oil or vitamin A supplements.

In addition, pregnant women are advised not to eat any type of pâté or undercooked meat to avoid the possible presence of harmful bacteria or viruses.

EFFECTS OF COOKING

The muscle protein *myoglobin*, which provides the red colour of raw meat, is changed by heat, and the brown colour associated with cooked meat develops at temperatures above 65°C. Heat causes the proteins in the muscle fibres to coagulate and the meat becomes firm; shrinkage occurs and this in turn causes release of meat juices and a loss of weight. Losses of fat and meat juices increase as the temperature rises, so the total weight loss is influenced by the cooking temperature and the internal temperature that the meat reaches as well as by the cooking time; thus the effects of grilling and frying are similar. The substantial variations that occur in the proportions of bone, muscle and fat in different parts of different carcasses also affect the nutrients that are actually available from a given weight of fresh meat. It is therefore very important, when estimating the contributions made by meat to the nutrient content of a diet, to weigh each cut after cooking and removal of any fat or bone.

Some cheaper cuts of meat which contain a higher proportion of connective tissue are more palatable if a slow moist method of cooking, such as stewing or braising, is used for the preparation; this allows the *collagen* in the connective tissue to be converted to *gelatin*, making the meat more tender. Pressure-cooking is also useful for this purpose.

Cooking does not affect the minerals present in meat but a proportion of those that are soluble pass into the exuded juices or the cooking water. Similarly, since the B vitamins are all water-soluble, varying amounts will be found in the drip, meat juice and stock. Losses of B vitamins from fried or grilled meat can be around 20%. Destruction of thiamin, niacin, pyridoxine and pantothenic acid in stewed meat varies between 30% and 70%, although overall losses are smaller if the gravy or liquid from a stew is consumed. About 30% of the folate is lost from stewed liver and kidney. After cooking, there are only small differences in the content of the B vitamins in fresh and frozen meat. Vitamin A is relatively stable when heated, and is not affected by most cooking procedures, although some loss occurs during frying at high temperatures (above 200°C).

There is no evidence of any significant loss of nutrients from meat during freezing, but the drip which collects on thawing will contain some soluble nutrients.

Meat juices are water-soluble substances from meat that include peptides, B vitamins and mineral salts. They provide, with fat, most of the flavour and aroma of meat and act as a stimulant to appetite and to the secretion of gastric juice.

Stock can be made by boiling meat bones in water. The hot water extracts a small amount of fat and gelatin from the bone marrow together with other minor components that provide the flavour. Stock is usually used as a basis for soup and it is the addition of other ingredients (e.g. milk, fat and flour in cream soups) which provides most of the nutritional value of the soup.

Meat products

The meat content of meat products such as sausages is controlled by government regulations (see Appendix 8). The contribution that meat products make to the nutrient content of the average adult diet is shown in Table 29; average consumption of meat products per head is greater than for carcass meat. The most usual methods of heat treatment which meat products undergo during manufacture before any further cooking in the home are roasting, baking and canning, all of which cause some loss of thiamin and a slight reduction in the quality of the meat protein. The loss of thiamin when meat is canned is generally slightly greater than in cooked meat. *Corned beef* is prepared from cured meat which is trimmed, coarsely cut and cooked before canning; after this process, very little thiamin remains in the finished product. Commercial *meat extract* is a by-product of the meat industry. The liquid in which meat and bone have been heated is concentrated after the removal of some of the fat. Such products, including stock cubes, may also be high in sodium. When the meat extract containing the dissolved solids is diluted again for consumption, the amount of protein and energy that it contributes to the soup or beverage is too small to be of importance in the diet; nevertheless, it contains minerals besides the salt and vitamins, and is a useful stimulant of appetite.

The nutrient losses that occur during the cooking of meat products are similar to those that occur during the cooking of carcass meat.

Fish and shellfish

IMPORTANCE IN THE DIET

Fish and shellfish are good sources of many vitamins, minerals and protein. The average content of fat in different kinds of fish varies widely; the flesh of white fish, such as cod, haddock, plaice, pollock and coley, contains very little fat (1–2%). Shellfish, including prawns, mussels and langoustine, are also low in fat. This is in contrast to oily fish, such as salmon, mackerel, sardines, trout and herring, the fat content of which varies from about 5% to about 20%. There can also be considerable variation within each type of oily fish, depending on the season of the year and the level of maturity attained by the individual fish.

In general, the vitamin content of white fish muscle is similar to that of lean meat. The fat-soluble vitamins A and D are present in the flesh of oily fish and in the livers of fish such as cod and halibut. Oils from the latter may therefore be used as concentrated vitamin supplements. However, pregnant women should avoid taking supplements containing fish liver oils, since these contain high levels of vitamin A which has been linked with some birth defects. Fish oils also contain long-chain *omega-3 fatty acids* which may help to prevent coronary heart disease (see 'Unsaturated fatty acids' in Chapter 3) by decreasing the tendency of the blood to clot and reducing inflammation. Some types of shellfish, such as mussels, oysters, squid and crab, are also good sources of long-chain omega-3 fatty acids, but they do not contain as much as oily fish. Taking fish oil capsules may help to protect against heart disease but it is preferable to eat fish because it is also an excellent source of other nutrients. For this reason, the UK health departments recommend that people should eat at least two portions of fish each week, one portion of which should be oily fish.

For certain types of fish, there are recommendations about the maximum amount that should be consumed. Pregnant or breastfeeding women and women planning a pregnancy have been advised by the Government to limit their consumption of tuna to no more than four medium-sized cans a week (drained weight 140 g per can) or two fresh tuna steaks a week (weighing 140 g cooked or 170 g raw), and to avoid eating shark, swordfish and marlin. This is because these types of fish can contain relatively high levels of *mercury*. It is also advisable for pregnant women to avoid having more than two portions of oily fish each week, since these types of fish contain pollutants such as *dioxins*. There is no problem with eating other types of fish during pregnancy as part of a healthy diet. Other adults have been advised to limit shark, swordfish and marlin to one portion a week, but do not need to limit tuna consumption. Children under 16 have also been advised to avoid shark, swordfish and marlin due to the mercury levels.

SUSTAINABILITY

When fish or shellfish are caught or produced in a way that allows stocks to replenish and that does not cause unnecessary damage to marine animals and plants, those fish or shellfish are called *sustainable*.

To ensure that there are enough fish to eat now and in the future, the Government encourages the consumption of a variety of fish, and that fish from sustainable sources are chosen. If only a few kinds of fish are eaten, then the numbers of these fish can fall very low due to overfishing of these stocks.

Overfishing endangers the future supply of the fish and can also cause damage to the environment from which the fish is caught.

Some organisations have produced lists of sustainable seafood, for example that found on the Marine Stewardship Council website (www.msc.org).

EFFECTS OF COOKING AND PROCESSING

The changes that occur when fish is cooked are similar to those in meat but the shrinkage is not so great; losses of mineral salts are proportional to the loss of water. Vitamins A and D in oily fish are both heat-stable. Canned tuna is a poor source of the long-chain omega-3 polyunsaturated fatty acids as processing reduces the fat content of the fish to a low level. Canning of other oily fish has little effect on their fat content, so that canned sardines, pilchards, mackerel and salmon remain good sources of long-chain omega-3 polyunsaturated fatty acids. When fish is canned or cured by smoking there is some loss of thiamin, but otherwise these processes have little adverse effect on the nutrients. Some fish that are cured and smoked or canned in brine can contain high levels of sodium (salt). Modern methods of freezing do not affect the nutritive value, and poaching and steaming incur only small losses of vitamins. Between 10% and 30% losses of B vitamins occur during baking, frying or grilling. For estimating the cooked weight of fish, a loss of about 15% may be assumed on gentle cooking unless frying is used: fish fried in batter and fish products that are fried will gain fat on cooking.

Eggs

IMPORTANCE IN THE DIET

The consumption of eggs has decreased significantly over the last 20 years. The current average consumption is about two eggs per person per week. Eggs therefore can still make a small but useful contribution to the daily intakes of vitamin D, vitamin A, riboflavin, iodine and protein in the average diet, and for the elderly they can be an important source of protein, vitamin B_{12} and vitamin D. It used to be thought that eggs were a good source of iron; however, it is now known that the body does not easily absorb the form in which iron occurs in egg yolk.

The shell colour is related to the breed of hen rather than to nutrient content and in this respect it is therefore unimportant; similarly, a deep-yellow yolk does not necessarily indicate a high vitamin A content since the pigment is not beta-carotene.

EFFECTS OF COOKING

When eggs are boiled or fried, the proteins coagulate first in the white, at approximately 60°C (140°F), then in the yolk. This property makes eggs suitable for binding dry ingredients together in cooking, and for thickening sauces and soups; the mixture of eggs and milk sets in baked egg custard. Over-cooking causes the proteins to curdle and contract slightly and a yellow watery fluid to separate out; this may occur when scrambling eggs or boiling sauces to which eggs have been added.

The black discoloration that is sometimes present around the yolk of hard-boiled eggs is *iron sulphide*. This is formed during cooking from hydrogen sulphide in the egg white and iron in the egg yolk. Cooling the eggs in water immediately after cooking can reduce the blackening.

When egg whites are beaten, the proteins hold air to form a stable foam which coagulates or sets at a very low temperature, as in meringues. Eggs are also used for aeration, for example in sponge cakes, and to promote the emulsification of fat, as in mayonnaise. Some of the heat-sensitive B vitamins are lost during cooking. For example, the average loss of thiamin which results from boiling, frying, poaching and scrambling is between 5% and 15%; similar losses of niacin also occur and slightly higher losses (15–30%) of these and other B vitamins take place in baked dishes. During frying, the fat content of eggs may be increased by about 50%.

Eggs should ideally be stored in the fridge. Eggs given to infants, pregnant women or frail older people should be cooked until both the yolk and white are solid to avoid the risk of food poisoning.

PULSES, NUTS AND SEEDS

Pulses (legumes) such as dried peas, beans, chickpeas and lentils, and the range of canned pulse products now available, are rich in protein and are an excellent source of fibre. They also contain *non-haem iron*. In general they are used as meat alternatives, especially by vegetarians and vegans. They provide more energy and B vitamins than many vegetables but do not contain vitamin C. Because their nutrient content differs from that of most other vegetables, it is recommended that, however much is eaten, they should only count once towards the recommended five portions of fruit and vegetables per day (see 'Fruit and vegetables' later in this chapter).

Soya drink derived from soya beans is used as an animal milk substitute and is sometimes fortified with calcium and sweetened with fruit juice. Soya flour and other products derived from soya are increasingly used in manufactured foods. They are nutritionally valuable but extra nutrients are added if they are intended to resemble or replace meat (see 'Novel sources of protein' in Chapter 4).

Nuts and peanuts (which are actually a type of legume) are rich in fat, especially monounsaturates, and are consequently a concentrated source of energy. They are an excellent source of protein and fibre and a good source of B vitamins and vitamin E, but contain no vitamin A or C.

Seeds from sunflowers, pumpkins and sesame, and products such as tahini paste from sesame seeds, have a nutritional value similar to nuts.

Cereals

IMPORTANCE IN THE DIET

Cereal grains are a major component of the human diet throughout the world. In the UK, wheat in the form of bread, flour, biscuits, cakes and pasta, together with other cereals such as rice, oatmeal and breakfast cereals, provide just under half of the carbohydrate – and about one-third of the total energy, protein, fibre and iron – in the average adult diet, although the iron is poorly absorbed. Cereals also make a substantial contribution to the intake of many other nutrients, particularly calcium, niacin and thiamin, which are currently added to most wheat flours, sodium from added salt, and fibre. In general, the common cereals (wheat, oats, barley, rye, maize and rice) contain 65–80% carbohydrate (starch), 7–13% protein, 1–9% fat, 2–15% fibre and approximately 12% water in the whole grain. Advances in plant breeding have led to the development of cereal varieties that are richer in *lysine*; some increases in protein levels may be obtained experimentally by the appropriate use of manures and fertilisers.

Cereals and their products, such as bread, pasta and noodles, together with tubers and roots such as yams and potatoes, are starchy foods that should make up about one-third of the diet (see the eatwell plate in Appendix 6).

NUTRIENT LOSSES IN MILLING AND THE COMPOSITION OF WHEAT FLOUR

The distribution of nutrients within the wheat grain is not uniform. The concentration of protein, vitamins and minerals is higher in the germ and outer layers of the grain than in the inner starchy *endosperm*; so, when wheat is milled to produce white flour, a proportion of the nutrients and fibre is discarded with the bran and germ. Owing to the continuing, if decreasing, preference for white flour in the British diet, those nutrients lost in the refining process that are of importance in relation to the diet as a whole are replaced through fortification. Similar losses of minerals and vitamins occur in the milling

Table 32. Minimum quantities of iron, thiamin and niacin in flour in the UK

	Weight (mg/100 g)
Iron	1.65
Thiamin (vitamin B$_1$)	0.24
Niacin	1.60

of rice unless it is parboiled, a process which causes nutrients to migrate from the outer to the inner parts of the grain.

The composition of flour in the UK is controlled by government regulations (see Appendix 8) which require that all flours contain minimum quantities of two B vitamins (thiamin and niacin) and iron, corresponding to the levels occurring naturally in 80% extraction flour.[21] These quantities are listed in Table 32.

All wheat flours, with the exception of wholemeal wheat flour, wheat malt flour and self-raising flour which has a calcium content of not less than 0.2%, have to be fortified with these nutrients to bring their concentrations to the prescribed levels; wholemeal flours contain more than the specified minimum quantities. In addition, calcium carbonate must be added to all flours except wholemeal, wheatmeal and certain self-raising flours at the rate of 235–390 mg per 100 g.

WHOLEMEAL, BROWN AND WHITE WHEAT FLOURS

The composition of each of these flours varies but, in general wholemeal flour contains somewhat greater amounts of most minerals and several vitamins, particularly of the B vitamins, but less calcium than the flours to which calcium has been added. Wholemeal flour also contains more fibre and phytates than brown or white flour. However, apart from the fibre content, nutritional differences between wholemeal and the fortified brown and white flours are unlikely to be of practical significance in a mixed diet.

Traditionally, flours which will produce a large loaf of good quality need to contain sufficient *gluten* (the protein which is responsible for the bread 'structure'), either from 'strong' varieties of wheat or else added separately. 'Weak' wheats, such as those grown in the UK, give flours which are more suitable for making biscuits and cakes (but see details of the Chorleywood Bread Process below).

---

[21] The weight of flour obtained from a given weight of cleaned grain, expressed as a percentage, is known as the *extraction rate*.

EFFECTS OF COOKING AND PROCESSING

Cooking causes the starch granules (of which cereal carbohydrate is composed) to swell and gelatinise, thus making the starch digestible; it also results in a tripling (approximately) of the weight of rice and pasta on boiling as they take up water.

Thiamin is the vitamin mainly affected during the baking or processing of cereal products because it is sensitive to heat and destroyed by alkali. The amount lost therefore varies with the cooking time and the final temperature of the cooked food, and whether or not baking powder is used, as for example in soda bread or scones. Riboflavin and niacin are more stable when heated and the loss on baking is small. Of the other unstable vitamins, folate is low in wheat, and vitamin C is only present if added as a flour improver before making bread. It is then destroyed on baking.

In bread-making, the yeast gradually ferments the sugars that are formed from the starch in the dough, breaking them down to alcohol and then to carbon dioxide and water, much of which is driven off. The carbon dioxide causes the bread to rise. When water is added to the flour in the preparation of the dough, the proteins *gliadin* and *glutenin* combine to form gluten. During baking, the yeast is killed and fermentation ceases. The gluten holds the pockets of gas and then coagulates as cooking proceeds, holding the bread in shape. The gelatinised starch in the bread also contributes to loaf structure. The average loss of thiamin in baking bread is about 15%.

About 80% of the bread sold in the UK is made by the *Chorleywood Bread Process* which decreases production time and allows UK and European wheats to be used through the addition of certain substances (improvers) to the mix and the replacement of conventional fermentation of the dough by a few minutes of intense mechanical agitation in special high-speed mixers. The process itself does not affect the nutritional value of bread significantly. However, UK and European wheat flours have lower levels of selenium than are found in the Canadian wheat flour used in conventional methods. This has resulted in decreased average selenium intakes by the UK population but the significance of this has yet to be determined.

Toast

When bread is toasted, the thiamin content is further reduced; the total loss on toasting is about 15%. The heat drives off water from the bread, so that the content of energy and most other nutrients per unit weight increases or remains the same.

Cakes and biscuits

When making a cake, such as a Victoria sponge cake, air is introduced into the mixture by creaming together the fat and sugar. The eggs are lightly beaten to incorporate air before being added to the creamed mixture and the flour is folded in lightly so that this air is not forced out. During cooking, the starch gelatinises and the flour and egg proteins coagulate. The loss of thiamin when making cakes and biscuits varies between 20% and 30%.

The relative proportions of fat and sugar to flour and other ingredients are important in giving different cakes and biscuits their characteristic textures and tastes.

Breakfast cereals

The heat treatment used in the preparation of breakfast cereals destroys a large proportion of the thiamin present in the whole grain. In puffed and flaked products, it is usually a total loss but the process used in the preparation of shredded wheat is less drastic and only about half the thiamin is destroyed. Many breakfast cereals are therefore enriched with thiamin, as well as a wide range of other vitamins including the synthetic form of folate (folic acid), vitamin B_{12} and iron, and these products are important sources of nutrients for many people. Sugar, salt and bran are also added to many products; muesli and some other cereal products also have a variety of dried fruits and nuts added. These, and bran-enriched products, provide an excellent source of fibre. Some types of processing lead to an increase in the proportion of starch that is resistant to digestion and which may have some functions similar to fibre. When porridge is made from coarse oatmeal, the cooking loss of thiamin is about 10%.

Tubers and plantains

POTATOES

Importance in the diet

In many diets, potatoes provide the main source of vitamin C, even though the vitamin content per unit weight is comparatively low. The amount is highest in new potatoes and falls gradually during post-harvest storage. Instant potato powder and potato flakes or granules are nutritionally equivalent alternatives to fresh potatoes only if the vitamin C and thiamin which are lost in processing are added back to the products. Because of the comparatively large amounts that are eaten, potatoes are a source of protein and iron and they are also useful sources of thiamin, niacin and several other nutrients including fibre. Potatoes, other roots, and tubers and cereals are starchy foods that should make up about one-third of the diet. Even though they are vegetables,

Table 33. Average loss of vitamin C from potatoes, by cooking method

Method of cooking potatoes	Vitamin C lost (%)
Boiled after peeling	20–50
Boiled in their skins	20–40
Baked in their skins	10–40
Roasted	15–50
Chipped or fried	15–30

potatoes are classified nutritionally as a starchy food because, when eaten as part of a meal in the UK, they are generally used in place of other sources of carbohydrate/starch, such as bread, pasta or rice. They do not count towards the recommended five portions of fruit and vegetables per day.

Effects of cooking

The digestibility of raw potato starch is very poor but is greatly improved by cooking. Peeling of potatoes that removes a significant proportion of the flesh along with the skin can result in the loss of vitamin C and some minerals. Water-soluble vitamins and some minerals are lost more readily from peeled potatoes than from potatoes cooked in their skins. Average losses of vitamin C from potatoes are shown in Table 33.

If cooked potatoes are mashed and then kept hot, the loss of vitamin C is greater than if they are left whole under similar conditions.

Potato whiteners or sulphite dips prevent the discoloration of raw pre-peeled potatoes (when they are commercially prepared) but the amount of thiamin that is lost when the treated potatoes are boiled or fried as chips and subsequently kept hot is greatly increased by this treatment.

The fat content of chips varies from less than 5% of their weight in some oven chips to more than 20% in fine-cut French fries. In home-prepared or retail chips, the fat content is lowest when the chips are cut large to reduce their surface area and when the frying oil is kept hot. Fat content can also be reduced by draining the chips on absorbent paper before serving. The amount of the different fatty acids they or other fried staples contain depends on the oil or fat in which they have been fried.

TROPICAL ROOTS AND TUBERS

In the UK, cassava and sweet potatoes (roots) and yams and eddoes (tubers) are at present eaten in quantity mainly in ethnic communities, particularly by people from Asia, Africa and the West Indies. Plantains (green bananas) are not roots, but fruits. However, they occupy a similar place in the diet of communities from Africa and the West Indies. Like potatoes, these foods provide moderate amounts of energy, fibre, vitamins and minerals. Cassava and sweet potato are similar to potatoes in their vitamin C content, and orange-fleshed, but not white-fleshed; sweet potatoes can contain substantial quantities of beta-carotene. Due to their nutrient composition, the current limited quantities in which most people in the UK eat them and the fact that they are largely consumed as a vegetable rather than a starchy food, orange-fleshed sweet potatoes can count towards the recommended five portions of fruit and vegetables per day.

Fruit and vegetables

IMPORTANCE IN THE DIET

It is recommended that people eat at least five portions of a wide variety of fruits and vegetables each day. This advice is based on many different studies. These have shown consistently that populations that have a high intake of fruit and vegetables have a lower incidence of heart disease, some cancers and other health problems.

However, it appears that it is the mixture of components in fruit and vegetables that is protective rather than any individual component. For this reason, it is preferable to eat fruits and vegetables rather than taking dietary supplements.

PORTION SIZES

All types of fruit and vegetables, whether fresh, frozen, canned, dried or pure juices (fruit, vegetable or smoothie), count towards the five or more daily portions.

The following is a guide to portion sizes of fruit and vegetables.[22]

ONE portion = 80 g = any of these

1 apple, banana, pear, orange or other similar sized fruit
2 plums or similar sized fruit
½ a grapefruit or avocado
1 slice of large fruit, such as melon or pineapple
3 heaped tablespoons of vegetables (raw, cooked, frozen or canned)
A dessert bowl of salad
3 heaped tablespoons of beans and pulses (more than this still counts as a
    maximum of one portion per day)

---

[22] Further details of portion sizes can be found at www.nhs.uk/LiveWell/5ADAY/Pages/5ADAYhome.aspx.

3 heaped tablespoons of fruit salad (fresh or canned in fruit juice) or stewed fruit

1 heaped tablespoon of dried fruit (such as raisins and apricots)

1 cupful of grapes, cherries or berries

A glass (150 ml) of fruit juice (more than this still counts as a maximum of one portion a day)

There are no epidemiological data to determine portion sizes of fruit or vegetables for children.

Since extraction of juice from fruits or vegetables reduces the fibre content and releases non-milk extrinsic sugars (see 'Health aspects of carbohydrates' in Chapter 2), fruit or vegetable juices should not be counted as more than one portion in a day, however much is drunk. Smoothies may only count as more than one portion if they contain all of the edible pulped fruit or vegetable. Puréed fruits and vegetables are among the first foods given to babies when they are weaned, and it is important that children eat a variety of fruits and vegetables every day. However, children should be introduced to five portions a day gradually between the ages of 2 and 5, adjusting portion sizes to be suitable for the child's age and capacity.

Vegetables

Although they contain 80–95% water, vegetables supply appreciable quantities of nutrients in the average diet. They are also an important source of fibre (see 'Non-starch polysaccharides' in Chapter 2). Many people do not eat nearly enough vegetables but their range of colours and textures can be exploited to prepare attractive, appetising and healthy meals. The composition of a selection of different vegetables is given in Appendix 3. Their nutrient content is influenced by a number of factors during growth and after harvesting, and different samples of the same vegetable can vary considerably. For example, the amount of vitamin C will vary with variety, maturity and exposure to sunlight, as well as with the method of handling, the temperature during transport and the delay before the 'fresh' produce is eaten.

GREEN AND SALAD VEGETABLES

Green vegetables, and salad items such as green peppers and tomatoes, are of nutritional importance because of their contribution to the daily intake of vitamin C, beta-carotene (which after absorption is converted to vitamin A in the body), folate, iron and other minerals, and fibre. They are especially valuable when eaten raw, as they will suffer no losses of nutrients due to cooking; there will, however, be considerable losses of vitamin C and folate in wilted vegetables.

ROOT VEGETABLES

Some 45% of the average daily intake of vitamin A (in the form of beta-carotene) for adults is provided by vegetables. Sweet potatoes with orange-coloured flesh are excellent sources of beta-carotene. Turnips, swedes and parsnips are comparatively good sources of vitamin C but they contain no beta-carotene.

Effects of cooking

The main purpose of cooking vegetables is to soften the cellular tissue and to gelatinise any starch that may be present so that they can be digested more easily.

Weight changes in preparation and cooking

Peeling and trimming may reduce the purchased weight of some vegetables by up to one-third or more (see Appendix 3); changes in the weight of most raw vegetables during boiling are small and may be ignored when making calculations from food tables.

Nutrient losses

After peeling or shredding, vitamin C is rapidly destroyed by oxidation either directly or by the action of an enzyme present in the plant tissues. This loss can be kept to a minimum by preparing vegetables immediately before use and by plunging them directly into boiling water (from which any dissolved oxygen will have been driven off) at the start of the cooking process, when the enzyme will be destroyed. During cooking, nutrient losses in vegetables (and to a smaller extent in fruit) are mainly caused by the passage of soluble mineral salts and vitamins from the tissues into the cooking water and by the destruction of some vitamins by heat. Thus, some of the vitamin C and thiamin are inevitably lost when water is used for cooking because they are both heat-sensitive and water-soluble. It is desirable to use small volumes of water for cooking to keep nutrient losses to a minimum.

Green vegetables, which have a large surface area, lose on average between 50% and 75% of their vitamin C during cooking. There is a further loss of vitamin C if vegetables are kept hot for any length of time. For example, after being kept hot for 30 minutes, cabbage will provide about 60% of its freshly cooked value and after an hour only 40% of its original vitamin C content. Adding sodium bicarbonate to the cooking water to maintain a bright green colour in vegetables accelerates losses of vitamin C. It is not necessary to use salt when boiling vegetables. Microwaving is a method of cooking vegetables which heats them rapidly using a minimum quantity of water and conserves their texture and colour.

Effects of processing

The general effects of processing on the nutritive value of foods are discussed in Chapter 10 (see 'Industrial processing'). Freezing does not in itself cause losses of vitamins but during canning there is some destruction of those vitamins that are unstable when heated (see 'Stability of individual nutrients' in Chapter 10).

When sulphite is added to dehydrated vegetables to preserve vitamin C and prevent deterioration of quality during storage, most of the thiamin is destroyed. In general, this loss is not serious because, in a mixed diet, thiamin is obtained from many other foods.

Fruit

Fruit and fruit juices are nutritionally most important as major sources of vitamin C. Fruit and fruit juices together now provide about 40% of all the vitamin C in the British diet. However, the vitamin C content of different fruits varies widely and will always be lower after cooking. Blackcurrants are exceptionally rich, followed by strawberries, kiwis, other soft fruits, oranges, grapefruit and many pure 100% fruit juices. Many canned fruits, such as pineapples, mandarin oranges and peaches, also supply moderate quantities of vitamin C. Eating apples, bananas, cherries and rhubarb are examples of fruits that contain much less of the vitamin and that do not in this respect compare favourably with green vegetables. Vitamins and minerals may be added to some fruit products such as apple juice and juice drinks. Fruit juice containers usually carry a nutritional panel in the labelling. Most fruits also contain sugars and small amounts of beta-carotene, other vitamins and minerals. The sugars in unprocessed fruit are considered to be intrinsic sugars and have not been shown to cause dental caries. However, sugars are released from the fruit cells during processing in products such as fruit juices and smoothies, and are therefore considered non-milk extrinsic sugars and are implicated in dental caries.

Most commercial *fruit juices* are made from concentrated juice and are preserved by a combination of heating during concentration and pasteurisation when diluted prior to filling the container. There is now also a fairly large production of freshly squeezed juices prepared directly from the fruit, given a mild pasteurisation treatment, and kept chilled before sale. Juice drinks consist of one or more fruit juices, water, sugar and preservatives. Fruit juices and juice drinks retain their vitamin C well during storage but once the package is opened the vitamin will slowly be lost through oxidation.

Fruit *smoothies* are blends of one or more puréed and/or pulped fruits; they sometimes have vanilla, honey or yogurt added. They are heat-treated and stored similarly to freshly squeezed fruit juices.

Dried fruits, such as currants, sultanas, raisins, dates and figs, provide energy principally in the form of sugar and are good sources of fibre. They do not contain vitamin C. Prunes and dried apricots are also useful sources of beta-carotene.

Dried apricots, figs, prunes, raisins and sultanas are good sources of iron. Dried fruit counts towards the recommended five portions of fruit and vegetables a day but more of the sugars in dried fruit are likely to be extrinsic (see 'Health aspects of carbohydrates' in Chapter 2) than in unprocessed fruit, since they will have been at least partly released from the cells by the drying process. Therefore, it is sensible not to eat them frequently during the day as snacks and to eat them preferably at meal times.

Fat spreads and oils

There is now a wide range of dairy spreads and reduced- and lower-fat spreads on the market, all of which can be used as butter substitutes. While some consist of a mixture of animal fats and vegetable oils, others contain vegetable oils with a significant proportion of polyunsaturated fatty acids. Almost any edible oil or fat can be used for making fat spreads.

Varying textures can be produced by mixing oils and fats with differing physical properties and by hydrogenation or hardening of oils. During manufacture, the mixture of oils and fats is emulsified with a salt solution and other constituents such as emulsifiers, flavouring and colouring.

Dairy spreads contain variable amounts (but less than 80%) of milk fat such as butter or cream. The fat of *blended spreads* is only partly milk fat. *Reduced- or low-fat* spreads generally vary in fat content from about 20% in a very-low-fat spread to about 40% in a low-fat spread and 60–70% in a reduced-fat spread. These contain a proportion of a fat replacer (see below). Some spreads now contain *stanol esters* (*plant sterols*), made from a plant extract, which can help to reduce blood low-density lipoprotein (LDL) cholesterol levels (see 'Health aspects of fats' in Chapter 3). Plant sterols lower blood cholesterol levels by reducing the absorption of cholesterol from the intestine. It is advisable for pregnant and breastfeeding women and children under 5 years of age not to consume plant sterols since they can interfere with fat-soluble vitamin absorption. Vitamins A and D are frequently added to other fat spreads but this is not obligatory.

Vegetable oils are produced from a variety of plant parts including seeds (e.g. sunflower, rape [canola]), grains (e.g. maize or corn), pulses (e.g. soya beans, peanuts), fruits (e.g. olive, palm) and fruit kernels (e.g. olive, palm, coconut). They are traditionally extracted by crushing or milling but nowadays these processes may be replaced or followed by solvent extraction. Vegetable oils vary in the composition of their fatty acids. They may be sold as a single type or as a blend of several oils. Some oils, such as sunflower, are high in polyunsaturated fatty acids, while others, such as olive and rape (canola) seed oils, are high in monounsaturated fatty acids.

FAT REPLACERS

Dietary advice to reduce the consumption of fat has stimulated research into ways of reducing the fat content of foods by developing fat replacers, which have some of the sensory characteristics of fats but a lower energy value. For example, Salatrim®, made from modified triglycerides, has been approved for use in the EU. Others, including protein-based, carbohydrate-based and sucrose polyester replacers, may be approved for food use in the future.

Sugars and preserves

Sugar provides energy and no other nutrient. Honey and some brown sugars include very small quantities of minerals and certain B vitamins but nowhere near enough of the latter to assist with the metabolism of the sugars present. Some preserves contain vitamin C, and chocolate contains iron and other nutrients. Table sugar, honey, syrups and the sugar added to preserves are all non-milk extrinsic sugars (see 'Health aspects of carbohydrates' in Chapter 2) that can cause dental caries if eaten frequently, especially between meals.

Alcohol

The alcohol in alcoholic drinks is rapidly absorbed from the digestive tract and utilised as a source of energy, 1 g of alcohol providing 29 kJ or 7 kcal. Carbohydrate may also be present in varying proportions and this provides additional energy. After an alcoholic drink is consumed, the alcohol content is rapidly absorbed and becomes a source of calories to the body. One *unit* of alcohol, which is the same as 8 g of pure alcohol (equivalent to a small single measure of spirits), contains 232 kJ (56 kcal). Any additional carbohydrates in an alcoholic drink will also be a source of energy and of calories, the exact amount varying with the type of drink and type of any mixer used.

The National Diet and Nutrition Survey (2008/09–2009/10) found that adult drinkers obtain a significant part of their energy intake from the alcoholic drinks they consume. The study found that, on average, adults aged 19–64 who consumed alcohol, over a four-day period of observation, obtained 9% of their energy intake from alcohol, while adult drinkers aged 65 and over in the study obtained 6% of their energy intake from the alcohol over the same period.

Table 34 gives the energy constituents of some alcoholic drinks.

Table 34. Energy constituents of some alcoholic drinks

	Average values per 100 ml			
	Alcohol (g)	Carbohydrate (g)	Energy (kJ)	(kcal)
Beer, draught, canned and bottled	2.9	2.2	124	30
Lager	4.0	0.0	121	29
Cider, sweet	3.7	4.3	176	42
Sherry, medium	13.3	5.9	482	116
Red wine	9.6	0.2	283	68
White wine, dry	9.1	0.6	275	66
White wine, sweet	10.2	5.9	394	94
Spirits	31.7	0.0	919	222
Liqueur, low–medium strength	19.8	32.8	1099	262

Source: McCance and Widdowson's Composition of Foods Integrated Dataset (COFIDS) published by the Food Standards Agency, 2008.
Note: 1 ml of pure alcohol weighs 0.79 g.

Heavy drinkers and those with alcohol dependence may eat very little food. They will get a large proportion of their energy intake from alcohol. This can cause a substantial fall in their intake of protein, vitamins and many other nutrients, which can cause very serious nerve and brain damage.

Studies have shown that alcohol both lowers inhibitions and stimulates appetite, and that certain patterns of drinking, especially episodes of heavy drinking or *binge* drinking, are linked to an increase in food intake – especially of convenience foods, which are often high in salt, fat and sugar.

Government guidance on drinking is based around the concept of the alcohol *unit*. A unit of alcohol is equivalent to 8 g (10 ml) of pure alcohol. The Government gives guidance on levels of drinking that are associated with a lower risk of developing future health harm. It is recommended that women should not regularly drink more than 2–3 units per day and men should not regularly drink more than 3–4 units per day.

National statistics for 2009 show that, while 90% of people had heard of units, only 63% of beer drinkers could actually correctly identify the volume of a unit of beer, and only 27% of wine drinkers could do the same for wine. Only 13% of survey respondents reported using units to keep a check on how much they were drinking (*Drinking: Adults' Behaviour and Knowledge in 2009*, Office for National Statistics, 2010).

It is estimated that 22% of adults (9.1 million) drink above the recommended levels for lower-risk drinking and that these drinkers consume over two-thirds (70%) of all the alcohol consumed in England. Furthermore, 2.2 million (7% of men and 4% of women) regularly drink more than double the recommended levels and these drinkers drink nearly a third (31%) of all the alcohol consumed in England.

12 Nutritional value of meals and the whole diet

In this chapter data are taken from *McCance and Widdowson's Composition of Foods Integrated Dataset* (COFIDS), published by the Food Standards Agency in 2008, and from *National Diet and Nutrition Survey: Headline Results from Years 1 and 2 (Combined) of the Rolling Programme 2008/9– 2009/10* published by the Department of Health in 2011, unless stated otherwise. Salt levels in processed foods reflect information from market leaders at the time of publishing.

The balanced diet

No single food contains all the essential nutrients that the body needs to be healthy and function efficiently, neither should a single food be considered intrinsically 'healthy' or 'unhealthy', although some foods are more likely to contribute beneficially to a healthy diet than others. It is the nutritional value of a person's diet as a whole that is important. This depends on the overall mixture or balance of foods that is eaten over a period of time, as well as on the needs of the individual eating them. That is why a healthy, balanced diet as outlined by the eatwell plate (see Appendix 6) is one that includes a wide variety of foods, so that adequate intakes of all the nutrients are achieved.

Many people are eating more saturated fat, salt and added sugar than government recommendations; and too little fruit, vegetables, oily fish and fibre. Diet can have a major impact on health, and evidence indicates that some common health problems, including heart disease, stroke and some cancers, can be diet-related. For example, eating a diet that is high in saturated fat can raise the level of cholesterol in the blood, and high cholesterol can increase the risk of heart disease. Consuming too many calories can result in overweight and obesity, and obesity can increase the risk of Type II diabetes, some cancers and heart disease; a diet high in salt (sodium) can raise blood pressure (see 'Sodium and chloride' in Chapter 7), which increases the risk of developing health problems such as heart disease and stroke.

Expert committees regularly review scientific evidence for the relationship between diet and disease. A person's genes can influence their risk of developing certain diet-related diseases, and other lifestyle factors are also regarded as being very important, particularly being physically active and not smoking as part of a healthier lifestyle.

Sound nutritional practice can help in preventing these diet-related diseases by developing eating habits that promote the maintenance of good health throughout life. For example, when someone is obese through persistent overeating, only a steady reduction in energy intake combined with an increase in energy expenditure, and not sporadic bouts of starvation or exercise, will lead to weight loss that can be maintained.

If a diet is low or lacking in a particular vitamin, the consequences of this deficiency may not become apparent for some period of time. However, the diet is much more likely to contain enough vitamins, especially vitamin C, if a variety of fruits and vegetables are eaten every day than if these foods are eaten only at infrequent intervals. It is also now being increasingly recognised that, in addition to vitamins, a large number of other components that occur naturally in fruits and vegetables may contribute towards their protective effect against diet-related diseases. For this reason it is recommended that at least five portions of a variety of fruits and vegetables should be eaten each day (see 'Fruit and vegetables' in Chapter 11).

Although heart disease will not result from eating the occasional fat-rich meal, it is wise not to consistently include large amounts of fat, especially saturated fat, in the diet. Over the long term, a person should ensure that their overall diet is balanced in the way shown by the eatwell plate in this manual (see Appendix 6). Apart from some vulnerable groups, most people can get all the nutrients they need from a healthy, balanced diet and do not need dietary supplements. Food is more likely to be enjoyed, rather than treated simply as something to fill up on, if people ensure that their diet is made up of a wide range of different foods, so that it is varied and interesting.

Meals and choice of foods

Although there is no single agreed definition of how many calories define a meal, it is assumed that a meal can be arbitrarily defined as the amount of food eaten at one period of time and which provides 2510 kJ (600 kcal) or more. This definition covers much more than the popular meaning of the word 'meal', which is that of hot, cooked food eaten while sitting down. Different people may eat quite different numbers of meals per day, the arrangements being determined by custom, lifestyle and working conditions. Many people now do not follow the traditional pattern of three main meals and one or more snacks, but 'graze' or 'snack' at frequent intervals throughout the day. There is evidence that the number of meals taken in a day (and consequently the amount of food eaten at one time) influences the pattern of utilisation of nutrients by the body. However, the balance of nutrients achieved over a period of time is undoubtedly more important in determining a person's nutritional status than the frequency of eating occasions. Nevertheless, it is sensible to try to eat one or more balanced meals each day. Although the amounts of nutrients in different meals may vary, the total intake of each nutrient should meet an individual's needs, ideally each day but certainly over the course of a week, if the food eaten is to be fully satisfactory for health.

Apart from breast milk, which satisfies all a baby's needs for the first six months of life, no single food provides all the nutrients we require. The easiest way of providing an adequate mixture and balance of all the nutrients is to eat a wide variety of foods chosen from among the four main groups shown in the eatwell plate (see Appendix 6):

- potatoes, bread, rice, pasta and other starchy foods
- fruit and vegetables
- milk and dairy products
- meat, fish, eggs, beans and other non-dairy sources of protein.

It is important to have some fat in the diet, but people do not need to consume any of the 'foods and drinks that are high in fat and/or sugar' as part of a healthy diet.

People who eat sweets, cakes, biscuits or chocolate between meals or as constant snacks and drink sugary soft drinks will be more prone to dental decay. Consuming large quantities of high-energy foods or drinks at or between meals can result in an undesirable increase in weight if the total daily energy intake exceeds the energy used up and, if these foods are high in saturated fat, may also lead to raised blood cholesterol levels and eventually to the development of heart disease. In addition, for adults, alcohol is high in calories, so reducing consumption can help to control weight.

BREAKFAST

Because of the length of time since the previous meal, and the consequent low blood sugar level in the morning, it is desirable to eat breakfast every morning. It is particularly important for children to have a good breakfast, as young children may not be able to satisfy their nutritional needs during the rest of the day if they miss breakfast; others may be tempted to fill up on nutrient-poor foods on the way to school or during the morning. Some people skip breakfast because they think it will help them to lose weight. However, research shows that eating breakfast can actually help people to control their weight.

Two possible breakfasts, both commonly eaten in Britain, are shown in Table 35. Both provide adequate amounts of energy, protein and a wide variety of vitamins and minerals (not shown). Breakfast 2 provides less fat and fewer saturated fatty acids and much more fibre and vitamin C than Breakfast 1. Breakfast 2 also provides two of the five recommended portions of fruit and

Table 35. Comparison of two breakfasts

	Weight (g)	Energy (kJ)	(kcal)	Total sugars (g)	Protein (g)	Fat (g)	Saturated fatty acids (g)	Fibre (g)	Sodium (mg)	Vitamin C (mg)
Breakfast 1										
Cornflakes	30	458	107	2.3	2.2	0.2	0.0	0.5	285	0
Sugar	10	168	39	10.5	0.0	0.0	0.0	0.0	1	0
Milk, whole	100	274	66	4.5	3.3	3.9	2.5	0.0	43	2
White bread (large loaf, 1 medium slice), toasted	27	307	72	1.1	2.6	0.5	0.1	0.6	132	0
Fat spread (60% fat), polyunsaturated	9	197	48	0.0	0.0	5.3	1.2	0.0	54	0
Marmalade	15	167	39	10.4	0.0	0.0	0.0	0.0	10	2
Milk (whole) in 2 cups of tea	50	137	33	2.3	1.7	2.0	1.3	0.0	21	1
Total		1708	404	31.1	9.8	11.9	5.1	1.1	546	5
Breakfast 2										
Wheat biscuits, 2	40	565	133	1.6	4.2	0.8	0.1	3.8	104	0
Milk, semi-skimmed	100	195	46	4.7	3.4	1.7	1.1	0.0	43	1
Banana, small	80	322	76	16.7	1.0	0.2	0.1	0.9	1	9
Wholemeal bread (large loaf, 1 thick slice), toasted	40	434	102	1.3	4.5	1.2	0.2	2.4	204	0
Low-fat spread (26–39% fat), polyunsaturated with olive oil	9	131	32	0.0	0.0	3.5	0.8	0.0	54	0
Marmalade	15	167	39	10.4	0.0	0.0	0.0	0.0	10	2
Milk (semi-skimmed) in 2 cups of tea	60	117	28	2.8	2.0	1.0	0.7	0.0	26	1
Orange juice, average glass	150	229	54	13.2	0.8	0.2	0.0	0.2	15	59
Total		2160	510	50.7	15.9	5.1	3.0	7.3	457	72

vegetables for the day (a banana and a glass of orange juice). Substituting a cereal with little or no sodium (salt), like shredded wholegrain wheat cereal or some types of muesli, for those shown in Table 35 can reduce the sodium content of these breakfasts. A person who feels unable to eat breakfast immediately on getting up should be encouraged to eat a nutrient-dense snack as soon as possible during the morning. Breakfast clubs in schools can help to alleviate the hunger felt by children who do not eat breakfast at home and, if healthier choices are provided, can help to improve the nutritional quality of their overall daily diet.

Calculation of nutrients in prepared dishes and meals, using food tables

DISHES

Appendix 3 gives the nutrient composition of many of the ingredients that may be used in mixed dishes. From the recipe, the approximate nutritional value of a dish can then be worked out by arithmetic. To illustrate this, the calculation of the nutritional value of a homemade quiche lorraine is shown in Table 36. An allowance has been made for the change in weight and probable loss of folate and vitamin C during cooking.

MEALS

It is not uncommon to have a choice between types of meal: for example, one could be a cooked meal and the other a sandwich-based meal. Many people may now eat the latter at lunchtime rather than the former. Some may not consider it a meal at all if they choose a sandwich. Table 37 compares the nutrient content of a ham sandwich, a low-fat fruit yogurt and a small glass of orange juice with that of roast chicken, oven chips, peas, canned pineapple and coffee with reduced-fat milk (as calculated from the figures given in Appendix 3). The sandwich meal has a lower energy, fat and saturated fat and vitamin D content than the cooked meal, but is richer in calcium and vitamin C. It has a similar folate content, but contains less fibre and will contain considerably more sodium unless the cooked meal is salted during cooking or at the table.

A cold or sandwich meal is thus not necessarily nutritionally inferior to a cooked meal; the nutritional values of both depend on the quantity and nutrient content of the items within them.

Table 36. Nutrients in a homemade quiche lorraine

	Weight (g)	Energy (kJ)	Energy (kcal)	Protein (g)	Fat (g)	Saturated fatty acids (g)	Carbohydrate (g)	Fibre (g)	Calcium (mg)	Iron (mg)	Sodium (mg)	Vitamin A (retinol equivalent) (µg)	Folate (µg)	Riboflavin (µg)	Niacin equivalent (mg)	Vitamin C (mg)
Flour mixture:																
White	67	1006	236	6.1	0.9	0.3	54.2	2.3	65	1.3	1.3	0	11	0.03	1.1	0
Wholemeal	67	931	218	7.8	1.3	0.2	46.8	5.9	22	1.7	1.3	0	18	0.07	3.4	0
Butter, salted	66	2019	491	0.4	54.3	34.4	0.4	0	12	0	400	632	0	0.05	0	0
Eggs	100	627	151	12.5	11.2	3.2	0	0	57	1.9	140	190	50	0.47	3.8	0
Milk, semi-skimmed	207	404	95	7	3.5	2.3	9.7	0	248	0	89	42	12	0.5	1.4	2
Streaky bacon	100	1142	276	15.8	23.6	8.2	0	0	6	0.5	1260	0	3	0.14	7.4	0
Cheddar cheese	100	1725	416	25.4	34.9	21.7	0.1	0	739	0.3	700	388	31	0.39	6.9	0
Whole quiche, cooked	527	7854	1883	75	129.7	70.3	111.2	8.2	1149	5.7	2592	1252	63	1.65	24	1
Per 100 g		1490	357	14.2	24.6	13.3	21.1	1.6	218	1.1	492	238	12	0.3	4.6	0.2

The quiche weight (527 g) is less than the sum of the ingredients (707 g) owing to the loss of moisture on cooking.
50% of folate is deducted to allow for loss on cooking; 50% of vitamin C is deducted to allow for loss on cooking.

Table 37. Comparison of the nutritional value of a sandwich meal and a cooked meal

	Weight (g)	Energy (kJ)	Energy (kcal)	Protein (g)	Fat (g)	Saturated fatty acids (g)	Carbohydrate (g)	Fibre (g)	Calcium (mg)	Iron (mg)	Sodium (mg)	Vitamin A (retinol equivalent) (µg)	Folate (µg)	Vitamin C (mg)
Sandwich meal														
Bread, wholemeal (2 slices)	72	664	156	6.8	1.8	0.4	30.2	3.6	76	1.7	302	0	29	0
Reduced-fat spread (41–62% fat), polyunsaturated	14	307	76	0	7.3	2.3	0	0	0	0	112	112	0	0
Ham, sliced (2 slices)	46	207	49	8.5	1.5	0.5	0.5	0	3	0.3	552	0	9	0
Pickle, sweet	20	121	28	0.1	0	0	7.2	0.2	3	0.1	322	8	0	0
Yogurt, low fat, fruit	125	414	97	5.3	1.4	1	17.1	0.3	175	0.1	78	13	20	1
Orange juice	150	230	54	0.8	0.1	0	13.2	0.2	15	0.3	15	4	27	59
Total		1942	460	21.4	12.1	4.1	68.2	4.3	273	2.6	1380	137	85	60
Cooked meal														
Roast chicken, meat only	100	742	177	27.3	7.5	2.9	0	0	17	0.8	100	24	10	0
Chips, oven baked	165	1320	312	5.3	8.1	1.3	58.2	4.5	20	1.3	87	0	35	20
Peas, frozen, boiled in unsalted water	80	233	55	4.8	0.7	0.2	7.8	4.1	28	1.3	2	76	26	10
Pineapple, canned in juice	80	160	38	0.2	0	0	9.8	0.4	6	0.4	1	2	1	9
Coffee, infusion, cup	190	15	4	0.4	0	0	0.6	0	6	0.2	0	0	0.2	0
Milk, semi-skimmed	30	59	14	1	0.5	0.3	1.4	0	36	0	13	6	2	0
Total		2529	599	39	16.8	4.7	77.7	8.9	113	4	203	108	74	39

ALLOWANCE FOR WASTE

The calculation of the nutritional value of a meal or a diet as actually eaten cannot be made directly from the total amounts of the foods bought from the shops, nor from the total food used in the kitchen. There is always a proportion of waste for which allowance must be made; that is:

- *inedible waste*, e.g. egg shells, potato peelings, outer leaves of cabbages, orange peel, bacon rinds, bones and gristle of meat etc. (see Table 38)
- *edible waste*:
  - preparation losses, e.g. batter left in mixing bowls, fat trimmed from meat or left in frying pans, crusts from bread, spilt milk
  - table waste, e.g. leftovers on plates
  - edible food which has 'gone bad' and is discarded.

Inedible waste

Average figures for the inedible waste associated with different foods are given in Table 38 as a percentage of the product as listed. For example, 34% of bananas (item 163), as purchased, consist of skin that is not eaten.

The food tables throughout this manual always give the nutrients per 100 g of 'edible portion' and, if they are used for calculating the nutritional value of foods where only the purchased weight is known, the percentage of inedible waste must be deducted. For example, to calculate the energy value of 1 kg (purchased weight) of bananas:

Edible weight = $(100 - 34) \times 10 = 660$ g

Energy value = $\frac{660}{100} \times$ (kJ per 100 g from Appendix 3)

$$= \frac{660}{100} \times 403 = 2660 \text{ kJ}$$

A similar calculation can be carried out using calories per 100 g from Appendix 3.

Typical values for the percentage of inedible waste in selected foods are shown in Table 38, but in reality values vary with the exact nature of the food and with its quality. For example, they vary between different cuts and joints of meat and between different sizes and varieties of orange. The values given must therefore be used with discretion.

Table 38. Percentage of inedible waste from food as purchased

Food	Percentage
Chicken, drumsticks, roasted	37
Lamb chop, loin	22
Kipper, grilled	37
Sardines, canned in oil, drained	18
Tuna, canned in brine, drained	19
Eggs, chicken, whole	11
Potatoes, new, with skin	11
Potatoes, old, with skin	20
Beans, red kidney, canned	36
Beetroot, boiled	20
Cabbage	23
Celery	9
Courgettes	12
Lettuce	26
Mushrooms, unpeeled	3
Onions	9
Peppers, capsicum, green	16
Peas, canned	35
Sweetcorn kernels, canned	18
Watercress	38
Apples, eating	11
Avocado	29
Bananas	34
Blackcurrants	2
Cherries	17
Dates, dried, with stones	16
Grapefruit	32
Grapes	5
Kiwi fruit	14
Mangoes	32
Melon, honeydew	37
Oranges	30
Peaches	10
Pears	9
Plums	6
Strawberries	5
Almonds, with shells	63

Fresh produce unless specified

Edible waste

It is often difficult for practical reasons to measure the weight of food actually eaten, for example by a particular individual in a large family or when a meal is eaten away from home. Estimates of portion sizes and of the loss of edible food may then need to be made before the nutritional adequacy of any diet can be worked out. The average wastage of food in the home in cooking, on plates and given to pets has been found to be between 5% and 10%, but of course the amount varies from food to food and from family to family. Wastage can also be high in some catering establishments.

Planning balanced meals and nutritionally adequate diets

The provision of palatable and acceptable meals must be the first consideration; only if foods are eaten, and not wasted, can planning for good nutrition be effective.

A balanced meal is one which provides adequate amounts of protein and all the vitamins and minerals, as well as energy. It should also provide fibre and should be limited in its fat, sugar and salt content.

The main sources of each nutrient are discussed in Chapters 2, 3, 4, 7 and 8, and the detailed composition of a range of foods is given in Appendix 3. Most foods contain a wide variety of nutrients, and most vitamins and minerals are present in a range of commonly available foods. Thus, the simplest way to meet nutritional requirements is to eat a varied diet containing a wide selection of different types of food.

To help make this easier, the Government has produced a set of eight tips for eating well and a pictorial guide to a healthy diet called the eatwell plate (see Appendix 6). In general, people should try to eat the following:

- *Plenty of potatoes, bread, rice, pasta and other starchy foods.* These provide energy, fibre, vitamins and minerals and should form the main part of most meals and snacks, making up about one-third of the total food intake.
- *Plenty of fruit and vegetables.* The daily diet should contain at least five portions of a variety of fruit and vegetables, which are good sources of some vitamins and minerals not commonly found in other foods and of fibre. These should also make up about one-third of the dietary intake.
- *Some milk and dairy foods.* This includes cheese, yogurt and fromage frais. These are good sources of protein and vitamins and they are also an important source of calcium. Lower-fat options should be chosen where appropriate.

- *Some meat, fish, eggs, beans and other non-dairy sources of protein.* These are a great source of protein and are rich in vitamins and minerals. The weekly diet should contain at least two portions of fish, including a portion of oily fish. Lower-fat options and/or cooking practices should be chosen where appropriate.
- *Just a small amount of foods and drinks that are high in fat and/or sugar,* such as butter, reduced-fat spreads, cream, fried foods, jam, cakes, pastries and biscuits.

Options that are lower in fat, salt and sugar should be chosen when possible.

Alcoholic drinks should be consumed infrequently or only in limited amounts.

The Reference Nutrient Intakes (RNIs) of selected major nutrients for groups of people of different ages are given in Table 27 (Chapter 9), and these figures may be used as a guide when planning diets. The Dietary Reference Values (DRVs) for fat and carbohydrate for adults are summarised in Table 28 (Chapter 9). As a rule of thumb, on average fat should not provide more than 35% of dietary energy for adults, and saturated fatty acids should not provide more than 10%. By implication, the total carbohydrate in the diet should provide about 50% of the food energy, with no more than about 10% coming from non-milk extrinsic (NME) sugars. Children under 5 years of age who are not able to eat large quantities of bulky foods may not obtain sufficient energy unless they are given energy-dense foods. It is therefore not wise to limit their fat intake too much (note that human breast milk derives 54% of its energy from fat and 26% from saturated fatty acids).

The adult diet should provide 18 g per day of fibre as non-starch polysaccharides. Wholemeal versions of cereals provide more fibre than refined products.

The RNI of sodium for adults is 1600 mg of sodium per day, which equates to 4 g of salt per day; babies and children have lower requirements (see Table 27 in Chapter 9). The RNI for sodium is easily achieved, as 75% of the salt that people eat is already in the food that they purchase. In fact, on average adults eat more than the recommended intake of no more than 6 g per day of salt, and children also eat more than their recommended intake. Individuals can try to cut down on their sodium intake by eating fewer processed salty foods, but also by using less salt in cooking and at the table. It is not always easy to tell by taste alone whether a food is high in salt. Checking the nutrition label on a product can be very helpful in choosing a lower-sodium food. For example, if a 500-g prepared meal contains 0.5 g of sodium (1.25 g salt) per 100 g, it will provide 2.5 g of sodium, or the maximum recommended daily amount of 6 g of salt. Other practical ways to help to reduce salt intakes include using herbs (fresh or dried) and spices to flavour dishes; choosing products that are marked 'reduced salt' or 'no added salt'; and cutting down on salty snacks and foods such as crisps, salted nuts, processed meats and prepared meals.

It is the total nutrient intake over at least one day (as in the example given in Table 42 in Chapter 13) and preferably a week which should be assessed. And even then it is the balance of the diet in the longer term which is most important for health.

Planning meals in relation to cost

Within this general framework it is usually necessary to consider the relative cost of different sources of nutrients. Allowance must also be made for the effects of cooking on the nutritional value of the food.

Great savings in the cost of eating can be made with a thorough knowledge of food composition and nutritional value for money. For example, cheaper cuts of lean meat have practically the same nutritional value as the more expensive cuts, although they may take longer to cook. Many meat products also provide good nutritional value for money. However, fatty meat and some meat products may prove relatively expensive if large quantities of fat have to be trimmed off before cooking or discarded after cooking. Again, a cheaper oily fish such as mackerel has a similar nutritional value to a more expensive oily fish such as salmon. Buying vegetables and fruit in season is usually less expensive; frozen vegetables can be good value, as there is no waste associated with preparing them and they often have a higher content of nutrients than fresh vegetables that have been stored at room temperature for some time. Fresh citrus fruits are very convenient sources of vitamin C and are also fairly cheap. Eggs, beans or pulses can take the place of meat in a main course.

It is important to understand that a cheap source of one nutrient may not be a cheap food in the context of the whole diet. For example, sugar supplies only one nutrient, whereas bread, pasta, rice, breakfast cereals, milk, oily fish, potatoes, peas and beans all supply several nutrients cheaply and are thus very good value for money.

Planning meals for the week ahead is really important in food budgeting. Careful shopping, preparation and storage of food, and a knowledge of basic cookery skills all play a part in using the available money to the best advantage.

13   Needs of particular groups of people

Infants and young children

Babies are unique in that they rely on a single food, milk, to satisfy all their nutritional needs for the first few months of their life. Breast milk is ideal for several reasons:

- All the nutrients are present in the right amount for human infants in a readily absorbed form and it changes daily, weekly and monthly to meet their growing needs.
- It contains several natural agents such as antibodies, which help protect the infant against infections and diseases.
- It cannot be prepared incorrectly.
- Breastfeeding has benefits for the mother, such as a reduced risk of breast and ovarian cancers, and can help mothers lose the weight they gained during their pregnancy.

It is therefore recommended that babies are exclusively breastfed (that is, given breast milk only, with no other food or drink) for around the first six months of their life. There are benefits from breastfeeding even if the mother breastfeeds for only a few weeks, but the longer breastfeeding can continue the greater the benefits. Some nutrients are present in low amounts in breast milk, such as iron and vitamin D. However, a store of these nutrients is built up in the developing baby's liver during pregnancy, supplying the newborn infant with an adequate amount until complementary foods are introduced at around 6 months of age. If there is doubt about the mother's vitamin D status (particularly if the mother did not take vitamin D supplements throughout pregnancy), then health professionals can recommend supplements for breastfed infants from the age of 1 month.

Those mothers who cannot or choose not to breastfeed should use infant formulas until their babies are 12 months of age. These are usually based on cow's milk, which has been modified so that its nutrient composition resembles that of human milk. Since the immature kidneys of young infants are unable to cope with high concentrations of protein and some minerals (such as sodium), it is very important to make up infant formula feeds exactly according to the manufacturer's instructions so that they are not too concentrated. Formula feeds should also not be diluted more than stated in the instructions because the feed will then not contain enough energy or nutrients for the baby's needs. Hydrolysed protein infant formulas can be prescribed by a GP if a baby has an allergy to cow's milk. Soya-based infant formulas should only be used on the advice of a GP or health visitor. Babies who are allergic to cow's milk proteins may also be allergic to goat's milk or soya proteins. Formulas based on goat's milk proteins have not been approved for use by the European Food Safety Authority for babies under 1 year old, and so should not be given to babies.

When a baby is around 6 months old, solid foods can be introduced alongside breast milk or infant formula. Before this, a baby's digestive system is still developing and they are probably not ready for solid food. Solid foods should not be introduced before 4 months of age. If parents decide to introduce solid foods into their baby's diet before the age of 6 months, then there are certain foods that should be avoided, as they may cause allergic reactions or make babies ill. These include wheat-based foods and other foods containing gluten, including bread, wheat flour, breakfast cereals and rusks; nuts and seeds, including peanuts, peanut butter and other nut spreads; eggs; fish and shellfish; liver; and soft unpasteurised cheeses. Children who have already been diagnosed with an allergy, such as a food allergy or eczema, or whose parents, brothers or sisters have an allergy (such as asthma, eczema, hay fever or other types of allergy) are at greater risk of developing a peanut allergy, and parents should talk to their GP, health visitor or a medical allergy specialist before giving foods containing peanuts to such children for the first time. Whole nuts should not be given to children under 5 years because of the risk of choking. Smooth nut butters or finely ground nuts can be given instead. There is no clear evidence to say whether eating or avoiding peanuts when pregnant or breastfeeding affects the chances of the child developing a peanut allergy.

From about 6 months of age onwards, parents can gradually introduce infant cereal foods, soft or cooked fruit and vegetables, eggs (cooked until both the white and the yolk are solid) and even finely blended or minced meat (using no added salt or sugar). By about 12–18 months, children can eat a mixed diet not very different from that of the rest of the family. However, salt should not be added to foods given to babies, as their kidneys cannot cope with it – too much salt can also give them a taste for salty foods and contribute to high blood pressure in later life. Foods high in salt, such as stocks, gravy, bacon or sausages, and processed foods, such as pasta sauces or breakfast cereals that are not made specifically for babies, should also be avoided. Infants up to the age of 1 year should have less than 1 g of salt per day. Avoiding sugary foods and drinks will help to prevent tooth decay – for young babies, mashed banana, breast milk or formula milk can be used to sweeten food if necessary. If sweet foods are given to toddlers, it is best to give them at mealtimes, as they will do less damage to their teeth. Honey can very occasionally contain bacteria that can multiply in the child's intestines, leading to infant botulism, so honey should not be given to children until they are 1 year old. Honey is a sugar, so avoiding it will also help to prevent tooth decay.

Cow's milk, goat's milk and sheep's milk do not contain the right balance of nutrients for infants and are particularly low in iron, so they should not be given as a main drink to children under the age of 1 year. They can, however, be used in cooking and preparing meals, as long as they are pasteurised. Whole milk and full-fat dairy products should be given, as they provide extra energy and higher levels of certain nutrients (such as vitamin A) that growing children need. Above the age of 2, semi-skimmed milk may be introduced as long as a child is eating well. Skimmed milk and 1%-fat milk are not suitable for children under the age of 5, as they do not contain enough energy. Once the diet has become more varied, infants can be given extra drinks of cooled, boiled water in hot weather, but sugary drinks and juices should be limited as they can harm developing teeth. Fruit juice should be diluted with water and given only at mealtimes, to prevent tooth decay.

Studies have shown that a significant proportion of infants and young children between 9 months and 3½ years of age have low iron intakes (below the Lower Reference Nutrient Intake [LRNI] – see Table 27 in Chapter 9). Although it has not yet been established whether children with habitually low intakes are deficient in iron, it is wise to include rich sources of iron among the foods provided for this age group. Some good sources of iron are listed in Table 12 (Chapter 7).

Children under 5 years should not be given only wholegrain foods such as high-fibre breakfast cereals, wholemeal bread or pasta, and brown rice, as they are too high in fibre. Young children have smaller stomachs, and high-fibre foods can fill them up before they have consumed enough calories.

Vitamin drops containing vitamins A, C and D should be given to children until they are 5 years old, unless they are good eaters of a varied diet. Drops are provided free under Healthy Start[23] for children aged 6 months to 4 years in those families who are on low incomes and are claiming certain benefits.

School-aged children

School-aged children are growing fast and are also very active. Tables 26 and 27 (Chapter 9) give the Estimated Average Requirements (EARs) for energy and Reference Nutrient Intakes (RNIs) for major nutrients for groups of children of different ages, and show that in some areas these are high in relation to their body size compared with those of adults. The big appetites of some children usually reflect a real nutritional need rather than greed. Because of their smaller size compared with adults, and their correspondingly smaller stomachs, it is important that children eat meals that are not too bulky and high in fibre (which may fill them up before they have consumed all the

---

[23] Healthy Start replaced the Welfare Food Scheme in 2006. It covers the whole of the UK.

calories and nutrients that they need). Bread, milk, cheese, meat, fish, liver, eggs, fruit, vegetables and potatoes are all excellent sources of a number of nutrients. Milk, whether whole, semi-skimmed, 1% fat or skimmed, is one of the best sources of calcium, riboflavin and protein.

The incidence of overweight and obesity in children has increased significantly in recent years. Therefore it is important that children are taught healthy-eating habits from an early age, both at home and at school: biscuits, sweets, sugary soft drinks, chips and crisps should not displace other more nutritious foods too often. In the school setting, children should receive a healthy-eating message right across the school, not only through the taught curriculum but also in the food provided in the school canteen, breakfast clubs, tuck shops and vending machines.

Children's dental health has significantly improved since the 1970s due to the increasing use of fluoride toothpaste. However, sweet and sticky foods, snacks and sugary soft drinks, consumed frequently between meals, are one cause of the dental decay still found in many British school children. Children should be encouraged to clean their teeth twice every day with a fluoride-containing toothpaste.

It is important that children are discouraged from acquiring a taste for salty foods, as too much salt can contribute to high blood pressure in later life. Children aged between 4 and 6 years should have no more than 3 g per day, 7–10-year-olds no more than 5 g per day and children of 11 years and over no more than 6 g per day (see also 'Sodium and chloride' in Chapter 7). At present, on average children are likely to be consuming significantly more than these daily recommended maximums.

Adolescents

The nutrient needs of adolescents are higher in many respects than those of any other group. Healthy adolescents have large appetites and it is important that they satisfy them with foods of high nutritional value in the form of well-balanced meals, rather than by too many snacks that are high in fat, sugar or salt. Overweight and obesity among school-aged children are increasing, and may continue into adult life. It is more sensible to prevent obesity than to try to correct it by periodically eating little or skipping meals; excessive dieting can be dangerous. Knowledge of nutrition and the incentive to apply this knowledge in practice are likely to benefit the health of young people for the rest of their lives.

Adolescents are known to have low intakes of several micronutrients, in particular iron for girls. Adolescents (both sexes) are also reported to have low vitamin D status.

Bone density increases during the late stages of adolescence, and a lack of calcium, magnesium and vitamin D at this crucial time may result in an increased likelihood of fracture later in life. It may be advisable for pregnant adolescents to have calcium intakes that are higher than the RNI (Table 27 in Chapter 9), although an increment above the RNI is not necessary for other pregnant women (see below). Poor intakes of micronutrients during adolescence and early adulthood can result in low stores of nutrients, which can subsequently put young women at greater risk of giving birth to a low-birthweight baby. Infants of adolescent mothers are more likely to be born small and are more at risk of several disabilities.[24]

Adults

The latest research shows that in England over 60% of adults are overweight or obese (see 'Obesity' in Chapter 5). Most adults, therefore, need to lose weight and to do so need to consume fewer calories. For adults who wish to reduce their intake of energy to help maintain a healthy weight or to decrease their intake of saturated fatty acids or salt to lessen their risk of premature heart disease, there is information throughout this manual which will help them to achieve this. Anyone needing to make changes to their diet will find it easier if they encourage family members or friends to support them by making similar changes. There is also information for those who wish to reduce their intake of sugars and to increase their intake of fruit, vegetables, oily fish and fibre.

In general, healthy, well-balanced diets are high in starchy foods and fruit and vegetables; contain some meat (or meat alternatives) and milk and dairy foods; and contain only small quantities of foods and drinks with high concentrations of fat (especially saturated fat), salt and sugar. Increasing the amount of starchy foods in the diet can help to reduce fats and sugars. Starchy foods also contribute fibre (particularly wholegrain varieties) to the diet and are important sources of several nutrients. In addition, it is also recommended that people eat at least two portions of fish a week, one of which should be oily fish. Fish is an excellent source of protein and contains essential vitamins and minerals such as selenium and iodine. White fish such as cod, haddock and plaice are very low in fat. Oily fish, however, is rich in beneficial long-chain omega-3 fatty acids and is a good source of vitamins A and D.

It is always wise to evaluate the whole diet before making any changes, so that the intakes of other nutrients, as well as the nutrient of concern, and the foods that chiefly contribute to these intakes are known. There would be little point, for example, in reducing an individual's fat intake further if their diet is already

---

[24] Under Healthy Start, all girls under 18 who become pregnant are entitled to free vitamin supplements and vouchers to purchase milk, fruit and vegetables, as well as infant formula milk when the baby is born.

low in fat, or in reducing their intake of a favourite food if this contributes little to their overall fat intake. It is recommended that reducing fat intakes should not result in higher intakes of foods that are rich in sugars or salt. Adults should aim to eat no more than 6 g of salt each day. Much of an individual's salt intake comes from manufactured foods, and care should be taken when purchasing prepared foods, as well as when adding salt at the table or in cooking.

It is also important to keep alcohol consumption limited, since the energy contained in alcohol can contribute significantly to overall energy intake. The Government gives guidance on levels of drinking that are associated with a lower risk of developing future health harm. It is recommended that women should not regularly drink more than 2–3 units a day and men should not regularly drink more than 3–4 units a day.

Pregnancy and lactation

A woman's requirements for some nutrients increase during pregnancy and lactation (the production of breast milk) (see Tables 26 and 27 in Chapter 9). This is not only because her diet must provide for the growth and development of her child, but also because new tissues are laid down in the woman's own body. The mother also needs to have enough energy to carry the extra weight. For some nutrients, there is no increment during pregnancy, as the body undergoes physiological changes to ensure that sufficient nutrients are available for the child without extra needing to be consumed in the diet. Much of the weight gain during pregnancy is due to the baby growing and to the accumulation of fat, which provides an energy store to meet the additional demands of the growing fetus and the breastfed infant.

Most women gain between 10 kg and 12.5 kg (22–28 lb) during pregnancy. Weight gain varies a great deal and depends on the woman's weight before pregnancy. If pregnant women put on too much weight, it can affect their health and can increase their blood pressure. However, it is important that pregnant women do not diet, but eat healthily (see Chapter 9). They may feel more hungry than normal but they do not need to 'eat for two', even if they are expecting twins or triplets.

The approximate weight of a fetus and infant at various ages is shown in Table 39.

Table 39. Approximate weight of a fetus and infant at various ages

Conception	0 kg
4½ months of pregnancy	0.5 kg
Birth	3.5 kg
4½ months after birth	7 kg

Pregnant women do not need to follow a special diet, but need to make sure that they eat a variety of different foods each day to get the right balance of nutrients. It is most important that the mother's diet contains sufficient energy, protein, iron, calcium, folate and vitamins C and D (and fluids during lactation) for building the baby's muscular tissues, bones and teeth, and for the formation of haemoglobin; if it does not, her own stores of nutrients may be reduced. Some good sources of these nutrients are given in Part 1. In practice, most of these extra nutrients will be obtained simply by satisfying the appetite with a good, mixed diet, including plenty of bread, fruit and vegetables, dairy products and meat (or its alternatives). Folic acid is important before and during pregnancy, as it can reduce the risk of the fetus developing a neural tube defect (NTD) such as spina bifida. All women planning a pregnancy are advised to take a daily supplement of 400 micrograms (µg) of folic acid before becoming pregnant and up until the 12th week of pregnancy, as well as eating more folate-rich foods. Those women who have already had a pregnancy affected by an NTD need a higher (5 mg) supplement of folic acid each day, available on prescription. In addition, those women who are diabetic or who take medication for epilepsy should talk to their GP, as it is likely that they will need to take a higher dose of folic acid. Pregnant women are also recommended to take a daily supplement of 10 µg of vitamin D throughout pregnancy and lactation (see 'Vitamin D' in Chapter 8). In the case of calcium, there is no increased requirement during pregnancy because the body undergoes various adaptations to ensure that it has an adequate supply, including increased calcium absorption from the diet (however, see 'Adolescents' above). Lactation increases a woman's calcium requirements by 550 mg per day.

A woman's GP or health visitor may recommend supplements of iron during pregnancy if she has a low iron status. Free vitamin supplements containing folic acid, vitamin C and vitamin D are available to pregnant women who are on certain benefits as part of the Healthy Start scheme.

However, pregnant women are advised not to take supplements containing vitamin A, including fish liver oil supplements, or to eat foods such as liver which may be extremely rich in vitamin A except on the advice of their doctor, due to the possible risk of birth defects.

Older people

There is very little difference between the nutritional requirements of most older people and those of the younger adult. However, as age progresses and body weight and energy expenditure decrease, people tend to eat less and hence may find it difficult to satisfy all their nutrient requirements. It is important, therefore, that older people are encouraged to maintain a good energy intake, unless they are overweight or obese. They should also have foods that are rich sources of protein, vitamins and minerals. The EARs for energy for populations of people aged 60 and over are shown in Table 26 (Chapter 9). A healthy weight can be more readily maintained and recovery from illness or injury will be more rapid if older people are also encouraged to take gentle exercise. As with younger adults, older people should not eat too much saturated fat, should aim to eat meals based on starchy foods and should try to eat at least five portions of a variety of fruit and vegetables a day. It is also recommended that, on average, older people should follow the Dietary Reference Value (DRV) for non-milk extrinsic sugars. This helps them to retain their own teeth (for those without dentures or with only partial dentures), consume a more varied diet and prevent possible disorders of their metabolism arising from a high glucose load. Foods that are rich in fibre can help to prevent constipation, which can be more common in older people.

Those who live alone may need to be encouraged to prepare a meal, but it may be helpful to stress that this does not necessarily have to be a hot meal. Including foods such as milk, cheese, yogurt, eggs, breakfast cereals, bread, and fruit or fruit juices rich in vitamin C which need little preparation helps to provide a healthy balance. It is a good idea, for those times when an elderly person is unwell or when the weather is bad and they are unable to shop, to have a store cupboard of essential items such as powdered or ultra-high-temperature treated (UHT) milk; breakfast cereals; cans of fish such as sardines; canned fruit, vegetables, pulses and milk puddings; UHT fruit juices; and dried fruit. Items such as frozen prepared meals and a supply of bread and vegetables can be kept, where a freezer is available.

Older people are at greater risk of osteoporosis; therefore it is important that they get sufficient vitamin D. All people aged 65 and over are advised to take a supplement of 10 µg of vitamin D each day. The main source of vitamin D is from the action of summer sunlight on the skin; consequently, supplements are especially important for older people who are completely housebound or who cover up with clothes when outdoors. Good dietary sources of vitamin D include fortified fat spreads and breakfast cereals, eggs and oily fish (e.g. sardines and mackerel). The importance of vitamin D and calcium for healthy bones is widely recognised, but other nutrients have been identified as being important for bones – many of these nutrients are found in fruit and vegetables. There is evidence to suggest that high intakes of vitamin A may increase the risk of bone fracture. Liver is a rich source of vitamin A, so older people should avoid eating liver or liver products such as pâté more than once a week, or should eat smaller portions. If they do eat liver once a week they should avoid taking any supplements containing vitamin A or fish liver oils (which contain high levels of vitamin A). Experts recommend that older people at risk of osteoporosis should not consume more than 1500 μg of vitamin A per day from diet and supplements combined.

Slimmers

Energy needs and food consumption have been discussed in Chapter 5. Most UK adults need to lose weight, and to do this they need to eat and drink fewer calories, even when following a balanced diet. Combining these changes with increased physical activity is the best way to achieve a healthier weight. A weight loss of about 0.5–1 kg (1–2 lb) a week should be aimed for, until a healthy weight for height is reached. This should be achievable if energy intake is reduced by 500–600 calories per day. Other nutrients should still reach recommended levels.

To reduce the number of calories in the diet, slimmers should make healthier choices when choosing food and drink. In practice, this can mean replacing high-fat or high-sugar foods or drinks for alternatives that contain fewer calories, or consuming these foods or drinks in smaller portions or less often. Alcohol is also high in calories, so reducing intake can help to control weight.

Portion size should also be reduced. Research suggests that people tend to eat more if they are served more, even when they do not need the extra calories. This can apply to the size of portions served at home as well as those selected when eating out. Knowing the calorie content of different foods and drinks can be useful when it comes to achieving or maintaining a healthy weight; it is a useful method of keeping track of the amount of energy consumed, and can help to avoid overconsumption. The calorie content of many foods and drinks is provided on the packaging as part of the nutrition label.

As it may take several months to reach the desired healthy weight, a slimming diet should be sensible and palatable enough to be tolerated for this length of time. After this, it is advisable to keep to the changes made to the diet while slimming and gradually increase the energy content until the new healthy weight is maintained. Diets that cut out whole food groups are not recommended. There is insufficient evidence to say whether such diets are free from negative health effects, nor whether they are effective and achieve sustainable weight loss in the long term. Diets based on only one or two foods may be successful in the short term but are hard to adhere to as they are unrealistic and dull, and do not teach healthy-eating habits; they can also be deficient in a range of nutrients and can therefore be dangerous. Very-low-calorie diets (VLCDs) (fewer than 3.4 MJ [800 kcal] per day) are unsuitable for infants, children, adolescents, pregnant or lactating women, elderly people and people with certain medical conditions, for example heart disease. VLCDs should be followed only for a short period (four to six weeks) and under the supervision of a health professional.

Keeping to a slimming diet can sometimes be made easier by joining a slimmers' group, and weight loss is improved by being physically active.

Vegetarians

Most vegetarians are lacto-ovo vegetarians and do not eat meat, fish, seafood or by-products of animal slaughter such as gelatin, but will eat milk, cheese and eggs. Such diets may be rather bulky and lower in energy than a mixed diet because most vegetables have a high water content but, in general, their nutritional values are very similar.

A much smaller group, *vegans*, eat no foods of animal origin at all. Human nutrient requirements, with the exception of vitamin B_{12} (see 'Vitamin B_{12}' in Chapter 8), can be met by a diet composed entirely of plant foods, but to do so it must be carefully planned using a wide selection of foods. A mixture of plant proteins derived from cereals, peas, beans and nuts will provide enough protein of good quality, but special care is needed to ensure that sufficient energy, calcium, iron, riboflavin, vitamin B_{12} and vitamin D are also available. Yeast extract is a good source of some of the B vitamins, including vitamin B_{12}, that are otherwise found mainly in foods of animal origin. In extreme cases, such as the Zen macrobiotic diet where little but wholegrain cereals are eaten, intakes of calcium, iron, vitamin B_{12} and vitamin C are likely to be too low.

Ethnic minority groups

In general, the traditional diets of ethnic minority communities provide adequate nourishment to those who consume them.

However, there are some specific health issues to be aware of (such as lactose intolerance in later life – see 'Disaccharides' in Chapter 2). In particular, people who have darker skin, such as people of African, African-Caribbean and South Asian origin, are at risk of becoming deficient in vitamin D because their skin produces less vitamin D than people with fairer complexions. Since vitamin D is mainly found in foods of animal origin (e.g. oily fish and eggs), South Asian vegetarians may also have low dietary intakes of vitamin D. Those who cover their skin when outdoors or are confined indoors are also at an increased risk of vitamin D deficiency because they lack exposure to the summer sun. A daily supplement of 10 µg of vitamin D is recommended for these groups of people.

Some people from ethnic minority communities appear to be at much greater risk of chronic diseases such as diabetes, coronary heart disease, stroke and hypertension than the general UK population. This is a result of a complex

Table 40. Dietary restrictions practised by religious and ethnic groups

Hindus	No beef	Mostly vegetarian; fish rarely eaten; no alcohol	Period of fasting common
Muslims	No pork	Meat must be 'halal';[a] no shellfish eaten; no alcohol	Regular fasting, including Ramadan for one month
Sikhs	No beef	Meat must be killed by 'one blow to the head'; no alcohol	Generally less rigid eating restrictions than Hindus and Muslims
Jews	No pork	Meat must be kosher;[b] only fish with scales and fins eaten	Meat and dairy foods must not be consumed together
Rastafarians	No animal products except milk may be consumed	Foods must be 'I-tal' or alive, so no canned or processed foods eaten; no salt added; no coffee or alcohol	Food should be organic

[a] Halal meat is dedicated to God by a Muslim priest present at the killing.
[b] Kosher meat must be slaughtered by a Rabbinical-licensed person and then soaked and salted.

interplay of many factors, including overweight and obesity. Some of these factors, such as diet (and physical activity), are modifiable, and therefore healthy-eating messages may be particularly pertinent to these groups.

South Asian groups, particularly women and children, may also be at an increased risk of iron deficiency anaemia.

Recent immigrants to the UK may have complex dietary problems depending on their country of departure and/or the circumstances in which they left.

The dietary restrictions practised by religious and ethnic groups are shown in Table 40.

Diabetics

Diabetes is a metabolic disorder which reduces the ability of the body to control the amount of glucose in the blood. It is important for diabetics to avoid the rapid rises in blood glucose that can result from eating readily absorbed carbohydrate, but this requires control rather than a reduction in total carbohydrate intake. People with diabetes can lead a full and active life. But, if uncontrolled, diabetes can cause a number of serious health problems over time, such as blindness, kidney failure, foot ulceration and nerve damage.

People with diabetes are also at greater risk of developing heart disease. It is therefore important that diabetics control their blood sugar levels and their blood pressure, eat healthily, are physically active and lose weight if necessary. The Government does not recommend products that are specifically aimed at diabetics. Foods that are labelled 'diabetic' are not necessarily healthier or more suitable for diabetics than other foods. All diabetics should be under medical supervision to ensure that the medical and dietary aspects of their conditions are well managed.

GLYCAEMIC INDEX

The Glycaemic Index (GI) ranks carbohydrate-containing foods based on their potential to raise blood glucose. Carbohydrates that are rapidly broken down cause a rapid increase in blood glucose and have a high GI rating. High-GI foods include sugar and sugary foods, soft drinks, white bread, potatoes, white rice etc. Low- and medium-GI foods include fruit and vegetables that have not been dried, pulses and wholegrain foods. Protein and fat slow down the absorption of carbohydrate, and mixing high-GI foods with foods with a low GI will give a meal with a medium GI. Some of the principles of GI-based diets follow the principles of the Government's current healthy-eating advice recommended for the whole population. Certainly, some low-GI foods such as wholegrains, pasta, fruit and vegetables, beans and lentils are foods of which we should be eating more. In addition, the GI concept encourages eating these foods in place of more refined carbohydrates and could discourage the consumption of foods that are high in added sugars. However, all foods with a high GI are not necessarily 'unhealthy'. Similarly, not all foods with a low GI are 'healthy'. For example, watermelon, bread, rice and potatoes are high-GI foods, while chocolate pudding has a low GI value. Consuming only foods with a low GI could result in a diet that is unbalanced and high in fat. Diabetics are advised to eat a healthy, balanced diet similar to that recommended for the population in general.

It is particularly important for diabetics to control their weight, as obesity can worsen diabetic control.

Other special diets

The principles set out in this manual hold in general for all healthy individuals. There are, however, some people who are allergic or intolerant to certain foods, for example peanuts, nuts, milk, eggs, shellfish or wheat gluten. Allergic reactions to such foods can lead to sudden anaphylactic shock which, unless treated immediately, can be fatal. People with conditions such as coeliac disease (see 'Other health aspects of proteins' in Chapter 4) or lactose intolerance (see 'Disaccharides' in Chapter 2) also need to avoid any foods containing gluten or milk respectively. These allergies and illnesses are a medical rather than a nutritional problem.

Summary: assessing the adequacy of a diet

It is important not only that all the essential nutrients are present in the foods eaten, but also that they are present in the amounts required by different people. To find out whether a particular diet is nutritionally adequate, three things must be known:

- What foods were eaten?
- How much of each food was eaten?
- What kind of person or people ate the foods? Were they men, women, adolescents or children, and were they very active or sedentary? What was their body mass index (BMI)? Were any of the women pregnant or breastfeeding a baby?

When the answers to these questions are known, daily nutrient intakes can then be compared with the DRVs and any other appropriate guidelines. It must, however, be emphasised that the RNIs for vitamins and minerals are high enough to cover the needs of practically all healthy people; someone who obtains less than the RNI is not necessarily deficient in that nutrient. An individual will only give cause for concern if they are consistently obtaining less than the LRNI.

Four important methods of measuring food consumption are as follows:

- The first is measuring the amount of food and drink purchased for eating both at home and outside the home by, for example, a family over one or two weeks. Surveys of food purchases at the household level, such as the family food module of the Living Costs and Food Survey,[25] provide estimates of the population's average food consumption, based on purchase information and the number of people in each household. It is important to note that this type of survey does not measure what individuals actually eat and may not take account of wastage.
- The second method is responding to a food frequency questionnaire to say how often each food from a list is eaten in terms of x times per day/ per week/per month. It may also include assessment of the quantity of

---

[25] The family food module of the Living Costs and Food Survey is a survey of household food purchases and expenditure which provides annual trend data on food expenditure, consumption and nutrient intakes at the population level. The Living Costs and Food Survey replaced the Expenditure and Food Survey, with the most recent publication being in 2010. More than 6000 households in the UK take part each year by recording purchases of household food and food eaten outside the home for a two-week period. The survey provides population average data on food consumption, expenditure and nutrient intake at the household level. Results can be broken down into various household characteristics such as region or income group.

food consumed on each eating occasion. A limited range of foods may be singled out for study if it is not necessary to assess the total diet. Food frequency questionnaires are quick and easy to complete, but do not provide precise estimates of food consumption.

- The third method is recalling, preferably with expert help, all the foods eaten in the previous 24 hours. This is the least time-consuming method, but it is easy to forget important foods and hard to estimate quantities accurately. Repeated 24-hour recalls may be used to get a better picture of usual diet. This method may be supplemented with a diet history that records a person's recollection of their 'typical' seven-day eating pattern.

- The final method involves recording details of (and sometimes weighing) all the food and drink consumed over a specified period (usually a week). Provided that the diet is not changed to accommodate the complex recording procedure, this should be the most precise method of assessing the value of anyone's diet. However, some people may, consciously or otherwise, make alterations to their normal diet during the survey week or omit to report some foods that were eaten. This method was used for the National Diet and Nutrition Survey[26] of adults aged 19 to 64, which furnished the nutrient intake data quoted throughout this manual, and for the national diet and nutrition surveys of other population groups referred to in Appendix 9.

It is easy to determine the weights of standard or pre-packaged items, and for meals served in some canteens or restaurants it may be possible to weigh all the components of duplicates of the meal. More care is needed to evaluate variable items such as stews in either the domestic or the catering context. It is also important to remember that the nutrient content of foods may vary from the average values shown in this manual.

As an example of the way in which a diet can be evaluated, the daily pattern of snacks and meals that might have been consumed by an adult man in a sedentary occupation has been set out in a systematic way in Table 41. The nutrients provided by these quantities of each of these foods must be calculated using food tables such as that set out in Appendix 3. The results can be summarised meal by meal as in Table 42, or the contribution of each food to each nutrient can be listed if the evaluation covers only a short period.

The intakes of nutrients can then be compared with the DRVs for such a person and, with an understanding of the principles set out in this manual, the significance of any departures from these values can be assessed. In the

---

[26] The National Diet and Nutrition Surveys constitute a programme of national surveys of various population groups with the aim of gathering information about the dietary habits and nutritional status of the British population. The results of these surveys are used to develop national nutrition policy and contribute to the evidence base for government advice on healthy eating.

Table 41. Example of a one-day diet diary for a young sedentary man

	Weight (g)		Weight (g)
Breakfast		*Evening meal*	
Orange juice, unsweetened	150	Spaghetti	230
Cornflakes	50	Bolognese sauce	240
Milk, semi-skimmed	146	Cheddar cheese	20
Sugar with cornflakes	10	Ice cream, dairy, vanilla	75
White bread, 2 slices, toasted	54	Peaches, canned in syrup	120
Reduced-fat spread (41–62%), polyunsaturated	18		
Marmalade	30		
1 cup of tea			
Milk, semi-skimmed, with tea	30		
Sugar with tea	10		
Lunch (sandwich)		*Snacks throughout the day*	
White baguette	120	2 cups of coffee	
Reduced-fat spread (41–62%), polyunsaturated	20	Milk, semi-skimmed, with coffee	60
		Sugar with coffee	20
Tuna, canned in brine	45	1 packet of crisps	35
Mayonnaise	15	1 apple	100
Banana	100	Chocolate bar	66
1 can of carbonated drink (cola, non-diet)	343		
		1 pint of lager	574

instance of the menu for this particular man (as seen in Table 42) the energy intake, at 14054 kJ (3359 kcal), exceeds the EAR (11500 kJ; 2749 kcal) for a 25–34-year-old man. When more calories are consumed than needed, our bodies store the excess as body fat. If this continues, over time it can lead to overweight and obesity. Ways of reducing this young man's calorie intake could include looking at lower-fat and/or sugar alternatives, or decreasing the quantity of snacks, sugary drinks and alcohol consumed, if this is his regular snacking and drinking behaviour. The portion size of the three meals could also be investigated.

The proportion of total energy derived from *protein* is 11.3%, which is acceptable. The proportion of the total energy intake derived from *fat* is 33.3%, from *saturated fat* 13.7% and from *carbohydrate* 50.6%. If the total fat intake was maintained at or at about this level over the course of time, the fat content of the whole diet would be at a very satisfactory level. The percentage of energy from saturated fat is above the recommended 10%

of food energy. If this higher intake of saturated fat was maintained, then it could have a detrimental effect on blood cholesterol and, over time, increase this man's risk of heart disease. Eating an evening meal of lean meat or fish without a cheese sauce, accompanied by a baked potato with a little low-fat spread and vegetables, would be one way of reducing his intake of saturated fatty acids. If he wished to treat himself to a chocolate bar, on another day he might want to substitute low-fat yogurt for ice cream in the evening and fresh fruit or salad items for the crisps or biscuits during snack times. An increase in his intake of starch-rich foods at the expense of sugar could improve his intake of *fibre* as non-starch polysaccharides (which is a little low), especially if wholegrain products were consumed. Alternatively, his fibre intake could be raised by, for example, substituting a high-fibre cereal for cornflakes at breakfast.

As previously discussed (see 'Fat' in Chapter 9), DRVs for fat, saturated fatty acids and carbohydrate are meant to be applied to population groups rather than individuals. Therefore, it is desirable for a group of men of this age and lifestyle (who, as individuals, vary in their nutrient needs) to consume on average over time a diet which achieves the DRVs, rather than each individual aiming to achieve the DRVs every day. Nevertheless, if each individual tries to make changes towards a more healthy diet, there is a greater likelihood that the population as a whole will achieve the DRVs.

Calcium, iron, folate and *vitamin C* intakes are well above the RNIs for these nutrients. In general it is easier for men to achieve these levels than women because they tend to eat larger quantities of food. The *sodium* content of the day's meals is more than twice the suggested RNI for an adult. This equates to about 9 g of salt and is much higher than the maximum daily adult intake of 6 g per day recommended by the Scientific Advisory Committee on Nutrition (SACN). It would be advisable for this young man to moderate his salt intake by, for example, comparing products and choosing those that are lower in salt, replacing a salty snack like crisps with a lower-salt alternative or fruit and adding less salt to the main dish during cooking.

Table 42. Nutrient content of a day's menu for a young sedentary man

	Energy (kJ)	Energy (kcal)	Protein (g)	Fat (g)	Satu-rated fat (g)	Carbo-hydrate (g)	Fibre (g)	Calcium (mg)	Iron (mg)	Sodium (mg)	Folate (µg)	Vitamin C (mg)
Breakfast	3046	719	15.6	15.3	4.6	138.6	2.5	354	8.8	742	245	64
Lunch	3397	805	22.7	25.9	4.9	128.2	4.0	177	2.5	1120	51	11
Evening meal	4148	987	46.5	42.4	18.6	111.8	6.0	327	4.3	933	59	14
Snacks	3502	835	11.2	31.7	13.9	92.1	4.4	262	1.6	357	91	19
Total	14092	3346	96.0	115.3	41.1	470.7	16.9	1120	17.1	3152	446	108
			11.5[a]	31.0[a]	11.0[a]	52.8[a]						
EAR (SACN, 2011)[b]	11500	2749										
EAR (DH, 1991)[c]			44.4	33[a]	10[a]	47[a]	18	525	6.7		150	25
RNI (DH, 1991)[c]			55.5					700	8.7	1600	200	40
LRNI (DH, 1991)[c]								400	4.7	575	100	10

[a] As a percentage of total energy.
[b] Data taken from the Dietary Reference Values for Energy 2011 report (SACN, 2012) for males aged 25–34 years.
[c] Data taken from the Dietary Reference Values for Food Energy and Nutrients for the United Kingdom, Department of Health, 1991.
See also Table 41.

APPENDICES

Appendix 1 Common measure and conversion factors

Although the labels of most pre-packed foods give their weight in grams, many fresh foods are weighed in imperial units and many people are more familiar with pounds (weight), pints (volume), inches (length) etc. Furthermore, energy has long been measured in calories, but the SI unit, the joule, is also used. The conversion factors in Table 1.1 show the relationships between these units.

Table 1.1. Common measure and conversion factors

Weight

1 milligram (mg)	= 1000 micrograms (µg)	
1 gram (g)	= 1000 mg	= 0.035 oz
1 kilogram (kg)	= 1000 g	= 2.20 lb
1 ounce (oz)	= 28.35 g	
1 pound (lb)	= 453.6 g	

Volume

1 litre	= 1000 millilitres (ml)	= 1.76 pt
1 pint (pt)	= 20 fluid oz	= 568 ml

Length

1 metre (m)	= 100 centimetres (cm)	
	= 1000 millimetres (mm)	= 39.4 in
1 inch (in)	= 2.54 cm	
1 foot (ft)	= 0.3048 m	

Energy

1 kilojoule (kJ)	= 1000 joules (J)	
1 megajoule (MJ)	= 1000 kJ	= 239 kcal
1 kilocalorie (kcal)	= 4.184 kJ	

Appendix 2   Equations for estimating the basal metabolic rate

Henry weight and height prediction equations can be used to calculate basal metabolic rate (BMR) in either MJ/day or kcal/day.

Table 2.1. Henry weight and height prediction equations

Gender	Age (years)	BMR (MJ/day)			BMR (kcal/day)		
		Weight coefficient (kg)	Height coefficient (m)	Constant	Weight coefficient (kg)	Height coefficient (m)	Constant
Male	<3	0.118	3.59	−1.55	28.2	859	−371
	3–10	0.0632	1.31	1.28	15.1	313	306
	10–18	0.0651	1.11	1.25	15.6	266	299
	18–30	0.0600	1.31	0.473	14.4	313	113
	30–60	0.0476	2.26	−0.574	11.4	541	−137
	>60	0.0478	2.26	−1.070	11.4	541	−256
Female	<3	0.127	2.94	−1.2	30.4	703	−287
	3–10	0.0666	0.878	1.46	15.9	210	349
	10–18	0.0393	1.04	1.93	9.40	249	462
	18–30	0.0433	2.57	−1.180	10.4	615	−282
	30–60	0.0342	2.1	−0.0486	8.18	502	−11.6
	>60	0.0356	1.76	0.0448	8.52	421	10.7

Use the equation below to calculate BMR for the appropriate gender and age.

BMR = (weight coefficient × weight) + (height coefficient × height) + constant

For example, in a woman who is aged 40, weighs 75 kg and is 1.65 m tall:

BMR = (0.0342 × 75) + (2.1 × 1.65) + −0.0486

= 2.565 + 3.465 − 0.0486

= 5.98 MJ/day

Or

BMR = (8.18 × 75) + (502 × 1.65) + −11.6

= 613.5 + 828.3 − 11.6

= 1430.2 kcal/day

The Scientific Advisory Committee on Nutrition (SACN) used a prescriptive approach to calculate the BMR for different age groups of the population when setting the Dietary Reference Values (DRVs) for energy (SACN, 2012). This means that the DRVs for energy were set at the levels of energy intake required to maintain healthy body weight, rather than existing body weight. In adults, the healthy body weight range is generally defined as equivalent to a body mass index (BMI) of between 18.5 kg/m² and 24.9 kg/m². However, for the purposes of calculating the DRVs for energy, SACN used the mean heights of the adult population to identify healthy body weights associated with a BMI of 22.5 kg/m², and applied these to calculate BMR values.

To employ this prescriptive approach to the example above, use a weight of 61.3 kg in the equation, which is equivalent to a BMI of 22.5 kg/m².

Appendix 3   Composition of food

The Department of Health publishes food composition data within *McCance and Widdowson's Composition of Foods Integrated Dataset* (COFIDS). The most recent analytical data within the current version of COFIDS date back to 2002 and, as manufacturers regularly reformulate recipes, some of the data published in COFIDS have now been superseded. In order to reflect the most up-to-date composition data, the information presented in this appendix is largely based on COFIDS but also includes data from analytical projects published since 2002 and some food-labelling data provided by manufacturers. All the data presented in this appendix are based on composite samples to give generic values for product types. For current nutritional information on specific products, food-labelling data provided by manufacturers should be used rather than the values provided in this appendix.

The current version of COFIDS is available for download (http://tna. europarchive.org/20110116113217/http://www.food.gov.uk/science/ dietarysurveys/dietsurveys/). The Department of Health plans to update COFIDS at regular intervals.

Table 3.1 shows typical values for the amounts of a range of nutrients in a wide variety of raw and cooked foods. Each value is the amount per 100 g of the edible part of the food as described. Individual samples of food can differ considerably depending on the season of the year; therefore, any information given on the label by the manufacturers should be more appropriate for that particular product than the more general values in this appendix.

Allowance may need to be made for wastage in foods that are weighed raw. The values given in Table 3.1 predict the proportion of each food as listed that cannot be eaten. Thus, for raw chicken, it is the amount of skin and bone likely to be in the whole or joint of a chicken to be cooked, but for slices of roast chicken there would be no wastage. Some individuals may, however, choose not to eat some of the fat or to discard those parts of a fruit that are bruised, and an additional allowance may have to be made for this.

The energy value of each food is given in kilojoules (kJ) and kilocalories (kcal), and both have been calculated from the protein, fat and carbohydrate content as listed in 'Energy value of food' in Chapter 5. The figures for vitamin A are given in the form of retinol equivalents (see 'Vitamin A' in Chapter 8). They are thus expressed in the same form as in the *Dietary Reference Values for Food Energy and Nutrients for the United Kingdom* (1991). Available carbohydrate is given as its monosaccharide equivalent (see Table 1 in Chapter 2). Appendix 4 provides examples of the use of Table 3.1.

Table 3.1. Composition per 100 g of edible portion

No.	Food	Inedible waste (%)	Water (g)	Energy kJ	Energy kcal	Protein (g)	Fat (g)	Saturated fatty acid (g)
	Cereals							
1	Flour, plain, white[a]	0	11.6	1501	352	9.1	1.4	0.4
2	Flour, wholemeal[a]	0	11.1	1389	326	11.6	2.0	0.3
3	Brown wholegrain rice, boiled[a]	0	67.0	563	132	3.6	0.9	0.2
4	White rice, easy cook, boiled[a]	0	66.8	590	138	3.5	0.4	0.1
5	Spaghetti, white, boiled[b]	0	64.9	601	141	4.4	0.6	0.1
6	Pizza, cheese and tomato, all bases (not stuffed crust)[c]	0	38.1	1148	272	12.2	9.8	4.1
7	Pasta, plain, fresh, cooked[b]	0	64.0	646	152	5.8	1.6	0.4
8	Pasta, fresh, cheese-and-vegetable stuffed, cooked[b]	0	56.2	823	195	8.7	5.8	3.2
	Breads							
9	Brown bread, average	0	41.2	882	207	7.9	2.0	0.4
10	White bread, sliced	0	38.6	931	219	7.9	1.6	0.3
11	White bread, 'with added fibre'	0	40.0	978	230	7.6	1.5	0.4
12	Ciabatta	0	29.2	1150	271	10.2	3.9	0.6
13	Wholemeal bread, average	0	41.2	922	217	9.4	2.5	0.5
14	Granary bread	0	34.9	1005	237	9.6	2.3	0.6
	Breakfast cereals							
15	Bran flakes[e]	0	4.0	1269	299	12.4	3.4	0.5
16	Cornflakes[e]	0	3.4	1526	358	7.1	0.8	0.1
17	Muesli, Swiss-style[e]	0	7.5	1515	357	9.2	6.3	1.3
18	Wheat biscuits[e]	0	6.0	1412	332	10.5	1.9	0.3
19	Frosted cornflakes[e]	0	3.1	1491	350	4.7	0.5	0.1
20	Porridge, made with semi-skimmed milk[e]	0	74.5	473	112	5.4	2.9	1.2
	Biscuits							
21	Short or sweet biscuits, full-chocolate coated[f]	0	1.9	2120	506	6.4	27.2	15.1
22	Cream crackers[f]	0	4.9	1874	445	8.9	16.4	7.4
23	Digestive biscuits, plain[f]	0	2.8	1943	463	6.2	21.3	7.7
24	Semi-sweet biscuits[f]	0	2.0	1874	444	6.4	15.1	5.1

Carbo-hydrate (g)	Total sugars (g)	Fibre (NSP) (g)	Calcium (mg)	Iron (mg)	Sodium (mg)	Vitamin A (µg)	Folate (µg)	Vitamin C (mg)	No.
80.9	0.6	3.4	96	1.9	2	0	16	0	1
69.9	1.4	10.1	32	2.5	2	0	27	0	2
29.2	0.1	0.9	17	0.53	4	0	7	0	3
32.2	0	<0.6	18	0.07	4	0	8	0	4
31.5	1.0	1.5	27	0.63	4	0	8	0	5
36.1	3.9	1.7	279	1.1	282	80	7	1	6
30.6	<0.1	0.9	29.4	0.6	8.9	0	6	0	7
28.7	0.1	1.6	110	0.8	239	75	12	<1	8
42.1	3.4	3.5	186	2.2	(410)[d]	0	45	0	9
46.1	3.4	1.9	177	1.6	461	0	25	0	10
49.6	3.3	3.1	150	2.3	450	0	(17)	0	11
52.0	3.1	2.3	(121)	(1.4)	(400)[d]	0	21	0	12
42.0	2.8	5.0	106	2.4	(420)[d]	0	40	0	13
47.4	2.9	3.3	209	1.9	(400)[d]	0	88	0	14
58.2	20.0	(14.4)[d]	329	16.2	(400)[d]	7	333	66	15
85.9	7.3	(2.1)[d]	3	14.5	(500)[d]	16	379	<1	16
72.6	21.3	6.7	93	3.3	138	<5	45	<1	17
72.7	3.9	7.3	30	12.6	260	<5	252	<1	18
87.0	38.3	(1.5)[d]	158	13.3	(350)[d]	0	241	0	19
17.1	3.7	0.8	119	0.7	38	17	10	<1	20
62.8	39.3	2.2	163	2.0	229	28	14	0	21
69.7	1.5	3.3	93	2.0	384	0	19	0	22
65.6	17.5	2.7	95	1.8	561	0	11	0	23
75.4	20.3	1.9	157	2.0	358	0	12	0	24

Table 3.1. Composition per 100 g of edible portion *continued*

No.	Food	Inedible waste (%)	Water (g)	Energy kJ	Energy kcal	Protein (g)	Fat (g)	Saturated fatty acids (g)
	Buns and cakes							
25	Currant buns	0	27.9	1185	280	8.0	5.6	1.9
26	Fruit cake[f]	0	21.8	1407	334	4.5	12.1	4.6
27	Flapjack, retail[f]	0	9.3	1821	434	5.1	22.8	10.3
28	Gateau, fruit, frozen	0	51.9	1042	248	3.2	12.3	7.0
29	Madeira cake	0	20.2	1585	377	5.4	15.1	8.4
30	Muffins, American-style, chocolate[g]	0	20.9	1713	409	5.5	22.1	4.5
31	Swiss roll, chocolate, individual[f]	0	13.4	1733	414	4.5	22.7	11.7
	Puddings and dairy desserts							
32	Crumble, fruit	0	49.1	924	219	2.4	8.3	4.0
33	Fruit pie, pastry top and bottom	0	47.8	1096	262	3.1	13.6	4.2
34	Cheesecake, fruit, individual	0	46.6	1111	264	6.1	12.3	7.5
35	Custard, made up with semi-skimmed milk	0	77.5	404	95	4.0	2.0	1.2
36	Rice pudding, canned	0	79.2	362	85	3.3	1.3	0.8
37	Trifle	0	66.5	696	166	2.6	8.1	2.4
38	Lemon meringue pie	0	42.1	1060	251	2.9	8.5	3.1
39	Mousse, chocolate	0	67.3	627	149	4.0	6.5	3.3
40	Mousse, chocolate, reduced fat	0	69.0	518	123	5.5	3.7	2.5
41	Ice cream, dairy, vanilla, soft scoop[c]	0	64.9	711	169	3.2	8.2	5.2
42	Ice cream, non-dairy, vanilla[c]	0	65.6	807	192	2.6	7.7	5.0
	Milk and cream							
43	Skimmed milk, average	0	90.9	136	32	3.4	0.2	0.1
44	Semi-skimmed milk, average	0	89.6	195	46	3.4	1.7	1.1
45	Whole milk, average	0	87.6	274	66	3.3	3.9	2.5
46	Dried skimmed milk	0	3.0	1482	348	36.1	0.6	0.4
47	Cream, single	0	77.0	798	193	3.3	19.1	12.2
48	Cream, double	0	46.9	2041	496	1.6	53.7	33.4
	Yogurt and fromage frais							
49	Whole-milk yogurt, plain	0	81.9	333	79	5.7	3.0	1.7
50	Whole-milk yogurt, twinpot, thick and creamy, with fruit	0	74.7	446	106	4.1	3.2	N

Carbo-hydrate (g)	Total sugars (g)	Fibre (NSP) (g)	Calcium (mg)	Iron (mg)	Sodium (mg)	Vitamin A (µg)	Folate (µg)	Vitamin C (mg)	No.
52.6	16.0	2.2	110	1.9	(220)[d]	0	12	1	25
55.2	39.6	2.4	74	1.6	193	39	<5	0	26
55.7	29.2	2.2	52	1.9	194	86	8	0	27
33.3	14.9	0.9	40	0.7	128	118	6	4	28
58.4	36.5	0.9	42	1.1	(310)[d]	N	N	0	29
50.1	31.1	1.4	70	3.0	(340)[d]	25	9	0	30
51.0	41.2	1.7	85	2.7	259	49	13	0	31
36.0	22.0	1.3	41	0.3	82	53	10	N	32
33.9	12.0	1.7	58	0.8	193	65	7	3	33
34.5	25.4	1.0	78	0.4	151	N	(7)	0	34
16.4	11.3	0	140	0.1	67	98	6	1	35
16.1	8.7	0.1	88	0.1	43	18	0	0	36
21.0	16.7	0.4	57	0.3	70	118	6	5	37
43.5	29.8	(0.7)	38	0	113	48	6	5	38
19.9	17.5	N	97	0.2	67	48	6	0	39
18.0	15.8	N	126	1.2	69	N	(0)	0	40
22.0	22.0	0	(100)	0	(60)	177	(6)	(1)	41
29.8	23.5	0	72	0.1	62	2	8	1	42
4.4	4.4	0	122	0.03	44	1	9	1	43
4.7	4.7	0	120	0.02	43	21	6	1	44
4.5	4.5	0	118	0.03	43	36	8	2	45
52.9	52.9	0	1280	0.27	550	351	51	13	46
2.2	2.2	0	89	0	29	319	5	1	47
1.7	1.7	0	49	0.1	22	860	7	1	48
7.8	7.8	N	200	0.1	80	28	18	1	49
16.2	15.6	N	130	0.2	53	(20)	(13)	(2)	50

Table 3.1. Composition per 100 g of edible portion *continued*

No.	Food	Inedible waste (%)	Water (g)	Energy kJ	Energy kcal	Protein (g)	Fat (g)	Saturated fatty acids (g)
51	Low-fat yogurt, fruit	0	78.9	331	78	4.2	1.1	(0.8)
52	Virtually fat-free/diet yogurt, fruit	0	85.4	201	47	4.8	0.2	(0.1)
53	Fromage frais, fruit	0	74.7	520	124	5.3	5.6	3.5
54	Milkshake, thick, takeaway	0	73.2	374	88	3.7	1.8	1.2
	Cheese							
55	Brie	31	48.7	1422	343	20.3	29.1	18.2
56	Cheddar cheese	0	36.6	1725	416	25.4	34.9	21.7
57	Cheddar-type, half fat	0	47.4	1141	273	32.7	15.8	9.9
58	Cheese spread, plain	0	58.8	1106	267	11.3	22.8	15.8
59	Spreadable cheese, soft white, full fat	0	58.6	1286	312	7.5	31.3	20.5
60	Cottage cheese, plain	0	78.6	423	101	12.6	4.3	2.3
61	Feta	0	56.5	1037	250	15.6	20.2	(13.7)
62	Mozzarella, fresh	0	57.4	1067	257	18.6	20.3	13.8
63	Processed cheese slices, plain	0	47.4	1234	297	17.8	23.0	14.3
64	Stilton, blue	0	38.0	1698	410	23.7	35.0	23.0
	Eggs							
65	Eggs, chicken, boiled	0	75.1	612	147	12.5	10.8	3.1
66	Eggs, chicken, fried in vegetable oil	0	70.1	745	179	13.6	13.9	4.0
	Fats and oils							
67	Butter, spreadable (75–80% fat)[c]	0	18.7	2941	715	0.4	79.1	34.2
68	Margarine, hard block[c]	0	22.2	2827	688	0	76.4	26.4
69	Fat spread (62–75% fat), not polyunsaturated[c]	0	24.6	2713	660	0.3	73.2	24.4
70	Reduced-fat spread (41–62% fat), polyunsaturated[c]	0	40.0	2190	533	0.0	59.2	13.2
71	Low-fat spread (26–39% fat), polyunsaturated[c]	0	52.5	1373	334	0.0	36.9	8.6
72	Sunflower oil	0	Tr	3696	899	0	99.9	12.0
73	Vegetable oil, blended, average	0	Tr	3696	899	0	99.9	11.7
74	Olive oil	0	0	3696	899	0	99.9	14.3

Carbo-hydrate (g)	Total sugars (g)	Fibre (NSP) (g)	Calcium (mg)	Iron (mg)	Sodium (mg)	Vitamin A (µg)	Folate (µg)	Vitamin C (mg)	No.
13.7	12.7	0.2	140	0.1	62	(10)	16	1	51
7.0	6.3	0	130	0.1	73	0	8	1	52
13.9	13.3	0	86	0.1	35	82	15	0	53
15.3	11.1	0	129	0.0	57	35	4	1	54
0	0	0	256	0	556	329	55	0	55
0.1	0.1	0	739	0.3	(700)[d]	388	31	0	56
0	0	0	840	0.2	670	210	56	0	57
4.4	4.4	0	498	0	(800)[d]	282	19	0	58
0	0	0	76	0	288	293	23	0	59
3.1	3.1	0	(127)	0	(300)	48	(22)	0	60
1.5	1.5	0	360	0.2	(1240)[d]	226	23	0	61
0	0	0	362	0	395	283	20	0	62
5.0	5.0	0	610	0.5	(600)[d]	286	15	0	63
0.1	0.1	0	326	0.2	788	390	78	0	64
0	0	0	57	1.9	140	190	39	0	65
0	0	0	65	2.2	160	215	40	0	66
0.5	0.5	0	18	0	(430)[d]	1059	0	0	67
0.0	0.0	0	4	0.3	680	733	0	0	68
0.0	0.0	0	N	0	(650)[d]	980	0	0	69
0.0	0.0	0	N	0	650	N	0	0	70
0.5	0.5	0	(39)	0	(550)[d]	(784)	0	0	71
0	0	0	0	0.1	0	0	0	0	72
0	0	0	0	0	0	0	0	0	73
0	0	0	0	0.4	0	0	0	0	74

Table 3.1. Composition per 100 g of edible portion *continued*

No.	Food	Inedible waste (%)	Water (g)	Energy kJ	Energy kcal	Protein (g)	Fat (g)	Saturated fatty acids (g)
	Meat and meat products							
75	Bacon rasher, lean and fat, grilled, back	0	50.4	1194	287	23.2	21.6	8.1
76	Bacon rasher, lean and fat, grilled, streaky	0	44.0	1400	337	23.8	26.9	9.8
77	Beef, mince, stewed	0	64.4	870	209	21.8	13.5	5.7
78	Beef, mince, extra lean, stewed	0	66.6	742	177	24.7	8.7	3.8
79	Beef, stewing steak, lean and fat, stewed	0	59.4	852	203	29.2	9.6	3.7
80	Beef, rump steak, fried, lean	0	61.7	770	183	30.9	6.6	2.4
81	Beefburgers, frozen, grilled	0	47.9	1355	326	26.5	24.4	10.9
82	Bolognese sauce, with meat	0	70.8	670	161	11.8	11.6	4.2
83	Chicken, roast, meat average	0	65.3	742	177	27.3	7.5	2.9
84	Chicken skin	0	31.1	2070	501	21.5	46.1	12.9
85	Chicken, stir-fried strips	0	65.9	677	161	29.7	4.6	N
86	Corned beef, canned	0	59.5	860	205	25.9	10.9	5.7
87	Ham, sliced	0	73.2	451	107	18.4	3.3	1.1
88	Kidney, pig, stewed	0	66.3	641	153	24.4	6.1	2.0
89	Lamb, roast, lean	0	54.4	1138	273	26.7	18.5	8.6
90	Lamb, loin chops, grilled, meat only	39	59.6	892	213	29.2	10.7	4.9
91	Liver, lamb's, fried	0	53.9	989	237	30.1	12.9	N
92	Pâté, liver	0	47.6	1437	348	12.6	32.7	9.5
93	Pork, loin chops, lean only, grilled	23	61.2	774	184	31.6	6.4	2.2
94	Pork, leg joint, roasted medium, lean	15	61.1	765	182	33.0	5.5	1.9
95	Salami	0	33.7	1814	438	20.9	39.2	14.6
96	Sausages, beef, grilled	0	48.0	1157	278	13.3	19.5	7.9
97	Sausages, pork, grilled	0	45.9	1221	294	14.5	22.1	8.0
98	Sausages, low fat, grilled	0	50.1	959	230	16.2	13.8	4.9
99	Steak and kidney/beef pie, individual, baked	0	41.4	1295	310	8.8	19.4	8.4
100	Turkey, roast, meat only	0	64.6	701	166	31.2	4.6	1.4
101	Lasagne, chilled/frozen, reheated	0	68.1	603	143	7.4	6.1	2.8
102	Chicken curry, average	0	70.2	603	145	11.7	9.8	2.9
103	Coated chicken pieces, takeaway[c]	0	44.5	1118	267	18.5	14.1	2.3

Carbo-hydrate (g)	Total sugars (g)	Fibre (NSP) (g)	Calcium (mg)	Iron (mg)	Sodium (mg)	Vitamin A (µg)	Folate (µg)	Vitamin C (mg)	No.
0	0	0	7	0.6	(1520)[d]	0	5	0	75
0	0	0	9	0.8	1680	0	3	0	76
0	0	0	20	2.7	73	13	17	0	77
0	0	0	14	2.3	75	1	20	0	78
0	0	0	15	2.3	51	1	11	0	79
0	0	0	5	3.0	78	1	5	0	80
0.1	0.1	0	10	2.5	400	0	10	0	81
2.5	2.1	0.6	16	1.06	306	123	9	3	82
0	0	0	17	0.8	100	24	10	0	83
0	0	0	16	1.3	80	N	N	0	84
0	0	0	6	0.5	61	0	5	0	85
1.0	1.0	0	27	2.4	860	0	5	0	86
1.0	1.0	0	7	0.7	(800)[d]	0	19	0	87
0	0	0	13	6.4	370	46	43	11	88
0	0	0	8	1.6	93	0	6	0	89
0	0	0	22	2.1	80	0	6	0	90
0	0	0	8	7.7	82	(19710)	207	19	91
(0.8)	0.4	0	16	5.9	750	7322	99	N	92
0	0	0	14	0.7	66	0	7	0	93
0	0	0	10	1.1	69	0	4	0	94
0.5	0.5	0.1	11	1.3	(1500)[d]	0	3	N	95
13.1	1.4	0.7	80	1.4	(590)[d]	0	7	N	96
9.8	1.5	0.7	110	1.1	(600)[d]	0	4	5	97
10.8	0.9	1.5	130	1.3	(590)[d]	0	32	37	98
26.7	1.5	0.5	60	1.3	460	8	(8)	0	99
0	0	0	11	0.8	90	0	17	0	100
15.7	3.0	0.7	80	1.0	390	N	11	N	101
2.5	1.2	2.0	41	2.32	356	35	N	0	102
17.6	0	1.1	25	0.6	(630)[d]	14	20	0	103

Table 3.1. Composition per 100 g of edible portion *continued*

No.	Food	Inedible waste (%)	Water (g)	Energy kJ	Energy kcal	Protein (g)	Fat (g)	Saturated fatty acid (g)
	Fish and fish products							
104	Cod in batter, fried in commercial oil[c]	0	57.3	1001	240	16.8	14.7	7.6
105	Fish fingers, grilled[c]	0	54.6	897	213	13.9	9.2	1.2
106	Haddock, steamed, flesh only	16	78.3	378	89	20.9	0.6	0.1
107	Mackerel, grilled	8	58.6	994	239	20.8	17.3	3.5
108	Pilchards, canned in tomato sauce	0	70.4	601	144	16.7	8.1	1.7
109	Prawns, boiled	62	70.0	418	99	22.6	0.9	0.2
110	Sardines, canned in oil, drained	18	58.6	918	220	23.3	14.1	2.9
111	Tuna, canned in brine, drained	19	74.6	422	99	23.5	0.6	0.2
112	Salmon, grilled[g]	18	60.4	995	239	24.6	15.6	2.9
	Potato and potato products							
113	Chips, homemade, fried in blended oil	0	56.5	796	189	3.9	6.7	0.6
114	Chips, fine cut (French fries), takeaway[c]	0	38.5	1219	290	3.5	14.2	2.5
115	Oven chips, no batter, frozen, baked[c]	0	54.2	800	189	3.2	4.9	0.8
116	Potato crisps fried in high olei[c] sunflower oil[c]	0	4.3	2064	493	6.2	28.8	2.5
117	Potatoes, new, average, boiled in unsalted water	0	80.5	321	75	1.5	0.3	0.1
118	Potatoes, old, average, raw, flesh only	20	79.0	318	75	2.1	0.2	0
119	Potatoes, old, baked, flesh and skin	0	62.6	581	136	3.9	0.2	0
120	Potatoes, old, boiled in unsalted water	0	80.3	306	72	1.8	0.1	0
121	Potatoes, old, roasted in blended oil	0	64.7	630	149	2.9	4.5	0.4
	Vegetables							
122	Beans, baked, canned in tomato sauce	0	71.5	355	84	5.2	0.6	0.1
123	Beans, red kidney, added salt, canned, drained	36	67.5	424	100	6.9	0.6	0.1
124	Beans, runner, boiled in unsalted water	0	92.8	76	18	1.2	0.5	0.1

Carbo-hydrate (g)	Total sugars (g)	Fibre (NSP) (g)	Calcium (mg)	Iron (mg)	Sodium (mg)	Vitamin A (µg)	Folate (µg)	Vitamin C (mg)	No.
10.7	1	0.5	67	0.5	160	N	57	0	104
20	1.3	1.6	92	0.8	(330)[d]	0	16	0	105
0	0	0	26	0.1	73	0	9	0	106
0	0	0	12	0.8	63	48	N	0	107
1.1	0.9	0	250	2.5	290	(30)	N	0	108
0	0	0	110	1.1	(640)[d]	0	N	0	109
0	0	0	500	2.3	450	7	8	0	110
0	0	0	8	1.0	320	N	4	0	111
0	0	0	11	0.4	49	18	9	0	112
30.1	0.6	2.2	11	0.8	12	0	43	9	113
39.7	0.3	3.2	14	1.0	(232)[d]	0	31	4	114
35.3	1	2.7	(12)	0.8	53	0	21	12	115
55.8	0.9	4.6	29	1.4	(660)[d]	0	30	35	116
17.8	1.1	1.1	5	0.3	9	0	18	15	117
17.2	0.6	1.3	5	0.4	7	0	35	11	118
31.7	1.2	2.7	11	0.7	12	0	44	14	119
17.0	0.7	1.2	5	0.4	7	0	19	6	120
25.9	0.6	1.8	8	0.7	9	0	36	8	121
15.3	(5)[d]	3.7	53	1.4	(300)[d]	12	22	0	122
17.8	3.6	6.2	71	2.0	(280)[d]	1	15	0	123
2.3	2.0	1.9	22	1.0	1	20	42	10	124

Table 3.1. Composition per 100 g of edible portion *continued*

No.	Food	Inedible waste (%)	Water (g)	Energy kJ	Energy kcal	Protein (g)	Fat (g)	Saturated fatty acids (g)
125	Beetroot, boiled in salted water	20	82.4	195	46	2.3	0.1	0
126	Broccoli, green, raw	39	88.2	138	33	4.4	0.9	0.2
127	Broccoli, boiled in unsalted water	0	91.1	100	24	3.1	0.8	0.2
128	Brussels sprouts, boiled in unsalted water	0	86.9	153	35	2.9	1.3	0.3
129	Cabbage, boiled in unsalted water, average	0	93.1	67	16	1.0	0.4	0.1
130	Cabbage, raw, average	23	90.1	109	26	1.7	0.4	0.1
131	Carrots, old, raw	30	89.8	146	35	0.6	0.3	0.1
132	Carrots, old, boiled in unsalted water	0	90.5	100	24	0.6	0.4	0.1
133	Cauliflower, boiled in unsalted water	0	90.6	117	28	2.9	0.9	0.2
134	Celery, raw	9	95.1	30	7	0.5	0.2	0
135	Courgette, boiled in unsalted water	0	93.0	81	19	2.0	0.4	0.1
136	Courgette, fried in corn oil	0	86.8	265	63	2.6	4.8	0.6
137	Cucumber	3	96.4	40	10	0.7	0.1	0
138	Hummus	0	61.4	781	187	7.6	12.6	N
139	Lentils (red, dried), boiled in unsalted water	0	72.1	424	100	7.6	0.4	0
140	Lettuce, average	26	95.1	59	14	0.8	0.5	0.1
141	Mycoprotein, Quorn®	0	74.2	389	92	14.1	3.2	0.6
142	Mushrooms, raw	3	92.6	55	13	1.8	0.5	0.1
143	Onions, raw	9	89.0	150	36	1.2	0.2	0
144	Onions, fried in corn oil	0	65.7	684	164	2.3	11.2	1.4
145	Parsnips, boiled in unsalted water	0	78.7	278	66	1.6	1.2	0.2
146	Peas, frozen, boiled in unsalted water	0	78.3	291	69	6.0	0.9	0.2
147	Peas, processed, canned, reheated, drained	35	69.6	423	99	6.9	0.7	0.1
148	Peppers, green, raw	16	93.3	65	15	0.8	0.3	0.1
149	Plantain, boiled in unsalted water	0	68.5	477	112	0.8	0.2	0.1
150	Spinach, frozen, boiled in unsalted water	0	91.6	90	21	3.1	(0.8)	0.1
151	Swede, boiled in unsalted water	0	95.8	46	11	0.3	0.1	0
152	Sweet potato, boiled in unsalted water	0	74.7	358	84	1.1	0.3	0.1

Carbo-hydrate (g)	Total sugars (g)	Fibre (NSP) (g)	Calcium (mg)	Iron (mg)	Sodium (mg)	Vitamin A (µg)	Folate (µg)	Vitamin C (mg)	No.
9.5	8.8	1.9	29	0.8	110	5	110	5	125
1.8	1.5	2.6	56	1.7	8	96	90	87	126
1.1	0.9	2.3	40	1.0	(13)	79	64	44	127
3.5	3.0	3.1	20	0.5	2	53	110	60	128
2.2	2.0	1.8	33	0.3	8	134	39	20	129
4.1	4.0	2.4	52	0.7	5	192	75	49	130
7.9	7.4	2.4	25	0.3	25	2079	12	6	131
4.9	4.6	2.5	24	0.4	50	2234	16	2	132
2.1	1.8	1.6	17	0.4	4	10	51	27	133
0.9	0.9	1.1	41	0.4	60	8	16	8	134
2.0	1.9	1.2	19	0.6	1	102	31	11	135
2.6	2.5	1.2	38	1.4	1	83	42	15	136
1.5	1.4	0.6	18	0.3	3	10	9	2	137
11.6	1.9	2.4	41	1.9	(300)[d]	N	N	1	138
17.5	0.8	1.9	16	2.4	12	(3)	33	0	139
1.7	1.7	0.9	28	0.7	3	171	55	5	140
1.9	0.8	4.8	29	0.6	348	0	21	0	141
0.4	0.2	1.1	6	0.6	5	0	44	1	142
7.9	5.6	1.4	25	0.3	3	2	17	5	143
14.1	10.0	3.1	47	0.8	4	7	38	3	144
12.9	5.9	4.7	50	0.6	4	5	41	10	145
9.7	2.7	5.1	35	1.6	2	95	33	12	146
17.5	1.5	4.8	33	1.8	380	10	11	0	147
2.6	2.4	1.6	8	0.4	4	29	36	120	148
28.5	5.5	1.2	5	0.5	4	(58)	22	9	149
0.5	0.3	(2.1)	150	1.7	16	(1101)	52	6	150
2.3	2.2	0.7	26	0.1	14	28	18	15	151
20.5	11.6	2.3	23	0.7	32	660	8	17	152

Table 3.1. Composition per 100 g of edible portion *continued*

No.	Food	Inedible waste (%)	Water (g)	Energy kJ	Energy kcal	Protein (g)	Fat (g)	Saturated fatty acids (g)
153	Sweetcorn kernels, canned, reheated, drained	18	72.3	519	122	2.9	1.2	0.2
154	Tofu, soya bean, steamed	0	85.0	304	73	8.1	4.2	0.5
155	Tomatoes, raw	0	93.1	73	17	0.7	0.3	0.1
156	Turnip, boiled in unsalted water	0	93.1	51	12	0.6	0.2	0
157	Veggie burger, retail, grilled	0	50.3	821	196	16.6	11.1	N
158	Watercress	38	92.5	94	22	3.0	1.0	0.3
159	Yam, boiled in unsalted water	0	64.4	568	133	1.7	0.3	0.1
	Fruit							
160	Apples, eating, average, raw, flesh and skin	11	84.5	199	47	0.4	0.1	0
161	Apricots, ready to eat (semi-dried)	0	29.7	674	158	4.0	0.6	N
162	Avocado, average, flesh only	29	72.5	784	190	1.9	19.5	4.1
163	Bananas, flesh only	34	75.1	403	95	1.2	0.3	0.1
164	Blackcurrants, stewed, with sugar	0	72.9	252	58	0.7	0	0
165	Cherries, raw, flesh and skin	17	82.8	203	48	0.9	0.1	0
166	Dates, raw, flesh and skin	16	14.6	1151	270	3.3	0.2	0.1
167	Figs, ready to eat	0	23.6	889	209	3.3	1.5	N
168	Grapefruit, raw, flesh only	32	89.0	126	30	0.8	0.1	0
169	Grapes, average	5	81.8	257	60	0.4	0.1	0
170	Kiwi fruit, flesh and seeds	14	84.0	207	49	1.1	0.5	N
171	Mangoes, ripe, raw, flesh only	32	82.4	245	57	0.7	0.2	0.1
172	Melon, honeydew, flesh only	37	92.2	119	28	0.6	0.1	0
173	Olives, in brine	20	76.5	422	103	0.9	11.0	1.7
174	Oranges, flesh only	30	86.1	158	37	1.1	0.1	0
175	Peaches, raw, flesh and skin	10	88.9	142	33	1.0	0.1	0
176	Peaches canned in syrup	0	81.1	233	55	0.5	0	0
177	Peaches, canned in juice	0	86.7	165	39	0.6	0	0
178	Pears, average, raw, flesh and skin	9	83.8	169	40	0.3	0.1	0
179	Pineapple, canned in juice	0	86.8	200	47	0.3	0	0
180	Plums, average, raw, flesh and skin	6	83.9	155	36	0.6	0.1	0
181	Prunes, ready to eat	14	31.1	601	141	2.5	0.4	N
182	Raisins	0	13.2	1159	272	2.1	0.4	N
183	Raspberries, raw	0	87.0	109	25	1.4	0.3	0.1
184	Rhubarb, stewed with sugar	0	84.6	203	48	0.9	0.1	0

Carbo-hydrate (g)	Total sugars (g)	Fibre (NSP) (g)	Calcium (mg)	Iron (mg)	Sodium (mg)	Vitamin A (µg)	Folate (µg)	Vitamin C (mg)	No.
26.6	9.6	1.4	4	0.5	270	18	20	1	153
0.7	0.3	N	510	1.2	4	0	15	0	154
3.1	3.1	1.0	7	0.5	9	94	22	17	155
2.0	1.9	1.9	45	0.2	28	3	8	10	156
8.0	3.6	4.2	100	4.5	490	N	95	N	157
0.4	0.4	1.5	170	2.2	49	420	45	62	158
33.0	0.7	1.4	12	0.4	17	0	6	4	159
11.8	11.8	1.8	4	0.1	3	3	1	6	160
36.5	36.5	6.3	73	3.4	14	91	11	1	161
1.9	0.5	3.4	11	0.4	6	3	11	6	162
23.2	20.9	1.1	6	0.3	1	4	14	11	163
15.0	15.0	2.8	47	1.0	2	13	N	115	164
11.5	11.5	0.9	13	0.2	1	4	5	11	165
68.0	68.0	4.0	45	1.3	10	7	13	0	166
48.6	48.6	6.9	230	3.9	57	10	8	1	167
6.8	6.8	1.3	23	0.1	3	3	26	36	168
15.4	15.4	0.7	13	0.3	2	3	2	3	169
10.6	10.3	1.9	25	0.4	4	7	N	59	170
14.1	13.8	2.6	12	0.7	2	116	N	37	171
6.6	6.6	0.6	9	0.1	32	8	2	9	172
0	0	2.9	61	1.0	2250	30	0	0	173
8.5	8.5	1.7	47	0.1	5	8	31	54	174
7.6	7.6	1.5	7	0.4	1	19	3	31	175
14.0	14.0	0.9	3	0.2	4	13	7	5	176
9.7	9.7	0.8	4	0.4	12	11	2	6	177
10.0	10.0	2.2	11	0.2	3	3	2	6	178
12.2	12.2	0.5	8	0.5	1	2	1	11	179
8.8	8.8	1.6	13	0.4	2	63	3	4	180
34.0	34.0	5.7	34	2.6	11	23	3	0	181
69.3	69.3	2.0	46	3.8	60	2	10	1	182
4.6	4.6	2.5	25	0.7	3	1	33	32	183
11.5	11.5	1.2	33	0.1	1	5	4	5	184

Table 3.1. Composition per 100 g of edible portion *continued*

No.	Food	Inedible waste (%)	Water (g)	Energy kJ	Energy kcal	Protein (g)	Fat (g)	Saturated fatty acids (g)
185	Satsumas	29	87.4	155	36	0.9	0.1	0
186	Strawberries, raw	5	89.5	113	27	0.8	0.1	0
	Nuts							
187	Almonds, flesh only	63	4.2	2534	612	21.1	55.8	4.4
188	Cashew nuts, roasted and salted	0	2.4	2533	611	20.5	50.9	10.1
189	Coconut, desiccated	0	2.3	2492	604	5.6	62.0	53.4
190	Peanut butter, smooth	0	1.1	2510	606	22.6	51.8	12.8
191	Peanuts, roasted and salted	0	1.9	2491	602	24.5	53.0	9.5
	Sugars and preserves							
192	Chocolate, milk[c]	0	1.6	2171	519	7.3	31.1	18.7
193	Honey	0	17.5	1229	288	0.4	0	0
194	Jam, fruit, with edible seeds	0	29.8	1114	261	0.6	0	0
195	Marmalade	0	28.0	1114	261	0.1	0	0
196	Peppermints	0	0.2	1678	393	0.5	0.7	N
197	Sugar, white	0	0	1680	394	0	0	0
198	Syrup, golden	0	20.0	1269	298	0.3	0	0
199	Toffees, mixed[c]	0	4	1630	387	2.1	15.9	8.6
	Beverages							
200	Cocoa powder	0	3.4	1301	312	18.5	21.7	12.8
201	Coffee, infusion, average	0	98.3	8	2	0.2	0	0
202	Drinking-chocolate powder	0	2.1	1582	373	5.4	5.8	3.4
203	Drinking chocolate, made up with semi-skimmed milk	0	82.3	310	73	3.6	2.0	1.3
204	Tea, black, infusion, average	0	99.5	0	0	0.1	0	0
	Soft drinks and juices							
205	Cola	0	89.7	174	41	0	0	0
206	Cola, diet	0	99.8	2	1	0	0	0
207	Lemonade, bottled	0	(95)[d]	(133)[d]	(31)[d]	0	0	0
208	Orange juice, unsweetened	0	89.2	(174)[d]	(41)[d]	0.5	0.1	0
209	Pineapple juice, unsweetened	0	87.8	177	41	0.3	0.1	0
210	Fruit drink/squash, undiluted	0	(88.1)[d]	(190)[d]	(44)[d]	0.1	0	0

Carbo-hydrate (g)	Total sugars (g)	Fibre (NSP) (g)	Calcium (mg)	Iron (mg)	Sodium (mg)	Vitamin A (µg)	Folate (µg)	Vitamin C (mg)	No.
8.5	8.5	1.3	31	0.1	4	13	33	27	185
6.0	6.0	1.1	16	0.4	6	1	20	77	186
6.9	4.2	(7.4)	240	3.0	14	0	48	0	187
18.8	5.6	3.2	35	6.2	290	1	68	0	188
6.4	6.4	13.7	23	3.6	28	0	9	0	189
13.1	(6.0)[d]	5.4	37	2.1	(400)[d]	0	53	0	190
7.1	3.8	6.0	37	1.3	400	0	52	0	191
56.0	56.0	1.3	220	1.4	85	27	11	0	192
76.4	76.4	0	5	0.4	11	0	N	0	193
69.0	69.0	N	12	0.2	29	0	0	10	194
69.5	69.5	(0.3)	26	0.2	64	8	5	10	195
102.7	102.7	0	7	0.2	9	0	0	0	196
105.0	105.0	0	(10)	(0.2)	5	0	0	0	197
79.0	79.0	0	16	0.4	270	0	0	0	198
62.9	39.1	0	73	0.2	340	0	0	0	199
11.5	0	12.1	130	10.5	950	(7)	38	0	200
0.3	0	0	3	0.1	0	0	0	0	201
79.7	77.7	N	39	3.5	228	N	7	0	202
10.9	10.7	0	114	0.3	58	18	5	1	203
0	0	0	0	0	0	0	3	0	204
10.9	10.9	0	6	0	5	0	0	0	205
0	0	0	(6)	0	0	0	0	0	206
(8.3)[d]	(8.3)[d]	0	5	0	7	0	0	0	207
(10.1)[d]	(10.1)[d]	0.1	10	0.2	10	3	18	39	208
10.5	10.5	0	8	0.2	8	1	8	11	209
(11.8)[d]	(11.8)[d]	0	6	0	(0)[d]	(35)[d]	2	(2)[d]	210

Table 3.1. Composition per 100 g of edible portion *continued*

No.	Food	Inedible waste (%)	Water (g)	Energy kJ	Energy kcal	Protein (g)	Fat (g)	Saturated fatty acids (g)
211	Fruit juice drink (25–49% fruit), ready to drink	0	(91.3)[d]	(182)[d]	(43)[d]	0.1	0	0
212	Fruit juice drink, low calorie, ready to drink	0	(99.1)[d]	(14)[d]	(3)[d]	0.2	0	0
	Miscellaneous							
213	Baking powder	0	6.3	693	163	5.2	0	0
214	Yeast extract	0	26.7	763	180	40.7	0.4	N
215	Mayonnaise, retail[c]	0	19.3	2824	686	1.1	74.8	5.7
216	Mayonnaise, retail, reduced fat	0	59.5	1188	288	1.0	28.1	4.2
217	Mustard, smooth	0	63.7	579	139	7.1	8.2	0.5
218	Pickle, sweet	0	60.7	604	141	0.6	0.1	0
219	Salad cream	0	47.2	1440	348	1.5	31.0	3.3
220	Soup, cream of tomato, canned, ready to serve[c]	0	89.0	215	51	0.9	2.0	0.3
221	Soy sauce	0	68.6	182	43	3.0	0	0
222	Tomato ketchup	0	68.0	489	115	1.6	0.1	0
223	French dressing	0	33.3	1902	462	0.1	49.4	8.0
224	Gravy, instant granules, made up	0	93.0	142	34	0.3	2.4	N
225	Pasta sauce, tomato based[b]	0	84.8	186	44	1.5	1.3	0.2
	Alcoholic drinks							
226	Beer, bitter, average	0	93.9	124	30	0.3	0	0
227	Cider, dry	0	92.5	152	36	0	0	0
228	Lager	0	93.0	121	29	0.3	0	0
229	Lager, alcohol free	0	96.3	31	7	0.4	0	0
230	Spirits, 40% volume	0	68.3	919	222	0	0	0
231	Wine, white, medium	0	(85.9)[d]	(321)[d]	(78)[d]	0.1	0	0
232	Wine, red	0	(88.6)[d]	(316)[d]	(76)[d]	0.1	0	0

[a] Source: *Nutrient Survey of Flours and Grains – Analytical Report,* Food Standards Agency, 2005.
[b] Source: *Nutrient Survey of Pasta and Pasta Sauces – Analytical Report,* Food Standards Agency, 2004.
[c] Source: *Nutrient Analysis of a Range of Processed Foods with Particular Reference to* Trans *Fatty Acids – Summary Report,* Department of Health, 2011. Macronutrients only.
[d] Source: Estimate based on label values of leading brands.
[e] Source: *Nutrient Survey of Breakfast Cereals – Analytical Report,* Food Standards Agency, 2004.

Carbo-hydrate (g)	Total sugars (g)	Fibre (NSP) (g)	Calcium (mg)	Iron (mg)	Sodium (mg)	Vitamin A (µg)	Folate (µg)	Vitamin C (mg)	No.
(11.3)[d]	(11.3)[d]	0	6	0	(0)[d]	N	2	(15)[d]	211
(0.7)[d]	(0.7)[d]	0	5	0	5	0	2	(15)[d]	212
37.8	0	0	1130	0	11800	0	0	0	213
3.5	1.6	0	70	2.9	(3900)[d]	0	2620	0	214
2.4	2.4	0	8	0.3	(620)[d]	103	4	0	215
8.2	4.6	0	N	N	(880)[d]	10	N	0	216
9.7	7.8	N	70	2.9	2950	N	0	0	217
36.0	(25.1)[d]	1.2	15	0.6	1610	42	0	0	218
16.7	16.7	N	18	0.5	(700)[d]	12	3	0	219
7.8	5.5	0.5	17	0.4	(270)[d]	(75)	12	0	220
8.2	7.3	0	17	2.4	(6100)[d]	0	11	0	221
28.6	(23.7)[d]	0.9	13	0.3	(900)[d]	79	1	2	222
4.5	4.5	0	N	N	460	0	0	0	223
3.0	0.1	0	1	0	460	N	0	0	224
6.9	6.1	1.3	30.9	0.65	(330)[d]	84	2	<1	225
2.2	2.2	0	8	0.1	6	0	5	0	226
2.6	2.6	0	8	0.5	7	0	N	0	227
0	0	0	5	0	7	0	12	0	228
1.5	1.2	0	3	0	2	0	5	0	229
0	0	0	0	0	0	0	0	0	230
3.0	3.0	0	12	0.8	11	0	0	0	231
0.2	0.2	0	7	0.9	7	0	1	0	232

[f] Source: *Nutrient Analysis Survey of Biscuits, Buns, Cakes and Pastries – Summary Report,* Department of Health, 2011.
[g] Source: *Nutrient Analysis Catch Up Project,* Food Standards Agency, 2004.
Source: unless otherwise stated, *McCance and Widdowson's Composition of Foods Integrated Dataset* (COFIDS), published by the Food Standards Agency 2008.

Appendix 4　The use of food tables for calculations of the nutritional value of foods

A great deal of useful information can be worked out from the food composition tables in Appendix 3. Examples of various types of calculation are given below.

Nutrient content

SIMPLE NUTRIENT CONTENT

The protein content of two grilled fish fingers is calculated as follows.

Fish fingers (food no. 105 in Appendix 3) contain 13.9 g of protein per 100 g.

Two fish fingers weigh 56 g (Appendix 5).

56 g of grilled fish fingers contain $13.9 \times \dfrac{56}{100} = 7.8$ g of protein.

NUTRIENT CONTENT ALLOWING FOR WASTAGE (INEDIBLE MATTER)

The carbohydrate content of one apple weighing 120 g is calculated as follows.

Eating apples (food no. 160 in Appendix 3) contain 11.8 g of carbohydrate per 100-g edible portion, and 11% waste.

An apple weighing 120 g contains $100 - \dfrac{11}{100} \times 120$ g of edible matter = 106.8 g of edible matter.

Therefore 106.8 g of apple (120 g whole apple) contains $11.8 \times \dfrac{106.8}{100}$ = 12.6 g of carbohydrate.

Portion sizes

400-kJ PORTIONS

A 400-kJ portion of Cheddar cheese is calculated as follows.

Cheddar cheese (food no. 56 in Appendix 3) has an energy value of 1725 kJ per 100 g.

400 kJ are contained in $\dfrac{100}{1725} \times 400 = 23.2$ g (a little less than 1 oz) of Cheddar cheese.

A 400-kJ portion of cottage cheese is calculated as follows.

Cottage cheese (food no. 60 in Appendix 3) has an energy value of 423 kJ per 100 g.

400 kJ are contained in $\dfrac{100}{423} \times 400 = 94.6$ g (or about 3½ oz) of cottage cheese.

100-kcal PORTIONS

(Note that the size of a 100-kcal portion will be slightly greater than a 400-kJ portion and slightly smaller than a 500-kJ portion.)

A 100-kcal portion of uncooked, old potatoes is calculated as follows.

Potatoes (old, average, raw, flesh only [food no. 118 in Table 3.1]) have an energy value of 75 kcal per 100-g edible portion.

100 kcal are contained in $\dfrac{100}{75} \times 100 = 133.3$ g of potato.

Cost of nutrients

NUTRIENTS PER PENNY

The nutrients obtained per penny from a large (800 g) loaf of sliced wholemeal bread costing £1.39 are calculated as follows.

1 p buys $\dfrac{1}{139} \times 800 = 5.7$ g.

Appendix 3 shows the nutrients in 100 g of wholemeal bread (food no. 13).

Therefore, multiply the values for each nutrient by $\dfrac{5.7}{100}$

  = 0.5 g of protein

  = 0.1 g of fat

  = 2.4 g of carbohydrate

  = 6.0 mg of calcium

  = 0.1 mg of iron etc.

COST PER NUTRIENT

The cost of 10 g of protein from baked beans is calculated as follows.

Baked beans (food no. 122 in Appendix 3) contain 5.2 g of protein per 100 g.

10 g of protein is contained in $10 \times \dfrac{100}{5.2} = 192.3$ g of baked beans.

A 410-g can of baked beans costs 59 p.

Therefore 192.3 g of baked beans cost $\dfrac{192.3}{410} \times 59 = 27.7$ p.

Percentage of energy from fat

BROWN BREAD

Brown bread (food no. 9 in Appendix 3) contains 2.0 g of fat and 882 kJ (207 kcal) per 100 g.

Each gram of fat provides 37 kJ (9 kcal).

The percentage of energy from fat is $2.0 \times \dfrac{37}{822} \times 100 = 8.4\%$

(or $2.0 \times \dfrac{9}{207} \times 100 = 8.7\%$).

MARGARINE

Margarine (food no. 68 in Appendix 3) contains 76.4 g of fat and 2827 kJ (688 kcal) per 100 g.

Each gram of fat provides 37 kJ (9 kcal).

The percentage of energy from fat is $76.4 \times \dfrac{37}{2827} \times 100 = 99.9\%$

(or $76.4 \times \dfrac{9}{688} \times 100 = 99.9\%$).

IN A COMBINATION OF FOODS

One slice of brown bread weighs 30 g, and 7 g of margarine is allowed for spreading on one slice.

One slice (30 g) of brown bread contains $(2.0 \times \dfrac{30}{100})$ g of fat and

$(882 \times \dfrac{30}{100})$ kJ = 0.6 g of fat and 264.6 kJ (63.2 kcal).

7 g of margarine contains $(76.4 \times \dfrac{7}{100})$ g of fat and

$(2827 \times \dfrac{7}{100})$ kJ = 5.3 g of fat and 197.9 kJ (47.3 kcal).

The combination of a slice of brown bread with margarine contains 0.6 + 5.3 g of fat = 5.9 g of fat and 264.6 + 197.9 kJ = 462.5 kJ (110.5 kcal).

Since each gram of fat provides 37 kJ or 9 kcal, the percentage of energy from fat in a slice of brown bread and margarine is $5.9 \times 37 \times \dfrac{100}{462.5} = 47.2\%$

(or $5.9 \times 9 \times \dfrac{100}{110.5} = 48.1\%$).

Adding baked beans, a banana or a drink such as fruit juice would further reduce the proportion of energy derived from fat.

Note that the values derived from kilojoules and kilocalories differ slightly because the conversion factor given in Appendix 1 is not exactly equivalent.

Appendix 5 Typical servings of commonly consumed foods

Milk, semi-skimmed	For 1 cup of tea or coffee	30 g
Milk	Average glass	200 g
Cheese, Cheddar type	'Matchbox-sized' piece	30 g
Yogurt, plain or fruit	Small carton	125 g
Chicken, roast	Medium portion	100 g
Pork chop	Average, with bone, fried or grilled	150 g
Minced beef	Medium portion, cooked	140 g
Bacon	Rasher back, average, fried or grilled	25 g
Sausage	Large, cooked	40 g
Beefburger, 100% beef	1 burger, fried or grilled	34 g
Fish finger	1 fish finger, fried or grilled	28 g
White fish	Medium fillet	150 g
Tuna	1 portion, for sandwich	45 g
Egg	Size 3, no shell	57 g
Baked beans	Medium portion	135 g
Butter, or fat spreads	For 1 medium slice of bread	7–10 g
Oil	1 tablespoon	11 g
Mayonnaise	1 heaped tablespoon	33 g
Peanut butter	Thickly spread on 1 slice of bread	20 g
Jam or marmalade	Average spreading on 1 slice of bread	15 g
Lettuce	Round, average serving in salad	30 g
Tomato	1 slice	17 g
	1 medium tomato	85 g
Peas	Medium portion	70 g
Carrots	Large portion	85 g
Orange	1 medium, without peel	160 g
Apple	1 medium, eating, without core	100 g
Banana	1 medium, without skin	100 g
Grapes	Small bunch	100 g
Peaches, canned in syrup or juice	Medium portion	120 g
Raisins/sultanas, dried	1 tablespoon	30 g

Fruit juice	Average glass	160 g
Potatoes, boiled	Medium portion	175 g
mashed	1 scoop	60g
baked, with skin	Medium	180g
Yam, boiled	Size of 1 medium potato	130 g
Bread, wholemeal, large loaf	1 medium slice	36 g
Flour	1 tablespoon, heaped	30 g
Porridge	Medium portion	160 g
Breakfast cereal	Cornflakes type, medium portion	30 g
	Muesli, medium portion	50g
Crispbread	1 crispbread, wholewheat	15 g
Biscuits, digestive	1 biscuit	13 g
Rice, boiled	Medium portion	180 g
Pasta, cooked	Medium portion	230 g
Coffee, instant	1 heaped teaspoon	2 g
Drinking chocolate	1 mug	18 g
Sugar	1 level teaspoon	4 g
Beer	Half pint	287 g (284 ml)
Wine	1 average glass	125 g (125 ml)

Source: *Food Portion Sizes*, Ministry of Agriculture, Fisheries and Food, 1993.

Appendix 6   The eatwell plate

The eatwell plate forms the basis of the Government's healthy-eating advice to the general population. As seen in Figure 3, it shows the types and proportions of foods needed to make up a well-balanced, healthy diet. This includes snacks as well as meals. The balance of foods to be achieved is shown by the different areas occupied by each of the five food groups:

- bread, rice, potatoes, pasta and other starchy foods
- fruit and vegetables
- meat, fish, eggs, beans and other sources of protein
- milk and dairy foods
- foods and drinks that are high in fat and/or sugar.

Choosing food groups in the approximate proportions shown and choosing a variety of different foods from within each group helps to ensure that all essential nutrients are consumed in adequate amounts. People differ in the amount of energy they need and hence in the amount of food they should eat, but whatever that may be, the proportions of foods from the different groups should remain the same. An individual is therefore advised to look at the plate and try to match the balance in their own diet. The approach recommended is to try to achieve the balance shown every day, but it can also be achieved over the course of a week or so. The eatwell plate applies to most people, including people whose weight is in the desired range for their height, those who are overweight,[27] vegetarians and people of all ethnic origins. Children under 2 years of age have different requirements; for example, they should be given full-fat milk and dairy products. People under medical supervision or with special dietary requirements should ask their doctor whether the eatwell plate applies to them.

Based on the eatwell plate, the healthy-eating messages are to try to:

- eat plenty of fruit and vegetables
- eat plenty of potatoes, bread, rice, pasta and other starchy foods – choose wholegrain varieties when you can
- consume some milk and dairy foods
- eat some meat, fish, eggs, beans and other non-dairy sources of protein
- consume just a small amount of foods and drinks that are high in fat and/ or sugar

---

[27] Most UK adults need to lose weight, and to do this they need to eat and drink fewer calories, even when following a balanced diet.

- choose options that are lower in fat, salt and sugar when you can.

In addition, the following eight tips for a healthy lifestyle complement the eatwell plate:

- Base your meals on starchy foods
- Eat lots of fruit and vegetables
- Eat more fish
- Cut down on saturated fat and sugar
- Eat less salt
- Get active and maintain a healthy weight
- Don't get thirsty
- Don't skip breakfast.

Further information on following a healthy diet is available from the NHS website (www.nhs.uk).

Further information on the eatwell plate, including guidelines for use and its reproduction, is available from the Department of Health website (www.dh.gov.uk/en/Publichealth/Nutrition/DH_126493).

Figure 3. The eatwell plate

The eatwell plate

Use the eatwell plate to help you get the balance right. It shows how much of what you eat should come from each food group.

Fruit and vegetables

Bread, rice, potatoes, pasta and other starchy foods

Meat, fish, eggs, beans and other non-dairy sources of protein

Milk and dairy foods

Foods and drinks high in fat and/or sugar

Department of Health in association with the Welsh Government, the Scottish Government and the Food Standards Agency in Northern Ireland

Appendix 7   Food additives

In addition to the expected ingredients of made-up foods, there are other
substances that may be added in small amounts to perform a specific
function in the food. These are called food additives. They fall into two broad
categories: those that are added to prevent food spoilage, and those that are
added to enhance the texture, flavour or appearance of food.

Preservatives and antioxidants

It is very important that every effort is made to prevent food being wasted.
Some forms of food spoilage, such as attacks on stored food by vermin, are
easily recognisable. Other forms of spoilage develop within the food itself
and give rise to off-flavours long before the visual appearance of the food
is noticeably affected; these may be caused either by the action of micro-
organisms (i.e. moulds and bacteria) or by chemical action. While some
micro-organisms merely make the food unpalatable, others such as *Clostridium
botulinum* produce highly poisonous toxins and present a considerable hazard
to health. Preservatives such as sulphur dioxide and sodium nitrite are added to
some foods to inhibit the growth of micro-organisms. The most common form
of chemical spoilage is rancidity.

Rancidity resulting from the oxidation of fat can be delayed by the addition of
antioxidants. Some antioxidants are natural compounds, but in order to protect
fats in foods that are baked (e.g. biscuits), heat-stable synthetic antioxidants
are required.

Other additives

The texture of food often depends on the ability of added emulsifiers to create
a uniform dispersion of fat and water (as in fat spreads and salad cream).
Similarly, stabilisers are added to prevent uniform dispersions separating out
(e.g. the setting of instant desserts).

The colour and flavour of foods are closely linked: consumers expect a food to
have a colour that matches the flavour. Therefore, if the natural colour is lost or
changed during processing, colouring matter may be added to restore the food
to the expected colour.

The law strictly controls the types and quantities of additives that may be
used in food (see also Appendix 8), and the list of ingredients must show the
additive category name (e.g. colour) and the serial number of the additive, or
its name, or both (e.g. E300 ascorbic acid, or E500 sodium bicarbonate).

Appendix 8 Legislation governing the composition and labelling of food

New EU food-labelling regulations have just been harmonised across Europe. Recommended Daily Amounts (RDAs) will be replaced with Nutrient Reference Values under the new Food Information Regulations (FIR), defined in Regulation 1169/2011. Although the FIR are in place at the time of publication of this manual, they will not become mandatory until December 2014.

The Government is also reviewing labelling legislation as part of the review set up to reduce burden on industry (the Red Tape Challenge). Given the changes that are ongoing, information on the labelling requirements have not been included in this edition of the manual.

European Regulation (EC) 1924/2006 controls the use of nutrition and health claims made on foods. It puts in place a list of authorised nutrition claims that can be made on food and the criteria a product must meet to use them. It also puts in place a process to establish a similar list of health claims. For a claim to be included or added to the list of health claims, it must be substantiated by supporting scientific evidence assessed by the European Food Safety Authority.

European Regulation (EC) 1925/2006 on the addition of vitamins and minerals and of certain other substances to foods controls which vitamins and minerals can voluntarily be added to food. This excludes mandatory fortified foods, such as flour and spreadable fats.

Consult the Department for Environment, Food and Rural Affairs and Department of Health websites for the most up-to-date information (www.defra.gov.uk; www.dh.gov.uk).

Appendix 9   Further reading

Government reviews and reports on nutrition

Committee on Medical Aspects of Food Policy. *Dietary Sugars and Human Disease*. Report on Health and Social Subjects No. 37. London: HMSO, 1989 (0 11 321255 0).

Committee on Medical Aspects of Food Policy. *Dietary Reference Values for Food Energy and Nutrients for the United Kingdom*. Report on Health and Social Subjects No. 41. London: HMSO, 1991 (Chapter 36 updated 1994) (ISBN 0 11 321397 2).

Committee on Medical Aspects of Food Policy. *Dietary Reference Values: A Guide. London*: HMSO, 1991 (ISBN 0 11 321396 4).

Committee on Medical Aspects of Food Policy. *The Nutrition of Elderly People*. Report on Health and Social Subjects No. 43. London: HMSO, 1992 (ISBN 0 11 321550 9).

Committee on Medical Aspects of Food Policy. *The Nutritional Assessment of Novel Foods and Processes. Report of the Panel on Novel Foods of the Committee on Medical Aspects of Food Policy*. Report on Health and Social Subjects No. 44. London: HMSO, 1993 (ISBN 0 11 321632 7).

Committee on Medical Aspects of Food Policy. *Nutritional Aspects of Cardiovascular Disease. Report of the Cardiovascular Review Group of the Committee on Medical Aspects of Food Policy*. Report on Health and Social Subjects No. 46. London: HMSO, 1994 (ISBN 0 11 321875 3).

Committee on Medical Aspects of Food Policy. *Weaning and the Weaning Diet*. Report on Health and Social Subjects No. 45. London: HMSO, 1994 (ISBN 0 11 321838 9).

Committee on Medical Aspects of Food Policy. *Nutrition and Bone Health: With Particular Reference to Calcium and Vitamin D*. Report on Health and Social Subjects No. 49. London: The Stationery Office, 1998 (ISBN 0 11 322262 9).

Committee on Medical Aspects of Food Policy. *Nutritional Aspects of the Development of Cancer*. Report on Health and Social Subjects No. 48. London: The Stationery Office, 1998 (ISBN 0 11 322089 8).

Department of Health. *Folic Acid and the Prevention of Neural Tube Defects: Report from an Expert Advisory Group*. Heywood, 1992.

Scientific Advisory Committee on Nutrition. *Salt and Health*. London: The Stationery Office, 2003 (ISBN 0 11 243075 9).

Scientific Advisory Committee on Nutrition. *Review of Dietary Advice on Vitamin A*. London: The Stationery Office, 2005 (ISBN 0 11 243088 0).

Scientific Advisory Committee on Nutrition. *Folate and Disease Prevention*. London: The Stationery Office, 2006 (ISBN 0 11 243111 9).

Scientific Advisory Committee on Nutrition. *Update on Trans Fatty Acids and Health. Position Statement by the Scientific Advisory Committee on Nutrition*. London: The Stationery Office, 2007 (ISBN 978 0 11 243117 7).

Scientific Advisory Committee on Nutrition. *Update on Vitamin D. Position Statement by the Scientific Advisory Committee on Nutrition*. London: The Stationery Office, 2007 (ISBN 978 0 11 243114 5).

Scientific Advisory Committee on Nutrition. *The Nutritional Wellbeing of the British Population*. London: The Stationery Office, 2008 (ISBN 978 0 11 243281).

Scientific Advisory Committee on Nutrition. *Iron and Health*. London: The Stationery Office, 2010 (ISBN 978 0 11 706992 3).

Scientific Advisory Committee on Nutrition. *The Influence of Maternal, Fetal and Child Nutrition on the Development of Chronic Disease Later in Life*. London: The Stationery Office, 2011 (ISBN 978 0 10 851064 9).

Scientific Advisory Committee on Nutrition. *Dietary Reference Values for Energy 2011*. The Stationery Office, 2012 (ISBN 978 0 10 851137 0).

Scientific Advisory Committee on Nutrition and Committee on Toxicity. *Advice on Fish Consumption: Benefits & Risks*. London: The Stationery Office, 2004 (ISBN 0 11 243083 X).

Scientific Advisory Committee on Nutrition and Royal College of Paediatrics and Child Health. *Application of WHO Growth Standards in the UK*. London: The Stationery Office, 2007 (ISBN 978 0 11 243280 7).

World Health Organization. *Diet, Nutrition and the Prevention of Chronic Diseases: Report of a Joint WHO/FAO Expert Consultation*. Geneva: World Health Organization, 2003 (ISBN 978 9 24120916 8).

Report on safety aspects of nutrients

Expert Group on Vitamins and Minerals. *Safe Upper Levels for Vitamins and Minerals*. London: Food Standards Agency, 2003 (ISBN 1 904026 11 7). http://cot.food.gov.uk/pdfs/vitmin2003.pdf

Government dietary and nutrition surveys

Department of Health. *National Diet and Nutrition Survey: Headline Results from Years 1 and 2 (Combined) of the Rolling Programme 2008/2009–2009/10*. Department of Health, 2011. www.dh.gov.uk/en/Publicationsandstatistics/Publications/PublicationsStatistics/DH_128166

Department of Health. *Nutrient Analysis of a Range of Processed Foods with Particular Reference to* Trans *Fatty Acids – Summary Report*, 2011.

Department of Health. *Nutrient Analysis Survey of Biscuits, Buns, Cakes and Pastries – Summary Report*, 2011.

Economic and Social Data Service. *Living Costs and Food Survey, 2010*. Economic and Social Data Service, 2012. www.esds.ac.uk/findingData/snDescription.asp?sn=6945

S Finch, W Doyle, C Lowe et al. *National Diet and Nutrition Survey: People Aged 65 Years and Over. Volume 1: Report of the Diet and Nutrition Survey*. London: The Stationery Office, 1998 (ISBN 0 11 243019 8).

Food Standards Agency. *1997 Total Diet Study – Fluorine, Bromine and Iodine*. Food Survey Information Sheet, 2000.

Food Standards Agency. *Nutrient Survey of Breakfast Cereals – Analytical Report*, 2004.

Food Standards Agency. *Nutrient Survey of Pasta and Pasta Sauces – Analytical Report*, 2004.

Food Standards Agency. *Nutrient Survey of Flours and Grains – Analytical Report*, 2005.

J R Gregory, D L Collins, P S W Davies et al. *National Diet and Nutrition Survey: Children Aged 1½ to 4½ years. Volume 1: Report of the Diet and Nutrition Survey*. London: HMSO, 1995 (ISBN 0 11 691611 7).

J Gregory, S Lowe, Bates C et al. *National Diet and Nutrition Survey: Young People Aged 4 to 18 years. Volume 1. Report of the Diet and Nutrition Survey*. London: The Stationery Office, 2000 (ISBN 0 11 621265 9).

L Henderson, J Gregory, K Irving and G Swan. *The National Diet and Nutrition Survey: Adults Aged 19 to 64 years. Energy, Protein, Carbohydrate, Fat and Alcohol Intake*. London: The Stationery Office, 2003 (ISBN 0 11 621567 4).

L Henderson, K Irving, Gregory J et al. *The National Diet and Nutrition Survey: Adults Aged 19 to 64 years. Vitamin and Mineral Intake and Urinary Analytes*. London, The Stationery Office, 2003 (ISBN 0 11 621568 2).

K Hinds and J R Gregory. *National Diet and Nutrition Survey: Children Aged 1½ to 4½ years. Volume 2: Report of the Dental Survey*. London: HMSO, 1995 (ISBN 0 11 691612 5).

Ministry of Agriculture, Fisheries and Food. *Total Diet Study 1994: Metals and Other Elements*. Food Surveillance Information Sheet No 131, 1997. http://tna.europarchive.org/20101209103637/http://archive.food.gov.uk/maff/archive/food/infsheet/1997/no131/131tds.htm

M Nelson, B Erens, B Bates et al. *Low Income Diet and Nutrition Survey. Volume 1: Background; Methods; Sample Characteristics, Volume 2: Food Consumption; Nutrient Intake, Volume 3: Nutritional Status; Physical Activity; Economic, Social and Other Factors*. London. The Stationery Office, 2007 (ISBN 978 0 11 703783 0).

National Centre for Social Research and Medical Research Council Human Nutrition Research. An assessment of dietary sodium levels among adults (aged 19–64) in the UK general population in 2008, based on analysis of dietary sodium in 24 hour urine samples. Food Standards Agency, 2008.

NHS Information Centre. *Infant Feeding Survey 2005*, Leeds: NHS Information Centre, 2007 (ISBN 1 84636 124 9). www.ic.nhs.uk/pubs/ifs2005

NHS Information Centre. *Health Survey for England – 2010: Trend Tables*. Leeds: NHS Information Centre, 2011. www.ic.nhs.uk/pubs/hse10trends

J Steele, A Sheiham, W Marcenes and A Walls. *National Diet and Nutrition Survey: People Aged 65 Years and Over. Volume 2: Report of the Oral Health Survey*. London: The Stationery Office, 1998 (ISBN 0 11 243017 9).

Food composition tables

Supplements to *McCance and Widdowson's The Composition of Foods*, listed in date order:

A A Paul, D A T Southgate and J Russell. *Amino Acids (mg per 100 g food), Fatty Acids (g per 100 g food)*. The first supplement to *McCance and Widdowson's The Composition of Foods*. London: HMSO, 1980 (ISBN 0 444 80220 7).

S P Tan, R W Wenlock and D H Buss. *Immigrant Foods*. The second supplement to *McCance and Widdowson's The Composition of Foods* (4th edn). London: HMSO, 1985 (ISBN 0 11 242717 0).

B Holland, I D Unwin and D H Buss. *Cereals and Cereal Products*. The third supplement to *McCance and Widdowson's The Composition of Foods* (4th edn). Nottingham: Royal Society of Chemistry, 1988 (ISBN 0 85186 743 X).

B Holland, I D Unwin and D H Buss. *Milk Products and Eggs*. The fourth supplement to *McCance and Widdowson's The Composition of Foods* (4th edn). Cambridge: Royal Society of Chemistry, 1989 (ISBN 0 85186 366 3).

B Holland, I D Unwin and D H Buss. *Vegetables, Herbs and Spices*. The fifth supplement to *McCance and Widdowson's The Composition of Foods* (4th edn). Cambridge: Royal Society of Chemistry, 1991 (ISBN 0 85186 376 0).

B Holland, I D Unwin and D H Buss. *Fruit and Nuts*. The first supplement to *McCance and Widdowson's The Composition of Foods* (5th edn). Cambridge: Royal Society of Chemistry, 1992 (ISBN 0 85186 386 8).

B Holland, A A Welch and D H Buss. *Vegetable Dishes*. The second supplement to *McCance and Widdowson's The Composition of Foods* (5th edn). Cambridge: Royal Society of Chemistry, 1992 (ISBN 0 85186 396 5).

B Holland, J Brown and D H Buss. *Fish and Fish Products*. The third supplement to *McCance and Widdowson's The Composition of Foods* (5th edn). Cambridge: Royal Society of Chemistry, 1993 (ISBN 085186 421 X).

W Chan, J Brown and D H Buss. *Miscellaneous Foods*. The fourth supplement to *McCance and Widdowson's The Composition of Foods* (5th edn). Cambridge: Royal Society of Chemistry, 1994 (ISBN 0 85186 360 4).

W Chan, J Brown, S M Lee and D H Buss. *Meat, Poultry and Game*. The fifth supplement to *McCance and Widdowson's The Composition of Foods* (5th edn), Cambridge: Royal Society of Chemistry, 1995 (ISBN 0 85186 380 9).

W Chan, J Brown, S M Church and D H Buss. *Meat Products and Dishes*. The sixth supplement to *McCance and Widdowson's The Composition of Foods* (5th edn), Cambridge: Royal Society of Chemistry, 1996 (ISBN 0 85404 809 X).

Ministry of Agriculture, Fisheries and Food. *Fatty Acids*. The seventh supplement to *McCance and Widdowson's The Composition of Foods* (5th edn) Cambridge: Royal Society of Chemistry, 1998 (ISBN 0 85404 819 7).

Food Standards Agency and Agricultural and Food Research Council Institute of Food Research. *McCance and Widdowson's The Composition of Foods*: *Sixth summary edition*. Cambridge: Royal Society of Chemistry, 2002 (ISBN 0 85404 428 0).

Food Standards Agency. *McCance and Widdowson's Composition of Foods Integrated Dataset* (COFIDS), 2008.

Food portion sizes

Ministry of Agriculture, Fisheries and Food. *Food Portion Sizes* (3rd edn). London: HMSO, 1994.

M Nelson, M Atkinson and J Meyer. *Food Portion Sizes: A Photographic Atlas*. London: Ministry of Agriculture, Fisheries and Food, 1997.

Policy

Department of Health. *Healthy Lives, Healthy People: A Call to Action on Obesity in England*. London: Department of Health, 2011. www.dh.gov.uk/ en/Publicationsandstatistics/Publications/PublicationsPolicyAndGuidance/ DH_130401

Department of Health. *The Public Health Responsibility Deal*. London: Department of Health, 2011. www.dh.gov.uk/en/Publichealth/ Publichealthresponsibilitydeal/index.htm

Department of Health. UK physical activity guidelines (a series of factsheets and reports). www.dh.gov.uk/en/Publicationsandstatistics/Publications/ PublicationsPolicyAndGuidance/DH_127931

Department of Health, Social Services and Public Safety (Northern Ireland). *A Fitter Future For All. Framework for Preventing and Addressing Overweight and Obesity in Northern Ireland 2012–2022*. Belfast: Department of Health, Social Services and Public Safety (2012).

HM Government. *Healthy Lives, Healthy People: Our Strategy for Public Health in England*. London: The Stationery Office, 2010 (ISBN 978 0 10 179852 5). www.dh.gov.uk/en/Publicationsandstatistics/Publications/ PublicationsPolicyAndGuidance/DH_121941

Scottish Government. *Healthy Eating, Active Living: An Action Plan to Improve Diet, Increase Physical Activity and Tackle Obesity (2008-2011)*. Edinburgh: Scottish Government, 2008 (ISBN 978 0 7559 5768 2). www.scotland.gov.uk/Resource/Doc/228860/0061963.pdf

Welsh Assembly Government. *Our Healthy Future – Technical Working Paper*. Cardiff: Welsh Assembly Government, 2009. http://wales.gov.uk/topics/ health/publications/health/guidance/technical/?lang=en

Healthy-eating advice

GENERAL

General advice is available on the NHS website at www.nhs.uk/LiveWell/ healthy-eating/Pages/Healthyeating.asp

SCHOOLS

Advice for caterers of school food is available on the Department for Education website at www.education.gov.uk and on the School Food Trust website at www.schoolfoodtrust.org.uk

Advice for schools on a whole-school approach to healthy eating is available on the Department for Education website at www.education.gov.uk/childrenandyoungpeople/healthandwellbeing/a0075278/healthy-schools

Expert Panel on School Meals. *Hungry for Success. A Whole School Approach to School Meals in Scotland. Final Report of the Expert Panel on School Meals.* Edinburgh: The Stationery Office, 2002 (ISBN 0 7559 0701 9). www.scotland.gov.uk/Publications/2003/02/16273/17566

Health Promotion Agency for Northern Ireland. *School Meals, Top Marks: Nutritional Standards for School Lunches – A Guide for Implementation.* Belfast: Health Promotion Agency for Northern Ireland, 2009 (ISBN 978 1 874602 67 5). www.healthpromotionagency.org.uk/Resources/nutrition/pdfs/food_in_school_09/Nutritional_Standard-1EEBDB.pdf

School Food Trust. *Eat Better Do Better. A Guide to Introducing the Government's Food-based and Nutrient-based Standards for School Lunches.* Sheffield: School Food Trust, 2007. www.schoolfoodtrust.org.uk/schools/resources/eat-better-do-better-january-2012

Welsh Assembly Government. *Appetite for Life Action Plan.* Cardiff: Welsh Assembly Government, 2008 (ISBN 978 0 7504 4198). http://wales.gov.uk/topics/educationandskills/schoolshome/foodanddrink/appetiteforlife/?lang=en

CATERING

Department for Environment, Food and Rural Affairs. *Government Buying Standards for Food and Catering Services.* http://sd.defra.gov.uk/advice/public/buying/products/food/

Department of Health. *Healthier and More Sustainable Catering: A Toolkit for Serving Foods to Adults.* London: Department of Health, 2011. www.dh.gov.uk/en/Publicationsandstatistics/Publications/PublicationsPolicyAndGuidance/DH_125579

BABIES AND INFANTS

Advice for parents on feeding babies and infants from birth to age 5 is available on the 'Birth to five' pages of the NHS Choices website at www.nhs.uk/planners/birthtofive/Pages/Birthtofivehome.aspx

General reading

S Canham-New, I Macdonald and H Roche (eds). *Nutrition and Metabolism* (2nd edn). Chichester: Wiley–Blackwell, 2011 (ISBN 978 1 4051 6808 3).

Chief Medical Officer. *At Least Five a Week: Evidence on the Impact of Physical Activity and its Relationship to Health*. Department of Health, 2004.

Chief Medical Officers of England, Scotland, Wales and Northern Ireland. *Start Active, Stay Active: A Report on Physical Activity for Health from the Four Home Countries' Chief Medical Officers*. Department of Health, 2011.

Department of Health, Social Services and Public Safety. *Northern Ireland Health and Social Wellbeing Survey 2005/06*. Central Survey Unit, Northern Ireland, 2007.

C Geisler and H Powers (eds). *Human Nutrition* (12th edn). Oxford: Elsevier, 2010.

M Gibney, B Margetts, J Kearney and L Arab (eds). *Public Health Nutrition*. Oxford: Blackwell Publishing, 2004 (ISBN 0 632 05627 4).

M Gibney, S Lanham-New, A Cassidy and H Vorster (eds). *Introduction to Human Nutrition* (2nd edn). Chichester: Wiley–Blackwell, 2009 (ISBN 978 1 4051 6807 6).

Office for National Statistics. *Drinking: Adults' Behaviour and Knowledge in 2009*. January 2010.

Scottish Government. *Scottish Health Survey 2010*. September 2011.

Welsh Assembly Government. *Welsh Health Survey 2009*. September 2010.

World Cancer Research Fund (WCRF) and American Institute for Cancer Research. *Food, Nutrition, Physical Activity and the Prevention of Cancer – A Global Perspective*. WCRF, 2007.

Useful information can also be found on the Department of Health and Scientific Advisory Committee on Nutrition websites (www.dh.gov.uk and www.sacn.gov.uk).

Acknowledgements

The 12th edition of the *Manual of Nutrition* was prepared by Samantha Montel, Farida Rahman and Louis Levy, with contributions from Alette Addison, Jamie Blackshaw, Penny Blair, Lynn Burns, Matthew Carden, Mary Day, Nimisha De Souza, Sakhi Dodhia, Rachel Elsom, Melanie Farron-Wilson, Lucy Jayne, Verity Kirkpatrick, Stephen Knight, Henry Odeje, Krishna Patel, Vicki Pyne, Sheela Reddy, Mamta Singh, William Stather, Elaine Stone, Rachel Stratton, Gillian Swan, Alison Tedstone, Elizabeth Tydeman and Rachel White.

Index

Page numbers in *italics* refer to tables or figures; the suffix 'n' indicates the reference is to a note.